THE HUSTLERS

Douglas Thompson

THE HUSTLERS

**An Explosive True Story of Gambling, Greed
and the Perfect Con**

Sidgwick & Jackson

First published 2007 by Sidgwick & Jackson
an imprint of Pan Macmillan Ltd
Pan Macmillan, 20 New Wharf Road, London N1 9RR
Basingstoke and Oxford
Associated companies throughout the world
www.panmacmillan.com

ISBN 978-0-283-07049-5 HB
ISBN 978-0-283-07055-6 TPB

1 3 5 7 9 8 6 4 2

A CIP catalogue record for this book is available from
the British Library.

Typeset by SetSystems Ltd, Saffron Walden, Essex
Printed and bound in Great Britain by
Mackays of Chatham plc, Chatham, Kent

Visit **www.panmacmillan.com** to read more about all our books
and to buy them. You will also find features, author interviews and
news of any author events, and you can sign up for e-newsletters
so that you're always first to hear about our new releases.

For Lesley and Dandy

– a winning double

Contents

Acknowledgements

Doc Holliday said, or was said to have said, that a 'friendly' game of cards was a misnomer: 'Play to win, or don't bother. Check friendship at the door. If what you want is camaraderie, there is the bar. If it is companionship you seek, there are any number of likely whores.'

I learned to play cards, three-card brag, usually 'blind' bets, in the bagpipe room of an Edinburgh higher education establishment. I was often lucky.

The luck stayed with me when I met John Burke and Bobby McKew. Doc was wrong: you can have a friendly game. I thank them both for their grand help, their inspiration, and, most of all, for their stories. I'd also like to thank Mark Sykes, Mark Birley, David Pritchett, Michael Caborn-Waterfield, Bobby Buchanan-Michaelson, Caroline Gray, Theresa Follet, Cathy Maxwell-Scott, Raymond Nash, Claus Von Bülow, Nancy Gillespie, Charlie Richardson, Frankie Fraser and Diane Guinan-Browne for their help and time.

As always, Ingrid Connell at Pan Macmillan was patient, polite and a superb help at all times, as was my agent Sheila Crowley. Thanks are also due to Bruno Vincent at Pan Macmillan for his inspired help with the manuscript and photographs.

Life is six-to-five against? It depends who you're playing with.

A big, winning hand for them all.

Picture Acknowledgements

Credits are by page number in order from left to right and top to bottom.

1: © PA Photos (both). 2: Courtesy Bobby McKew; Mirrorpix. 3: Courtesy Bobby McKew (both). 4: Getty Images (both). 5: © PA Photos; Getty Images. 6: Getty Images; Topfoto. 7: Getty Images; Topfoto. 8: Getty Images. 9: Getty Images; courtesy John Burke. 10–11: Courtesy John Burke. 12: Topfoto; Mirrorpix. 13: Mirrorpix; Emma Giacon. 14: Desmond O'Neill Features; @ popperfoto.com; Mirrorpix. 15: Courtesy Bobby McKew (both). 16: Getty Images.

Preface

**The race is not always to the swift,
nor the battle to the strong,
but that's the way to bet.**

DAMON RUNYON'S PARAPHRASE OF ECCLESIASTES

More than a dozen years or so ago I wrote a series of newspaper articles about the ongoing mystery of Lord Lucan. At the time my inquiries involved the Clermont Club, and I heard the name John Burke mentioned. A one-time director of the club, he knew all the famous and infamous members and their stories but had 'retired; the word was he wanted to protect his secrets. There were 'reasons'.

Later, when I worked with Christine Keeler on her bestselling autobiography, *The Truth At Last*, she told me of the characters who inhabited the Star Tavern in Belgravia, including John Burke, whom she liked. He was, she said, a gentleman, who knew everybody but also knew how to keep secrets. At the same time a series of rather racy drawings by Stephen Ward, considered by some the most important and central character in the Profumo affair, were put up for sale.

I traced the seller, Michael 'Dandy Kim' Caborn-Waterfield. One of the more colourful characters in the country, he told me endless stories of London in the 1950s, 1960s, and 1970s. One involved a man called Bobby McKew with whom Kim had spent time in jail in the South of France – a little something to do with a robbery at Hollywood film tycoon Jack Warner's Riviera mansion.

McKew, it transpired, was as legendary as Kim, but in a far less flamboyant way. He knew people that people didn't want to know. He played his cards quietly, kept his own counsel. Against all his instincts Bobby joined me and Kim for lunch on the King's Road in Chelsea. With him was his long-time friend and fellow Irishman John Burke.

It was then that the two men, who had met in Dublin, began to tell me the story of the 'Big Edge', one of the most outrageous but brilliant crooked schemes of the twentieth century. It was also hugely successful, generating tens of millions of pounds in profits in today's money. As John Burke put it: 'It was brilliantly designed. It was psychologically and mathematically brilliant. Einstein would have been proud of it.'

The story involved a colourful cast of characters: rogues, villains, chancers, con men, aristocrats, people who delighted in devilment. Almost all were gamblers of one sort of another, a gallery of eccentrics worthy of Dickens at his most ingenious and Damon Runyon at his most fanciful.

In truth, it was a tale not just stranger but far more fascinating than fiction, more intriguing than the legend so far recorded about the people and events involved.

This, then, is the story of the 'Big Edge'.

Douglas Thompson, 2007
www.dougiethompson.com

Under the influence of uncontrollable ecstasy,
the players gamble their wives, their children
and ultimately themselves into captivity.

TACITUS, *GERMANIA*

Chemin de Fer

The Rules for Those Who Wish to Follow Them

Chemin de fer, known as chemmy, is utterly extravagant in its madness. It is a game of daring and nerve, of impetuosity – a true game of chance. It's as simple as betting on which number of bus will come around the corner first.

All face cards and tens count as zero. The aces count as one, and the rest as they are numbered: two, three, four, five, six, seven, eight, and nine.

If in counting the cards the total amounted to double figures, the ten would be dropped, a seven and six would count as three, a six and four as zero.

Nine is the best number, and called, along with a count of eight, as a 'natural'. The gamble is an even-money bet on which of two players is closest to nine.

Even if a player draws a third card, that decision involves no talent. The rules of the game, the tableau, which in casinos must be followed exactly, dictates mathematically correct play: whether to draw or rest.

Six packs of cards are normally used for a shoe. The croupier never handles the cards directly before a 'coup', a hand; he may move them down the table with his palette. Before the start of every shoe he shuffles the cards, a player cuts them by placing one card at random in the deck (something a clever croupier can 'break'), and places them in the shoe.

The cards in each coup, initially two each, are dealt by whichever player holds the 'bank'; he strokes them singly from the wooden shoe, which has a weight at the back and a metal mesh in front. He is gambling against whoever at the table calls '*banco*', and any player can do that. If the player who calls '*banco*' loses he can immediately call '*suivi*' and play again. This can go on until the bank loses.

Chemin de fer (French for 'railway' – the image of the shoe as a train travelling around the table) is the companion game of baccarat, once the grand gambling game in French casinos. The house provides a croupier to advise players of the rules. It also supplies all the necessary gaming equipment: table, chairs, the shoe (called the *sabot*) and the cards. For that, the house takes a percentage commission (the *cagnotte*, or rake) of 5 per cent on all winning bank hands. The house also guarantees to pay the winners.

Each player can be a banker in turn. The player who is acting as the bank is responsible with his/her own money for all losing bets, as well as collecting all winning bank bets.

The instructions and terms used in the game are in French. In a casino or gambling club chemmy is played on a kidney-shaped table covered with a green beige cloth. The croupier sits in the middle; there are nine seats for the players, the space on the table in front of them being marked with the numbers one to nine. There can be fewer players seated at the table, but never more than nine.

There is a slot in the table beside the croupier's place leading to a cabinet locked into the table into which the croupier drops the *cagnotte* (later a table charge). There is also a nine-inch-diameter hole in the centre of the table into which a removable, cylindrical metal container, flat on top and about two feet deep under the table, is placed. It has a slit into which the cards are dropped by the croupier after each coup.

The first bank goes to the player sitting at the right of the croupier, at number one. He puts in the middle of the table chips (cash is never seen in smart games) to the value for which he wishes to open his bank (his bet).

The player sitting at number two seat has first choice of taking the bet and after that precedence to do so moves anticlockwise – but anyone at the table can call the bet by saying '*banco*'.

The bank deals two cards alternately to his opponent and himself. They are dealt face down. The caller looks at his cards and if the joint count is either eight or nine he turns them over, as does the bank. There is then no further action; the better hand wins.

If there are no 'naturals', the caller can stay put – *reste* – or ask for a third card. The bank has exactly the same judgement to make.

The tableau, a copy of which is usually attached to the chemmy shoe, tells both players what is mathematically the correct strategy to adopt in almost every situation. There are a few situations where mathematically the alternatives of resting or drawing (*avalante*) make no difference to the chance of winning, and the gambler makes a choice. In casinos it was obligatory to adhere strictly to the tableau; in London, the games did not always hold as closely to the rules.

After a winning coup or coups the bank remains with the same person; after the first losing coup it passes automatically one place to the right – the train moves around the table.

Prologue: The Edge of Wonderland

Cheats don't prosper, but they have a big edge.

SYDNEY SUMMERS, 1955

They led the American Ray Ryan up the exquisite staircase, one of architect William Kent's most applauded achievements, to the *Salle Privée* which sat off a landing between the first and second floor at 44 Berkeley Square, London.

It was after dinner at the Clermont Club, and by 10.20 p.m. some of the other card players, in dinner jackets and dark lounge suits, had already arrived. Chatter, thick unfiltered cigarette smoke and the clink of iced drinks drifted around the classically elegant room.

Ryan was the tough, laconic 'founder' of Palm Springs in California. Once an oil wildcatter, he was now a wealthy man, the friend of movie stars, co-owner (with Oscar-winner William Holden) of the Mount Kenya Safari Club and boy-friend of Princess Alexander Hohenlohe (one-time actress and society playgirl Patricia 'Honeychile' Wilder). This par-ticular evening he was extremely relaxed. He was a regular player when in London and was regarded by everybody at the Clermont as an all-round good guy.

Yet the plan that Christmastime in 1963 was not just to lead him up Kent's architectural wonder of a staircase, but up the garden path; to cheat him of £50,000, the equivalent in 2007 of £1 million.

It was a question, John Aspinall, the owner of the Clermont, told his fellow director and long-time gambling partner John Burke, of 'needs must'. At that time gambling clubs were allowed to give long-term credit, so, despite the extravagantly affluent appearance of the Clermont, the company's cash profit was poor.

John Aspinall had borrowed $200,000 from Ryan in May 1963, to cement the Clermont's reputation as the city's most exclusive gambling club and support his own position in London society. He had assumed that when Ryan returned to London he would ask for the loan to be repaid. The snag was that Aspinall could not afford to pay Ryan back. Instead he would 'win' back his debt, with some interest.

Which was why when Ryan took his seat to the right of the croupier, at number one, at the *chemin de fer* table in the *Salle Privée*, an Italian card sharp called Biondi sat at the croupier's left, at number nine. The salon had been turned into a private gaming area that evening for the first time.

Around the table, Ryan could see John Aspinall and other players like John Ambler, publisher John 'Mike' Ryan, the stockbroker Stephen Raphael and his protégé Richard John Bingham, the future 7th Earl of Lucan, whom Raphael had taught to play poker at the Hamilton Club in Park Lane. But tonight, 20 December 1963, it was chemmy, the game of choice in the London of the day, the ultimate game of chance when players went one to one. Players can swiftly win – or lose – enormous amounts of money.

The table set-up had been arranged so that Ryan couldn't make much eye contact with Biondi, who Aspinall had recruited through an international businessman, a questionable golf gambler and shady precious metals dealer who was said to be the inspiration for Ian Fleming's Bond villain Goldfinger. With his agile imagination Aspinall had introduced Biondi, who looked like a sleek, middle-aged, mild-mannered European businessman, as a friend of the Italian car tycoon Gianni Agnelli.

Biondi had collected the specially patterned, cellophaned Caro playing cards (every casino had its own upmarket 'brand' delivered regularly from the company's headquarters at 252 Boulevard Voltaire, Paris) from his contact at the Clermont on 19 December. He then 'treated' the cards so he could 'read' them and they were returned, seemingly innocent and untampered with, on the day of the private game.

For Ray Ryan it was meant to be a night of fun. He was an easy-going, colourful character; a seasoned gambler, he'd been around. Aspinall kept up the conversation at the table with typical embellishments. Biondi was a professional, and when he took the bank he stroked the cards out of the shoe with a practised, pink and manicured hand.

The cards turned for around ninety minutes in the private salon while downstairs in the stunning, splendid Grand Salon, other players, overseen by John Burke on this busy evening, chanced their luck at two chemmy tables.

In the Ray Ryan game, luck had nothing to do with it. Every play made by Biondi was dictated by his ability to 'read' the cards. He creamed off the winning coups and left the losing ones to his victim. With everyone playing on credit in the small, exclusive casino, Ryan began to call for more credit slip 'markers' and only a short time into the game had signed four, each for £5,000. (He had originally staked himself with a £5,000 'marker' for playing chips.)

But Ryan was no easy 'mark'. He'd been involved in the early days of gambling in Las Vegas when most of the desert town was controlled by the Mob. He'd grown up ·in the toughest gambling schools and had played with sharks before. Biondi just wasn't a good enough mechanic to fool and steal £50,000 from this man who had won, and lost, massive sums of money at gaming tables around the world. Less than two hours had gone by when Ryan sensed something was wrong. Or maybe he spotted a wrong movement. Perhaps it was simply his gambler's antennae warning him that all was not as it should be. He put down his cards and with his hands flat on the table raised himself from his chair. His grey eyes narrowed and he looked over at John Aspinall, who still wore his shameless, engaging smile. Quietly, he said: 'Can I have a word, John?'

The two men left the private salon. Ryan took Aspinall downstairs and into a little room at the back of the *caisse*, the cashier's office. In a quiet voice he told Aspinall that he knew what was going on. Aspinall said nothing, made no attempt to deny it.

Then Ryan asked for his 'markers'. There was a lot going on around the *caisse*. Aspinall called to John Burke and asked him to retrieve them from the *caissier*, the cashier Jim Gore, who had just returned from a tea break. Nearby was a watchful, helpful man who lent the cashier a hand on busy nights like this, allowing Gore to take short breaks.

The part-time cashier was not a man to whom John Aspinall or John Burke paid much attention, although he was very useful. To them, to Aspinall especially, he had the status of a well-connected concierge. Certainly this night Aspinall, as he was confronted by Ray Ryan, did not notice him in the background, his eyes constantly frisking the casino. Neither did John Burke, who was busily explaining to the concerned Jim Gore – who didn't just dish out signed papers to anybody and was nervous because he had to keep exact books – that Aspinall would take responsibility.

Aspinall, still silent, handed the markers to Ryan, who tore them up and put them in his pocket. A careful man, he didn't like the idea of having his signature even on torn pieces of paper in the Clermont. Aspinall remained quiet. What could he say?

Ryan looked at him and said, 'John, steal whatever you want, but don't rob the man who saved your life.'

With that Ryan walked out into the cold night air. He made no fuss. If he had done so it could have been the end of the Clermont, then arguably Europe's most glamorous gambling club, and of Aspinall's social and financial ambitions: Ryan, had he wanted, could have brought down the whole house of cards.

'He was an amazing man,' said John Burke. 'He could have caused a major scandal but he just shrugged it off; he had been around and expected people to try and cheat him in casinos, but John Aspinall he considered a friend. That annoyed him but he never once raised his voice. His attitude was one of disappointment, of being let down. He had a remarkable philosophy.'

As did Aspinall. He was a tough guy. Although badly shaken by what had happened, his first concern was that the show must go on. There was still a game to play upstairs, where there were two empty seats. Biondi, fearful that he was going to be caught up in a scandal, had vanished. The Clermont's star 'house' player, Peter West, was recruited to take his place at the table, and Aspinall rejoined the game and played on as if nothing at all had happened.

Biondi took with him £7,550 worth of Clermont chips that he had 'won'. He returned to the Clermont on 23 December and attempted to cash in. A furious Aspinall – Biondi had failed in his mission – instructed the cashiers to refuse to pay.

A week later the Secretary of the Clermont Club received a solicitor's letter, from Summer and Co., 25 Dover Street, Piccadilly, demanding payment of the £7,550. It was ignored.

Another letter was delivered by hand on 10 January 1964. It, too, was ignored, but behind the scenes a £1,000 payoff was made to Biondi in return for his 'chips'.

The settlement was engineered by a gambler called Leslie Price but known to Aspinall and Burke and everyone else in the gambling world as the Vicar. Price had his own reason for enjoying Aspinall's discomfort and it was he who had introduced Biondi to the West End legal firm. When that got no result he made a phone call to the Clermont:

'Aspers, I hear you're in a spot of bother.'

'What would that be, Vicar?'

'Difficult chaps, these Italians.'

'What can you do about it, Vicar?'

'I can fix that for a couple of grand. That'll get your chips back and you'll never be bothered about it again.'

'Five hundred pounds.'

'Let's call it a grand and be friends.'

'A thousand pounds it is.'

Biondi accepted this. He also, somewhat reluctantly, accepted some advice to leave the country and never return to England again. It was, in the circumstances, astute of him. The man who had told him to get out of town was the quietly intimidating Billy Hill, the controller of London's underworld and one of the most powerful gangsters in Europe.

One of his senior henchmen drove former boxer and 'minder' Bobby Warren to call on Biondi at the flat he was staying at in Chelsea Reach with some travel hints. Biondi didn't require any more encouragement to find his passport.

'Perhaps Biondi wasn't much of a card cheat,' said John Burke, 'but he wasn't a total fool. Better to get out than end up in the Thames.'

Hill, who looked as sleek as Humphrey Bogart in his gangster movie heyday, was quietly spoken but could be so chilling it was said he peed iced water. Like the screen idol, he almost always had a cigarette, a Capstan Full Strength, in his hand or in the corner of his mouth. He was 14 when he committed his first stabbing, and since then he had bullied and battered and cut his way to the top of London's gangland; had carved his place in crime history, often using his shiv to place a V for Victory on his victim's face. He specialized in protection rackets earning from West End nightclubs, drinking dens, bookmakers and illegal gambling joints known as spielers. He had powerful connections with the French and American Mafia.

Now, at the age of fifty-three, he was supposedly 'retired'. The reality was that from his home in Moscow Road, Bayswater, he was simply more careful and corporate in his dealings; he was London crime's chief executive officer, who would advise and finance robberies and other enterprises but found even richer pickings available from Britain's growing casino culture.

Which is why Biondi had to be thrown out of the country. What if there had been a scandal at the Clermont? It would just have drawn unwanted attention to Hill's own endeavours at other gambling clubs in London and Glasgow. The Italian had to go, before he messed up on the doorstep again.

The Ray Ryan debacle had seriously annoyed Billy Hill, something sensible people did not do, because he himself had always wanted to operate within the Clermont. Previously, he had asked his number two, Bobby McKew, to contact his friend and fellow Irishman John Burke. Hill also knew Aspinall's confidante from drinking with him at the Star Tavern in Belgravia where spivs, questionable toffs and Scotland Yard officers mingled most evenings with the pub's rich and respectable clientele.

'I told Bill that John Burke would never go for it, that he

was six-and-eight, straight,' said Bobby McKew. 'Bill accepted that and we pursued our business elsewhere. He didn't put it out of his mind though.'

Hill knew all about the Ray Ryan affair because he had a man inside the Clermont Club who monitored everything, as he had everywhere there was profit to be made. This was the part-time cashier, a clever shadow of a player, whose motivation was never compromized. It was always financial. He changed name according to country, and had so many different ones that they just called him Mr Money. That was his business: making money, moving money. Mr Money connected those who inherited wealth, those who got lucky with it and even some who earned it, with those who would casually take it away from them.

A refugee from Hitler's regime, with almost perfect English, he was a currency operator and jewellery fence. Aspinall was one of his better customers for stolen items, bought for the 'fence' price but insured for the full price against a rainy day.

Mr Money had first established his financial credentials in London, making his first big stake though a simple con. His girlfriend worked as maid to the wife of a shipping tycoon who liked to gamble in Monte Carlo. There was strict currency control at the time, and it was a serious criminal offence to break the rules. Yet, for a fee, Mr Money could do just that. His girlfriend introduced the tycoon to her 'Swiss banker', who was given £25,000 – a vast sum in the 1950s – to transfer to the South of France. When Mr Money and the cash vanished the victim could not go to the police. He was an accessory to a crime, and was not the kind of person to employ gangsters to retrieve his cash from the con man, so he had to accept what had happened.

Although a stocky figure, Mr Money was clever at remaining in the background, an unpretentious chameleon; working both sides of the street, as it were, he was on Billy Hill's weekly payroll as well as the Clermont's. Neither Aspinall nor John Burke was aware of his underworld connection.

Mr Money lived only a short walk from Moscow Road. He would visit Billy Hill regularly – Hill often didn't leave his flat for weeks at a time – to offer information and to be rewarded with two or three hundred pounds: the amount always depended on Hill's mood rather than on the information itself. Still, on the morning of 21 December as he rushed over to Moscow Road, Mr Money anticipated much profit in the news he had to share about the previous evening's entertainment at the Clermont. He knew that, although the Clermont was smaller than other London casinos, the enormous amounts of money gambled there every evening made it the ultimate prize.

Hill was enjoying a pot of tea when his breathless informant arrived. The gangster called for another cup as Mr Money hurriedly made him aware of Aspinall's attempt to rob Ryan and his desperation for cash.

Over that midmorning pot of tea, the wily Billy Hill sensed an opportunity.

1. THE PLAYERS

Trust everybody, but always cut the cards.

MR DOOLEY, 1950S DUBLIN PUB PHILOSOPHER

Picturing a teenaged Bobby McKew digging up turf board to fuel the fires of his home city of Dublin, it's difficult to imagine he'd later be known as 'the Chelsea Scallywag': dapper, with perfect manners, clever, quick-witted, a man whose sociability and tact would allow him to be Billy Hill's lieutenant, the son-in-law of South African millionaire industrialist 'Lucky' Jack Gerber and the close friend of movie stars and aristocrats. Yet he's always been a man of single-minded enterprise. Whatever has been thrown at him he has dealt with in a no-nonsense, practical way. He has accepted the knocks – and there have been a few, mostly self-inflicted – and ridden them out.

His father was in the movies. Robert McKew Senior worked for Rank and was in charge of the distribution of films to Irish cinemas. The powerful film executive thought his son might follow him into show business, which, in some ways, he eventually did. He lived with his father and his mother, Iris, and his two older sisters, Joy and Paddy, in the highly respectable Dublin suburb of Blackrock. The adored only boy in this comfortable, successful family went to Mountjoy College, a prominent Protestant school, but says his father got fed up with paying for him to do little but play sport and told him: 'I'm not sending you to Trinity College to play bloody rugby.'

The solid-thinking businessman hoped his son would join him at Rank, but instead Robert Junior got a job as a labourer, taking what work came around, but especially digging turf board, which kept him fit and put money in his pocket. When not working, he'd meet up with friends in the pubs around town, usually Davy Byrne's just off Grafton Street. Bobby often encountered John Burke, as they moved in a similar set. They were both restless young men, keen for company and intrigued with the world. Bobby McKew wasn't sure what he wanted, other than more excitement than he was getting in Dublin. John Burke simply wanted to play cards, to socialize, but also yearned for a bigger playing board. Among the friends they'd meet most evenings was John Ryan, the brother of the actress Kathleen Ryan.

Kathleen was renowned as a great beauty of her time. Her prominent Tipperary family had opened a shop on Dublin's Parnell Street in the 1920s, the first of a chain known as the 'Monument Creamery'. She was a prize in every way. In her decade-long career she appeared in several films, including her 1947 debut opposite James Mason in Carol Reed's eloquent classic, *Odd Man Out.*

One of her admirers was the gifted safe-cracker and Second World War double agent Eddie Chapman, who was more colourful than a rainbow and a dab hand with gelignite and the ladies. He treated them both delicately and to good effect. The safe-cracker came to Ireland to pursue Kathleen Ryan and one evening in Davy Byrne's her brother introduced Chapman to his 19-year-old friend Bobby McKew.

'Eddie always wanted the best,' said McKew. 'She was an utterly gorgeous, long-red-haired girl and Eddie was friendly with her. She lived with her mother Agnes Veronica and Eddie had to be careful with his courtship. But he didn't mind. He was a handsome man and had great charm and birds used to throw themselves at him.'

The young Dubliner was fascinated by Chapman and his incredible, seductive stories of events which were still fresh in everybody's minds. This was contemporary excitement, lavish true-life adventure. Eddie Chapman, the only Englishman to have been awarded the Iron Cross, directly from Hitler, had much to teach. He'd worked for Winston Churchill stealing Nazi secrets, and MI5 regularly had to decline his offers to assassinate Hitler. In 1997, his MI5 wartime files were released by the UK Public Records Office. Christopher Plummer had played Chapman in the rather wooden 1966 film, *Triple Cross*. The British Intelligence file on the agent codenamed 'ZigZag' is much more entertaining:

'The story of many a spy is commonplace and drab; the story of Chapman is different. In fiction it would be rejected as improbable. The subject is a crook, but as a crook he is by no means a failure and in his own estimation is something of a prince of the underworld. He plays for high stakes and would have the world know it. Of fear he knows nothing. Adventure to Chapman is the breath of life. Given adventure, he has the courage to achieve the unbelievable.'

Chapman, who was born in a village near Newcastle, had deserted from the Coldstream Guards in the 1930s and metamorphosed from a professional soldier into a highly successful professional crook, leader of London's infamous 'Gelignite Gang', whose trademark was to use the newly popular American chewing gum to attach the explosives. His MI5 personal file disclosed new details of his life before he became a spy. He had served a series of prison sentences, mostly for robberies, although one came after 'he behaved in Hyde Park in a manner likely to offend the virtuous public and was caught in flagrante delicto'.

He was arrested in Scotland after blowing the half-ton Chubb safe of the headquarters of the Edinburgh Cooperative Society. After endless scrapes and scraps he fled to Jersey, where he was eventually jailed for cracking the safe of a large dance hall. In prison he used his burglary knack to make keys that allowed him to move freely at night between the men's and the women's prisons and pursue the only thing he enjoyed more than blowing up safes.

After the Germans occupied the Channel Islands in 1940, he saw an opportunity for some form of freedom and offered his services to the Germans as a spy. He was convincing enough for the German authorities to move him from Jersey to France, where he was trained in the dark arts of espionage. As a subterfuge, the Nazis pretended to have executed him. In reality, he was sent back into Britain with orders to blow up the De Havilland aircraft factory in Hatfield, Hertfordshire. He handed himself over to MI5, who decided to play him back against the Germans, using him to provide false information as part of the Double Cross system. They staged a fake explosion at the aircraft factory and Chapman returned to Germany a hero. He was then sent back to England as an agent for the second time and fed his German handlers false information about the effects of the V-1 and V-2 rockets blitzing Britain. He is credited with saving the lives of many, many Londoners.

'The Germans came to love Chapman but although he went cynically through all the forms he did not reciprocate. Chapman loved himself, loved adventure and loved his country, probably in that order.' His MI5 file continues, 'The outstanding feature of the case is the courage of Chapman.'

Bobby McKew, who in 2007 regularly visited Chapman's widow Betty, has no doubts about that: 'They never admitted how good he was. My goodness, he went back to Germany! How crazy was that! And then he returned supposedly to guide in the V-bombs. He misled the Nazis and saved thousands of lives. To me he was a big hero. Yet the authorities didn't even give him a pension until 1994 – three years before he died.'

The charges against Chapman (for emptying more than forty safes) were dropped after the war, saving him a possible twenty-year prison term. In time, Chapman became the young Bobby McKew's mentor. Bobby told me the story over afternoon tea at a hotel near his home in Chelsea: 'Eddie became like an older brother to me. I stayed friendly with him all his life. He taught me how to blow up safes, dope greyhounds and a lot more.'

Much, much more.

Chapman was also tough, as Bobby McKew learned early on in their friendship. In those early days in Dublin it was common for young men to get into a fight after a pint too many, but it was carried out in a gentlemanly way. The two combatants would take their coats off, go outside, knock the hell out of each other, and then go back into the pub with missing teeth or a bust-up nose, but the best of friends. It was, Bobby acknowledges now, pointless and stupid. Yet there would be more serious arguments in his life with which he learned to deal more effectively. The lesson came from Chapman.

'One night, I was 21 then, I was in the bar with Eddie and I got into a ruck with this fella about I don't remember what, and we did the usual and went outside. He was a big lad but big people have never frightened me – you can't miss 'em. We were standing off before going at it when Eddie appeared. He had a tyre iron in his hand and he just bounced it off the side of the other guy's head. He dropped like a sack of potatoes. People were watching, had never seen anything like it. Eddie said, "Now, that'll save you a lot of trouble." He was right, and I've never forgotten that. What's the point of getting broken about and your teeth knocked out? Better to get in first and get it over and done with.'

In the weeks that followed Bobby felt stifled by Dublin, and to ease his boredom – and to please his parents – he agreed to take a job with the publicity department of the Rank Organization in London. He found it less than fascinating, but lasted nine months.

Bobby knew few people in London but he would meet Eddie Chapman for a drink. Chapman made some introductions, one of them to Billy Hill.

John Burke was 6 years old when he first picked up a pack of playing cards at the family home in the south of County Tipperary, and the mathematics and thrill of games of chance became a lifelong obsession.

He was born into a prominent Irish family, many of whose members devoted a large part of their lives to horses, racing and hunting. The family money came from business and property investments. His father, Richard Burke, was Master of the Tipperary Fox Hounds, one the premier packs in the country, for more than thirty years.

It was still the nineteenth century when Richard Burke graduated in law from Trinity College and took the long trip to San Francisco to practise. His only connection there was his former nanny, Helen O'Brien, who was now working for a wealthy Californian family. He decided to visit her. It proved to be a romantic decision. Her charge then was the 18-year-old beauty Margaret Donahue, daughter of one of the founders of the Bay city. It was, say the family, love at first sight and they were soon married.

The Donahues owned a bank and many of the streets of San Francisco. A superb horseman, Richard Burke introduced fox-hunting to California, in the Donahue-owned Menlow Park which is now part of Silicon Valley. However, says his son, Richard Burke MFH was not a man of business, and despite all the opportunities offered by the Donahue family yearned to hunt back home in County Tipperary. With his new wife he returned to Ireland and they set up home and enjoyed a financially carefree life. They had four children, but tragically Margaret Donahue died giving birth to their last child.

Richard Burke married again in 1913 and had another four children, and John Burke, born in September 1926, was the youngest. His father was nearly 70 years old when he was born. His highly intelligent Irish mother, Sheila Geoghegan, was a suffragette who had worked with Emily Pankhurst; she was living in London when she married Richard Burke. Her youngest son was rather doted upon and would sit, as a boy, playing bridge with his father.

John's brother Edward became a chartered accountant and in 2007 was retired in France; his sister Eve married Arthur Goodbody, an academic who inherited a series of businesses. He sold them and bought an Irish estate, where he took up farming. His sister Sheila kept her maiden name by marrying a namesake. After her marriage to Ulick Burke the couple established their own estate, and in 2007 she was training and racing horses in County Tipperary.

John, who was given an excellent education and studied engineering, did not overly concern himself with acquiring a profession. After an exceptional life, in 2007 he was living with his partner Caroline in the mists of Ireland, where we talked for dozens of hours:

'I was always thought of as something of a ne'er-do-well. I loved gambling and I was a good bridge player. I suppose I was a layabout. I was studying engineering but didn't find it that fascinating. The cards were much more intriguing. For me, from early on, it was always about percentages. It rather blinded me to being what people would regard as sensible in terms of career and future.

'I was fooling around in Dublin. I got a job at one point

selling calculators, which I rather enjoyed because I do like numbers – life really is all about odds. Yes, there is luck but it is percentages, often tiny ones, which count most.

'I shared a flat in Dublin with Richard Parkes. He was one of the nicest people I have ever known. He was English but his family lived near Dublin and we were great friends. I played a lot of cards, often at Trinity College, with, among others, two divinity students, who would leave the game on a Saturday night and Sunday morning for about an hour to do God, and then gamble again. I suppose they were hedging their bets.' John Burke's talent at the card table won him a place on the Irish Bridge Team and he represented his country in international matches. Each year there was the opportunity to play at the top level in European capitals. One year, aged 22, he attended a bridge congress in Copenhagen. On the way back to Dublin he stopped off in London. He liked it, and stayed for a week.

Five years later, in 1953, the International Congress was in Finland. On the way home from Helsinki he again stopped in London. 'It turned into a fifty-year holiday . . .'

Today, London society is much changed from the circles he mixed in then, where the characters he met could have been drawn from the novels of Evelyn Waugh and were, in some cases, the inspiration for Waugh and other writers. It was a world inhabited by the gifted and the deluded, the famous and the infamous; where you could be rich one day and poor the next and vice versa: you couldn't bet on it either way. There could never be any odds available. Or much public gambling.

As the nation struggled out of the lingering aura of austerity there were no casinos or betting shops (cash betting except at the tracks was illegal); no one-armed bandits, no spread betting or betting exchanges like Betfair (where more than £300 million was wagered via their website on the 2006 World

Cup). Even the housewife's choice, bingo halls, had not yet arrived on a scene governed by gaming laws established more than a century earlier. Under the 1854 Gaming Act groups could gather and play cards, and gamble on anything they liked, but the hosts or organizers of the games could not charge for providing the facilities. That was illegal. Of course, that didn't prevent such enterprises.

For John Burke and Bobby McKew, London in the 1950s was like two cities: there was the rarified world of Belgravia, Mayfair and Chelsea, where the inhabitants had money and glamour and double-barrelled names. Gentlemen were still gentlemen, with their sacred code of honour. A gentleman would always honour a gambling debt, whereas his tailor or wine merchant might have to wait to be paid. Tradesmen were, well, tradesmen. At the same time, the capital was also a city of myriad dark corners and double-barrelled shotguns, of bohemian Soho with its spivs, pubs and clubs and its clip joints where tinsel and morality were casually stripped off. Gangsters would cut, shoot and kill – often each other – for power and profit. Each territory had its own rules and risks. Yet they often made a compatible connection.

That London was a village compared to the sprawling metropolis of the twenty-first century; Hampstead was an out-of-town trip, and there was no congestion on the roads to charge for. Of course, few people had cars. The average price of a house was £2,081. A skilled worker took home about £11 a week – the equivalent in today's money of £161. An income tax rate of 45 per cent did not help. Foreign travel was unheard of for most people. A flight between London and Paris cost £10 – nearly a week's wages. Trains still ran on steam, but a programme of electrification was being introduced.

London had the intrigue of wartime Lisbon and the action of pre-war Berlin. It was a potent mix. It wasn't so much *Who's Who* as Who was Really Who? There was certainly a sense of anything goes, an overspill of the Blitz mentality, of the blackout; for the wide boys, the chancers at every level, there were many opportunities. The cold war was chilling nicely and many ordinary people were still suffering post-war deprivation; food rationing did not end until midnight on 4 July 1954. Yet an extraordinary mix of aristocracy, landown-ers and villains were rolling in cash.

John Burke, a tall, elegant man who quietly kept his own counsel, found friends in both camps – as did many others. Mark Sykes, a man of aristocratic connections and a leading rascal of the times (he was the inspiration for Robin Cook's landmark 1962 novel, *The Crust on its Uppers*), is certain the connection followed on from the war, where officers and other ranks relied so tremendously on each other.

'It was a very positive thing at that time,' he says today. 'It hadn't happened since the days of William Crockford, since Regency times – and it hasn't happened since. It was a time of toffs and spivs, the other lot didn't matter one bit. The upper classes and the lower classes always get on well because they hate the middle classes. They regarded them as terribly preten-tious. Which they are, of course, they are.'

Indeed, 'suburban' appeared to be the dirtiest word of that time; John Osborne's plays, the Northern novels, and real-life dramas of the 1950s and into the 1960s reflected a view that the only lives worth living were ones of privilege or those of the working class. It was working-class lads, actors like Albert Finney (*Saturday Night and Sunday Morning*) and Tom Courtenay (*The Loneliness of the Long Distance Runner*), who brought them to life when they were celebrated in the cinema. It was a time of Shakespeare or the kitchen sink. 'It was an extraordinary time. Fun, always fun, even when things did get a little shaky,' observed the ever-ebullient Sykes.

When he arrived in London, in Belgravia of course, John Burke found life intriguing, although there were to be 'shaky' moments for him too. It was a time of change but also a time where everything appeared to offer a financial opportunity. People were smarter and sharper, and most of all the con men and hustlers, scam artists, the gangsters and the gamblers. It was a time for opportunists, for players.

John met two sets of people: as a professional bridge player he mixed with world-class bridge masters like Boris Shapiro and Terence Reece, and bridge players like Michael Alachouzos, Eric Leigh-Howard, Emilio Schisa, Stephen Raphael, and the Frenchman who ran an illegal poker room at Crockford's (the original Hellfire Club) in Curzon House Terrace. Through his friend Richard Parkes (owner of three dog stadiums), who was also now living in London, he met a racier circle, men like 20-year-old already buccaneering entrepreneur Jimmy Goldsmith, and Peter Sargent, the son of hugely popular conductor Sir Malcolm Sargent. Peter was fond of the horses and was known to the bookies, then and later, as 'the bandleader's boy'.

Parkes' close crowd also included the 26-year-old Ian Maxwell-Scott, a well-connected aristocrat (he called the Duke of Norfolk 'Uncle Bernard'). With the help of a family trust, he would happily gamble around the clock, at the racetrack (horses and dogs) and card tables. The great-great-great-grandson of Sir Walter Scott, he was calm, enervated, ever confident, never fazed by anything, and to John Burke likeable in the extreme. He also liked the more energetic John Aspinall, then aged 27, who was Maxwell-Scott's great friend and fellow gambler at Oxford University. The smart set called him 'Aspers', but he was almost a stranger in this confident crowd of men, people who were rich and connected to the upper classes in a 1950s Britain still ruled by grandees. Aspinall was the new boy on the block; he was an *arriviste*.

He was also the most outré of men, an iconoclast who wanted to join the party, in his case the Establishment, at the same time as he was giving it an enormous thumping. In the military manner, he carried a rolled umbrella with a gold pencil built into it with which he would mark his race card. One day at the races a punter watched him and exclaimed, 'Blimey! The Count of Monte Cristo!' Certainly for Aspinall, as with Dumas's Monte Cristo, there were other people's treasures to be enjoyed.

Aspinall worked at the image. He was tall with blond hair and an athletic figure and cut quite a dash around town. He has been called a maverick but he wasn't: he was a wide boy on the make. He just spoke a little differently from his counterparts on the other side of the game. And, when he wanted to be, he was egocentrically charming, a brilliant and amusing raconteur, which all helped create the myth. John Burke found him splendid company from the moment they first met at the offices of Sydney Summers, who ran an illegal SP (starting price) betting shop from a flat in Jermyn Street.

Sydney Summers was a near-sighted East End Jew who spoke like Henry Kissinger and wore thick glasses which gave him a sinister look at odds with his kindly nature. A master of understatement, he would have squeezed perfectly into a corner booth of a Damon Runyon speakeasy with Harry the Horse and Bookie Bob. He was a character, and he ran a thriving business. Bookmakers had offices, rather drab affairs, where you could ring up and place a bet, and they were 100 per cent legal. But places like Sydney Summers', where you could go and hang about with friends, have drinks and place a cash bet, were not. Of course, they were far more convivial and far more popular.

As always, John Burke was well groomed and smartly dressed – good suit, polished shoes (Fosters of Jermyn Street) – when he first met John Aspinall. He was also with the wealthy Richard Parkes and known as someone who played bridge for high stakes. Aspinall took this to mean that his new acquaintance had money. Of course, he didn't.

Aspinall invited John Burke to lunch at Wheeler's in Knightsbridge. He was not yet the sophisticate he would learn to be but he wanted to impress Burke so when he ordered white wine to go with the fish he picked the most expensive, Chateau d'Yquem. It was a sweet dessert wine. Yet by a remarkable metamorphasis, within two years Aspinall was hosting lavish dinner parties where everything was perfect. He was a quick learner – at everything, including how to cheat at cards.

John Burke found himself enjoying Aspinall's company: 'Occasionally I played poker with him. We used go to the races together or to Sydney Summers' office and then on to tea at the Ritz, which was only a short walk away. Sydney had his marvellous connections; many policemen won on the horses without even placing a bet. There was never any trouble and always lots of fun.'

As the new friends gambled around town, John Burke repeatedly heard stories about an amazing card 'mechanic' called Bruce, an Australian who had displayed his proficiency in London at the start of the decade. As a young man, Bruce had murdered his wife and spent nine years in jail in Tasmania. Every day, all day, in his prison cell he had developed his skill with cards. By the time John Burke arrived in London the card sharp had flown home, but the legend of his expertise remained.

John Aspinall had met Bruce through an agreeable East Ender called Joe Dagle who ran a poker game with Bruce. The Australian could arrange cards in a certain way without being spotted as he shuffled the pack (or, in the case of *chemin de fer*, packs). Bruce taught Aspinall, and presumably others, some simple card tricks. The legend of Bruce would live on in all sorts of establishments, usually of the gambling variety. It moved along like falling dominoes . . .

Dagle lived with Pauline Wallace, who was an appealing,

charismatic lady. She would graduate in the club/gambling trade with some associates at the Mount Street Bridge Club in Mayfair, once a fashionable card club where John Burke played. Her brother Aubrey once acted as a 'runner' for Aspinall and Maxwell-Scott when they ran a short-lived SP office – half a dozen telephones and two rooms – at 33 Dryden Chambers near Oxford Street, an operation financed by Richard Parkes.

The influence of Bruce on Aspinall and subsequent events cannot be stressed too much: he gave him not just the know-how but the intent and the callous application of it. The willingness to take an edge – if not, yet, the big one.

From Bruce, Aspinall learned one simple card trick which, cleverly used in five-card stud poker games, was to separate wealthy young bucks around town from their generous allowances. The poker games, which were not illegal as no charge was made, were staged in hotels and flats in central London locations by Aspinall, though not in any organized way. If he and Ian Maxwell-Scott saw a mug poker player they would get him into a game. An opportunity was an opportunity; it was casual but calculated.

Which is how the great con man George Denison-Webster found himself a little short of readies. Something of a toff, Denison-Webster, at this time in the money, was wandering through the foyer of the Ritz when he was spotted by Aspinall and Maxwell-Scott. Early in the evening they inveigled him into a poker game in their hotel room, the cost of which they almost always recovered. By 5 a.m. the next morning the inevitable had happened – their guest was a huge loser.

Denison-Webster wrote out a big cheque and left. Aspinall spotted that it had been drawn on a bank in his victim's home town of Moreton-in-the-Marsh in Gloucestershire. Aspinall knew that Denison-Webster, although he had money, was highly likely to stop the cheque when he realized what he had done. So he got Maxwell-Scott to drive off in the early hours to be on the doorstep of the Cotswolds bank at 9.30 a.m. with the cheque and to lodge it to Aspinall's bank in London. At 10 a.m. Aspinall instructed his bank to call Moreton-in-the-Marsh and find out if the cheque had been cleared and it had. By then, it could not be stopped by Denison-Webster when he woke up at lunchtime after his costly night.

It was in those early days of their friendship that John Burke identified what the Duke of Devonshire called the 'amoral' aspect of Aspinall's character. 'I reflect now that John Aspinall was pathologically dishonest. I think it was through Bruce that he first "practised to deceive". He certainly defrauded a young man called Rory McKechnie. I witnessed some of the game. John was desperate for money, and Rory had inherited £100,000 or something like that.

'I'd called to visit him and a game of stud poker was in progress. There were four players – Aspinall, Maxwell-Scott, another friend of his and McKechnie. Somewhat to my surprise, I noticed that on one hand when John was the dealer he arranged the cards in such a way that he would win the hand at the expense of McKechnie; in other words, he cheated. His method of doing so was simple. There were four players and the victim was sitting opposite to him. The game was five-card stud, in which the first card each player receives is dealt face down and the remaining four cards are dealt face up. While shuffling the cards before dealing, Aspinall arranged the top eight cards so that the second and sixth cards (McKechnie's hand) would both be kings and that the fourth and eighth cards (his) were aces. Since one ace and one king were hidden and John bet sportingly and freely without even looking at his hole card – good psychology – a large pot built up before the inevitable, though apparently and mathematically improbable, denouement took place when full five-card hands were revealed.'

John Burke's reaction was to be slightly shocked – gentlemen did not cheat at cards! It was beyond the pale. Apart
from the drudgery of honest toil there were other methods of
keeping the wolf from the door, such as getting very long-term
credit from landlords, tradesmen and others, knocking bookmakers, skilful honest card play, being economical with the
truth and charming to bank managers and, *in extremis*, bounc-
ing the odd cheque – issuing what Ian Maxwell-Scott called
'nasties'. Now he had seen Aspinall, who had the appearance
and manner of a gentleman, behaving like a card sharp –
actions condoned by his aristocratic friend Maxwell-Scott.

Burke confronted his friend, asking him what was going
on and what he was up to. Aspinall smiled calmly back at him.
'Burkie, it's all just as needs must. A necessity.'

'Necessity?'

'I've written a couple of important cheques and if they
turn into nasties I'll be homeless. Didn't want them to bounce,
so I had to get the money.'

Burke nodded and said nothing.

Aspinall went on: 'And it's big enough stuff to get me
taken to Tattersalls and warned off all racecourses.'

John Burke understood the implications, and also understood that for Aspinall there was an even stronger reason to
cheat.

'I've been tipped about an unraced two-year-old which is
going to do the business. I needed the money for that.'

'For John this was an extremely plausible explanation,' says
Burke, 'to have wind of a pending coup. He wanted, needed,
all the financial firepower he could get. It would never have
been in his nature not to go after it.

'John's attitude was that he had stolen a few hundred
pounds which was nothing to the amount the lad had been
gifted. It was not going to damage him financially. That
summed up John Aspinall's morality. John was a determined

and charismatic character and he made those reasons difficult to argue with. He often talked of his ambition and his perfect evening. He dreamed he was playing poker in a luxurious, upper-class club and saying: "Your monkey, Duke, and up a grand."'

John Burke admits he could have objected to Aspinall's devious methods and simply walked off. He didn't. Instead, he witnessed other victims being taken, including one important company chairman.

Why? Ambitious politicians often find it helpful to their advancement not to be burdened with sincere, rigid principles and beliefs; gamblers and entrepreneurs also find an advantage in having a flexible moral code.

One game led to another, the stakes and, increasingly, the chances taken, ever higher. At the Westbury Hotel, in that affable cul-de-sac off Bond Street, a poker game was taking place in the fourth-floor room of John Burke's good friend Stephen O'Flaherty. The ebullient O'Flaherty was a superb and enormously rich businessman with the Volkswagen and Mercedes car concessions in Ireland and England. At 4 a.m. the management objected to the gambling, rather grossly pointing out that they were acting illegally on the premises. O'Flaherty booked out and never stayed at the hotel again. There were other hotels, and lots and lots of other games.

Mark Sykes attended many of them and ran some himself. He was not an Aspinall fan: 'People always thought he was a tremendous sport because he'd offer to cut the pack at the end of an evening for the total winnings, which could easily be in excess of £1,000 – in the 1950s, quite an amount. The helpful Aspinall was always the first to cut the pack.

'What all these people didn't know is that it's one of the easiest things in the world to win, usually with a card that is a very slightly different shape and in the shuffle put next to an ace. A card player like Aspinall could perform that trick in a second – he didn't need to tamper with the cards before the cut.

'He always sought the upper hand no matter what. He could be very disagreeable. I went out with his half-sister at one time and I don't think she had much time for him. Aspinall was an absolute world-class shit, but he was good company. That's the story, really. He was a world-class shit. A very good phrase which I will always remember in conjunction with Aspinall is, "It's very easy to steal from your friends."'

Unfortunately, even with the card tricks, John Victor Aspinall was not making enough money at poker to satisfy his expectations. As the perceptive John Burke – an eyewitness and primary connection to all that happened – has pointed out, Aspinall was quick to learn the rules and terms of engagement, and to use them fully to his own advantage.

Which he did when he first met the Vicar.

2. PREACHING TO THE CONVERTED

**For what we are about to receive,
may the Lord make us truly thankful . . .**

TRADITIONAL DINNER GRACE

He was middle aged, middle class, plump from good food and red in the face from the bottle of claret he normally had with dinner. He was tough, told risqué stories, was foul-mouthed in general conversation, and they called him the Vicar in the way that classroom giants are known as Tiny.

Leslie Price, the Vicar, had no illusions about humanity. It was there to be fed off. He had a voice, but not one for sermons. He was a grand storyteller, spouting his tales above a chequered waistcoat bursting with good living. He was also an extremely clever gambler with gangland connections. Indeed, blessed wcrc the strong.

John Aspinall first encountered the Vicar in the early 1950s. It was a 'road to Damascus' moment. They were both on the make, Aspinall with his poker parties and Price running highly lucrative gambling evenings.

Aspinall's connections were immaculate even before he saw the light; he knew people who were happy to gamble and, so much more importantly, reliable in paying up. As well as the trusted Ian Maxwell-Scott, his crowd included people like Anthony Blond of the Marks & Spencer family; Johnnie Holbeach, the future powerhouse of Gordon's Gin; the affable but naughty Peter West; Richard Parkes; Dominick Elwes; newspaper heir Vere Harmsworth; Alan and Colin Clark (sons of Lord *Civilisation* Clark); and wealthy American Gerry Albertini. It was a glamorous set, enlivened by the presence of people like Lady Jane and Lady Annabel Vane-Tempest-Stewart, daughters of the Marquess of Londonderry, and Lady Annabel's future husbands, the tall Old Etonian Mark Birley (first) and Jimmy Goldsmith (second), and Jimmy's brother Teddy. Princess Margaret's crowd hovered and added another cloak of sophistication. When the veneer was stripped away, all that was there was more veneer. For the majority it was all jolly fun; for Aspinall it was a deadly serious business.

Perhaps appropriately, his life up to that point had been something of a lottery. He was born in Delhi on 11 June 1926. His father – or so he believed – was Robert (Robby) Aspinall, a medical officer in the Indian Army. His mother, originally Mary Grace Horn, was the daughter of a civil engineer. Robby and Mary Grace had married just two weeks after they had met on the dance floor where Robby was a star turn. Their first son Robert, always known as 'Chips', was born in 1924.

John, the second son, was very much his mother's favourite. At the age of 6 he was sent with his brother to a boarding school at Eastbourne and the boys saw their parents only once a year for the next half-dozen years. They spent their holidays either with their maternal grandparents or with a local farmer, Jack Pring, who became a surrogate father and taught young John the lore of the countryside.

His parents divorced when John was 12 but it wasn't until he was 26 years old that he discovered one effect of his mother's unhappy marriage and another influential 'Bruce' in his life. He found out that his true father was an Army officer, later Major-General George Bruce, and that he had been conceived under a tamarisk tree beside a lake in Uttar Pradesh after a regimental ball. Mrs Aspinall's extramarital lover had then been a young captain in the infantry with something of a reputation, being apparently a useful swordsman privately as well as professionally.

In 1938, Aspinall's mother had remarried George Osborne, who had beautiful home in Sussex. When her husband inherited a baronetcy, his mother, who could never conceal her delight at such a thing, became Lady Osborne, forever known in the Aspinall circle as Lady O.

Much of John Aspinall's ruthlessness and determination was inherited from his mother; Lady O. was a keen gambler and a remarkable woman. Once she opened a credit account with Charlie Matthews, a well-known Irish gypsy bookmaker who also ran a second-hand car business at Warren Street and a huge tyre business, Matthews of Brixton. Charlie, who bet under the name 'Monk', was himself a dodgy character noted for his 'strokes'. For once, he met his match.

Lady O.'s weekly racing account went the way that such accounts frequently do – she had a sequence of small winning weeks and duly received her modest cheque on the following Tuesday. Then one week everything went wrong; the get-out bets, small at first, got bigger and bigger and all of them lost, right up to the final plunge on Saturday. So, for the first time, in her Ladyship's mail on the Tuesday morning, instead of a cheque from Monk, a large bill arrived. Charlie waited confidently to reclaim everything he had already paid Lady O., plus some more.

John Burke recalls it well: 'Perhaps he waited patiently – knowing Charlie I doubt this – but he certainly waited. After about a week he began to get a trifle worried and so he telephoned Lady O. to ask for his cheque. Charlie's telephone manner was, of course, superficially the most friendly. "'Ow

about a little kite, love – 'ave you forgot?" He was not, however, prepared for the effect that his friendly words had on
Lady O.

'Adopting a majestically haughty tone, the "Lady" verbally
tore a strip off the unfortunate bookie – never before or since
has a message so full of disdainful contempt been carried over
the telephone wires between East Sussex and Brixton.

'"Matthews! How dare you telephone up your social
superiors and ask for money; I will have the law on you!" was
the final outburst before Lady O. slammed down the receiver.
The account remained unpaid, and when we wanted to wind
Matthews up we'd only have to ask, "Have you seen Lady O.
recently?" The air would immediately turn blue.'

The one driving force in her life was the intense devotion
and protective urge she felt for her son, John. The she-tiger
guarding her cubs from danger was as harmless as a teddy
bear compared to Lady O. when she felt that her darling
needed support. John Burke knew her well and was often in
awe at how calculating she could be: 'Though not overly
intelligent, she had a devious, totally crooked mind and was an
accomplished schemer.' The famous Whites Club description
of Lady O. was that she had 'the mind of a Borgia in the body
of a cook'. The remark has been attributed variously to the
Duke of Devonshire, Bernard van Cutsem and Henry Vyner.
Whoever said it was spot on.

However she behaved to others, Lady O. looked after her
youngest son as far as she could. Yet the great influential event
for the teenaged John Aspinall was his reading of H. Rider
Haggard's *Nada the Lily*, the tale of Umslopogaas, illegitimate
son of an admired Zulu king, Shaka. Against all odds, and
standing alone, Umslopogaas becomes a magnificent warrior
and triumphs; the book began for Aspinall a lifelong obsession
with the Zulus and with tribalism.

Many others have tried to explain the psychology and the workings of Aspinall's mind, yet even as they do, it's clear they have never totally grasped it. John Aspinall was a curious, complex character. He firmly believed in the survival of the fittest, that the strong would rule the world, the weak go to the wall. He was an unmatched mixture of good and evil. John Burke saw his man in glory and in desperation, often as startled as a rabbit in the headlights. He explained:

'He had very definite set views about some things. Once he got them into his mind, he would convince himself that he was right, then no power on earth would make him change his mind. I know that he would justify his conduct in his own mind, saying it was like a tiger's entitlement to kill deer.

'Following from that, he was entitled to rob the rich, the decadent, and weak and useless people in order that he had the funds to do what was important in the world. In his eyes. In his eyes alone.'

Lady O. arranged the more secular aspects of her favoured son's upbringing with the help of the always kindly and generous Sir George, who paid for him to go to Rugby. In 1943 the school suggested he did not return for another term. After Rugby, he spent three years in the Royal Marines.

In 1947, aged 21, he went up to Jesus College, Oxford, where the first thing he learned was guilt-free gambling fever. It was there that he established his life-long friendship with Jimmy Goldsmith. They were kindred spirits: Goldsmith had left Eton as a 16-year-old following an extraordinary gambling success, an accumulator bet on three horses, Merry Dance, Bartisan and Your Fancy at Lewes, a roll-up, which netted him £8,000. So when Jimmy Goldsmith turned up at Oxford to visit his brother Teddy and met John Aspinall and his set, he was in financially sharper shape than the others. But it was determination, single-minded attitude and poker playing which made Aspinall warm to him, though Aspinall was seven years older. It was a mutual attraction.

Mirroring his new friend's audacious gambling, Aspinall risked his entire term's grant of £70 on a horse called Palestine in the 2,000 Guineas. It won in a photo finish at 7–2 on, and Aspinall's faith in himself soared – even with short odds.

The winnings were as short-lived as the odds. He was sent down for missing his 1950 finals, feigning illness and slipping away, with the ever-ready Ian Maxwell-Scott, by hired Daimler to Royal Ascot, which had the bad luck to clash with the examinations.

The affable Maxwell-Scott was most certainly a leading star in the gambling set. At Grand National time in May 1956, he and John Burke were staying as house guests of Richard and Angela Parkes at their flat in Wellbeck Street. The two young men were in financially embarrassing circumstances – they were broke.

Maxwell-Scott was a long-odds player at the horses; he always bet on outsiders. For the Grand National he worked out that ESB (Electricity Supply Board in Ireland), quoted at 66–1, represented the best value in this tricky lottery. A borrowed two pounds was his total gambling capital, and he courageously wagered it all on ESB to win. John Burke recounts the story still with some amazement in his voice:

'Two pounds may sound a paltry sum of money. However, fifty years ago and in the prevailing financial climate of the Parkes' house guests, it was far from paltry, in fact, we considered Maxwell to be brave to the point of foolhardiness for betting his all on such a long shot. The race is well documented in the history books. The Queen Mother's horse Devon Loch came over the last jump well in front of all the other horses still remaining in the race and was striding out to win easily, when, just before the winning post, he slipped and slithered down onto his belly.

'This allowed ESB, who was a long way behind in second place, to gallop slowly past the prone Devon Loch and win the Grand National. We were listening to the race; the commentator was Raymond Glendenning. Glendenning pulled out all the oratorical stops in order to describe this royal equine tragedy with due solemnity. In measured funereal tones, his commentary continued:

'"A hushed silence has fallen over this vast crowd, stunned by the enormity of the tragedy they have just witnessed. While all our thoughts, our hearts and our sympathy go out to the most gallant of ladies, our Queen Mother . . ."

'At just about this point, when ESB had safely passed the post and was confirmed as winner, the Parkes' drawing room was shattered by an eruption of raucous laughter. It was Ian braying, in his own inimitable aristocratic tongue.

'"Wup! Wup! Wup Wup!" he thundered. "Fuck the Queen Mother; I had a two-er on ESB!"

'Financial reality totally scuppered Glendenning's eloquent bathos.'

Financial reality was not something which interfered with John Aspinall's lifestyle. He never took to regular employment, despite the efforts of his stepfather Sir George to help him with his 'connections'; instead he spent his days at the racecourses and his evenings, when possible, gambling at cards. He was often lucky at the races and was regarded as a good judge – of rich men as well as of horses.

He became friends with Gerry Albertini, a rainbow of genetics but American by birth and wealthy from his family's clever US business investments with Reynolds/Veitch. 'Gerry was always kind and generous, to all of us, not just John,' remembers John Burke. 'With Gerry's financial help, John had a few spectacular coups at the races. But he would lose just as spectacularly. Gerry or Richard Parkes would usually bail him out but that was not a balance John liked at all.'

What could Aspinall do? The ongoing drawback for a man with irregular income was the lack of regular funds.

'Yet, whenever he had a "sure thing" he was able to get the money to bet; he would never miss an opportunity. It didn't matter who had to lose their money, or how they lost it,' recalls John Burke, who would become a friend of the Vicar.

John Burke would play poker with Leslie Price but was never invited to his professional chemmy games – for the obvious reasons that he was too good and canny a card player and, more importantly, was not rich. With the chemmy games, the Vicar had picked a winner. It made him rich, bought him a spectacular home in Esher. There he had installed a slot machine, a one-armed bandit. It was intended to distract not his card players, but his staff. The gamblers tipped generously and the Vicar calculated, correctly, that he'd get that money too, with the waiters and others playing the machine. He did not miss much.

His success was built not on a grand idea but a clever one: convenience for his clientele. In the late 1940s and early 1950s Britain's wealthy gamblers would fly from Lydd airport in Kent to France, to the casino of Le Touquet, to feed their gambling habit and perhaps play golf during the day. Deauville was also close by. There, of course, the game of choice was chemmy. When he published *Casino Royale* in 1953, Ian Fleming had James Bond gambling in north-eastern France, in the fictional town of Royale-les-Eaux, because that's exactly where the action was at the time the book was set, in 1950.

The Vicar decided, correctly, that if the games were closer to home there would be even more action and, for him, profit. Of that he was certain. For with chemmy there was a crucial advantage to the host – there was a 5 per cent charge, the *cagnotte*, on every winning bank. No matter how the players prospered, with the French rules – that 5 per cent charge on at least 50 per cent of hands – the house always won. In Leslie Price's games, he, the Vicar, was blessed with profit at every evening's gambling.

Still, he made one error. After he had begun running his so highly lucrative chemmy games on a carousel basis at friends' and associates' flats and homes in the West End and Belgravia, he went, as he often did, to the Star Tavern, the fiefdom of the late and lunatic landlord Paddy Kennedy.

The Star stands on a quiet cobbled mews at the end of Belgrave Square. An early nineteenth-century building, it was created to house the servants from the rich homes of Belgravia. When Paddy Kennedy took over the house, the catacomb of domestic rooms had been opened up, with scrubbed pine tables and two fireplaces in the downstairs bar and the kitchen upstairs with another bar. Upstairs was, de facto, private, in that if Kennedy took a dislike to a customer he or she was told to get lost. Indeed, the only thing extraordinary or spectacular about the place was the landlord.

The Star, although a little obscured by the arch framing the northern entrance to Belgrave Mews West, was a magnet for an eclectic cast of characters, many of whom considered luck itself a skill – or maybe an art form. Rather like life. John Burke often played spoof at the bar with the great painter and, as a young man, highly enthusiastic gambler, Lucian Freud. They were regulars, as were Bobby McKew and, in the mid 1950s, John Aspinall. Over time they chatted with glamorous characters like Chelsea-set leader, the well-connected Michael 'Dandy Kim' Caborn-Waterfield, and soon-to-be Great Train Robber Bruce Reynolds. There would be Billy Hill at one end of the bar and Wally Virgo, Commander of Scotland Yard's Serious Crime Squad, at the other, a case in those quiescent days of law and disorder, and vice versa. Between them would be the man all the regulars called 'Boss', once the richest man in the world. The Eton-educated Sandhurst graduate and newly divorced Maharaja of Baroda, Sir Pratap Sinh Gaikwad, enjoyed the cut and thrust of the company.

When he was at Eton he'd been approached by a master and reprimanded for not attending church.

'But why would I?' asked 'Boss'.

'To pray to God,' boomed the pompous master.

'Sir, in my country, I am God.'

He didn't act the part at the Star, however. He was also always happy to buy a round, ordering in his soft, agreeable English–Indian accent, which endeared him even more to the crowd. Eddie Chapman reckoned 'Boss' was the nicest foreign person he ever met.

Paddy Kennedy, the landlord, a biggish, often exhausting man with dark hair, dark humour and either a grin or a scowl on his red Irish face, was as much an attraction as the customers. He was tough, loud, and if anyone – it didn't matter who – upset him, he would physically eject them from the premises. But his bark could be worse than his bite. One evening Eddie Chapman was there with his friend and associate Jim Hunt. Kennedy placed his chin on the bar and challenged Hunt: 'Go on, hit me!'

Hunt's fist moved about three inches; Kennedy was out for twenty minutes.

Kennedy said he wouldn't allow the Kray Twins, then fledgling gangsters, through the door, but the reality was that they would not have tried to drink there because Billy Hill did, and he was the guv'nor. John Burke met one of the Krays one evening when he was at dinner with Kennedy at a nearby restaurant. Not long afterwards at the Star he inquired of Billy

Hill what their status was and got the quiet reply: 'I let them do little jobs for me sometimes.'

Paddy Kennedy always got on well with John Burke, Bobby McKew and the Vicar – as he did with Billy Hill, who used to sit in a corner of the pub playing cards for astronomical stakes with Peter Rachman. Rachman's protégé Raymond Nash, a large, gregarious, clever and colourful Lebanese, would sit watchfully at another table.

Peter Rachman's name cast a notorious shadow over London in the 1950s and early 1960s. Part of his infamous legacy was to the English language. The *Concise Oxford Dictionary* defines Rachmanism as: 'Exploitation of slum tenants by unscrupulous landlords. From P. Rachman, London landlord of the early 1960s.'

'What used to astonish us,' recalls Bobby McKew, 'was that Bill sat with a pack of cards on his lap and openly cheated Rachman. There wasn't much of an attempt to disguise what he was doing. He'd sometimes drop cards, aces and kings, on the floor and pick them up. There was no attempt at subtlety.

'It was all about Rachman not losing face. He didn't want to be known as a man paying protection money, but if you didn't look after Bill, whatever you were up to quickly got shut down. This way Bill got his money and Rachman got to get on with what he was doing.'

It was an eccentric environment. Paddy Kennedy did not let much upset him, perhaps because his own behaviour was not always to order. To get Elizabeth Taylor to move seats, when she was on a visit to London promoting her movie *Beau Brummell*, he ordered: 'Get your fat arse off that stool and let my friend sit down.' She happily obliged.

John Burke recalls the ambassador from an African nation being rather more flummoxed than the Hollywood star by Kennedy. The ambassador and his retinue had arrived for lunch. It was busy. He enquired several times what the always short-fused Kennedy would recommend from the menu to be finally startled by a bellowed: 'Try the roast missionary, you black heathen bastard!'

The Star was a refuge for many, including genuine refugees. 'Achtung' Alfie was an Austrian Jew who had escaped Hitler's regime, and was well liked. One evening in the Star he went on and on about his brother who had fled to America and made his fortune after the war. 'I should have gone to America,' moaned Achtung. Kennedy was getting irritated, but still Achtung whinged on: 'I should never have bothered with bloody London, a waste of time.'

That did it. Kennedy cracked down a pint glass on the bar and turned on Achtung Alfie: 'You snivelling bastard – you should have stayed in Germany: you'd 've been a grand lampshade.'

'There's no doubt what Paddy was,' says John Burke. 'An argumentative, intolerant, racist, sexist chauvinist. He was also the kindest and most generous man I've ever had the pleasure to get drunk with.'

Kennedy employed a superb barman who called his boss 'Sir' and gave the customers their titles and due reverence. When 'Boss' Baroda saw Kennedy in a dreadfully hungover state he offered to buy him some salvation.

'His Royal Highness would like to buy you a drink, sir.'

'Tell the cannibal to make it a large one.'

Yes, he could be affable when he wanted. Kennedy owned a beautiful Alsatian called Danny who had a famous trick. When the pub was full, the dog would bound down the stairs and Kennedy would command: 'Danny! Show us what girls do to get fur coats.' Danny would roll over on his back with his paws in the air. Danny knew the score, as did the girls in the minks.

It was at the Star that the Vicar met his match, though of

course he didn't realize that he was about to be screwed. He allowed John Aspinall to, as it were, look up his cassock.

'Another drink, Vicar?' asked Aspinall in the upstairs room, nodding for top-up gin and tonics for himself, John Burke and their companion. The Vicar was clearly prospering. On occasion, Burke and Aspinall had met him at the afternoon races, but Leslie Price usually kept vampire hours.

'You're looking in great form,' Aspinall told the Vicar. He then went on to enthuse about Leslie Price's success and his own more precarious gambling life. The Vicar, overcome either by the gin or the charm, quietly explained in the crowded, smoke-filled bar that his upmarket evenings of *chemin de fer* were always odds-on winners.

Then he made his mistake: 'Aspers, why don't you come along one evening. Burkie here is a poker man, but you come, you'll like it.'

The chemmy evening was on the upper floor of a house, since knocked down and redeveloped, off Park Lane. Aspinall pointed it out to John Burke as the place where he hit the jackpot, although his funds were in 'a spot of bother' that first night and he lost.

Aspinall told John Burke he had gone to the game with the casually charming court jester Dominick Elwes who, in company, softened Aspinall's sharper edges. Elwes's girlfriend Sarah Chester-Beatty was there too, and she, as bad luck required, provided the cash to pay off the two men's losses at the Vicar's evening.

Aspinall immediately spotted the secret of the Vicar's affluence – the *cagnotte*, the table slot into which went 5 per cent of every winning bank. The *cagnotte* depended on the bravado and the bankroll of the player who had called 'banco'. As the evening progressed it steadily mounted, shoe after shoe, hour after hour. Some shoes could accrue a *cagnotte* of £100. If you were the host, like the Vicar, then chemmy was that curious and supposed impossibility, a sure thing. With the *cagnotte* in play life was, without any complaint, a cabaret.

John Aspinall grasped the possibilities immediately.

'Come again next week,' said the Vicar. 'Sorry you lost.'

John Burke was told what happened next: 'John rushed away with no intention of ever returning. The Vicar probably reckoned John would be back with more of his friends and boost the profits. Not a bit of it. John was already working out what food to serve at his own chemmy parties. One of his first stopping points was to see Paddy Kennedy who he did a deal with to provide booze on credit for the first parties. Paddy liked John, enjoyed the chancer in him.

'But with these games John played it straight. Why not? Eventually, if the debts were honoured, the money would roll in.'

The Vicar was much greedier and liked more than a little edge with his chemmy. One evening at a pub called the Bunch of Grapes in Knightsbridge he explained to John Burke how that had become a problem at his big Ascot week game:

'The Vicar had just had his big game of the year during that important racing week and quite deadpan he told me his tale of woe. The right sort of people were playing, all right, but the wrong people were winning. People who settled immediately on the dot when they lost were winning and people who were slow payers were losing. House players were getting drunk and making fools of themselves and *banco*-ing when they should be keeping quiet. Everything that could go wrong, went wrong. Leslie Price had one thing in his favour though. He had one line of defence: he employed a very experienced French croupier, a man in his sixties called Louis.

'I knew him, as did others, as "Louis the Rat". He was quite able to arrange the cards to the Vicar's advantage. After one disastrous shoe the Vicar announced, "Well, now we'll go next door and have champagne and caviar and we'll have a little relaxation and then we'll carry on playing the next shoe."

'They left the table and went into the next room to be served with the best-quality champagne and caviar and all the trimmings. One player, Lord Willoughby de Broke, who was extremely rich and the star player of the evening, did not indulge. He just came from the chemmy table for a moment and then he said to Price: "Leslie, that croupier of yours looks very tired, I think I'll give him a hand."

'Price, of course, was horrified. He had to stop this happening. I can still hear him saying: "I tried to explain to His Lordship that the croupier wasn't really tired, it was just the way he happened to look."

'He couldn't stop him and his lordship went back to the table where "Louis the Rat" had already "prepared" quite a lot of the cards. They were stacked up nicely, in every sense. Willoughby de Broke took the cards and thoroughly reshuffled them, to the total horror of the Vicar, who moaned, "All this good work done for nothing!"

Good 'mechanics' could swell the proprietor's profits. Considering that in French casinos chemmy croupiers spend hours every day for years of their lives shuffling cards and putting them into a wooden shoe, it's not difficult to imagine how, with ingenuity and more practice, they can attain quite spectacular skills. Yet, like the fastest guns of the Old West, there is always someone quicker. Or with a better idea.

It most certainly looked as if the Vicar had blessed John Aspinall, who, it appeared, had never had it so good.

3. DUCKING AND DIVING

**So we beat on, boats against the current,
borne back ceaselessly into the past.**

F. SCOTT FITZGERALD, *THE GREAT GATSBY*, 1925

When he finally got fed up with being a publicity shill for the
Rank Organization – he felt confined by the job, the hours and
by office life – Bobby McKew found himself being happily
drawn into Chapman's inner circle of associates. There was
always a scheme, a scam, a way to earn a guinea or two; there
was plenty of work outside the nine-to-five parameters,
especially in the gambling arenas.

In this world without betting shops, there were the bookmakers' allocated spots at the point-to-points and racecourses
which offered opportunistic betting, and a shaping of the odds
at times; they had long been controlled by 'Italian' Albert
Dimes, who had a justifiable reputation as a killer. He was the
official minder to Maxie Parker, one of two brothers who
bought Ladbrokes from its previous gentlemanly owners.
One had to be careful, but the young McKew's new friends
were older and more experienced, especially Billy Hill who
had overall control. They went where there was money,
not trouble. Which included the greyhound tracks, as Bobby
McKew recalled:

'At one meeting we doped five of the runners. We used
something called Luminol which was hard to detect. What we

didn't know was that the trainer, for his own reasons, had doped the sixth dog, the one the bent money was going to be on. All the dogs staggered out of the traps. It wasn't a race but an endurance test.

'Once we went to West Ham where they had a great sweeping racetrack. It was in the middle of winter and one of the dogs was drugged up so much it couldn't take the bend – it went straight into the straw bales at the side of the track. Doping certainly wasn't an art form.'

Nor were his escapades with gelignite: 'Eddie was still blowing safes and I'd go along with him. Just for company, you understand. On one particular safe in a London office I said to Eddie: "Can I do it?"

'"Go on then, have a go," he told me.

'I was very young and silly. It was a small wall safe. I put in far more gelignite than you should, and when we touched it off the door came off and it went through three walls. Each one getting bigger; you could see right outside. And there was all this confetti flying up and down in the air. The money. There was a lot of money in there. We were covered in dust and tiny bits of banknotes and I was upset at making a mess of it, but Eddie just laughed and shrugged: "Don't fuss, there's lots of other safes."

'That was Eddie, a real man.'

Bobby McKew found that Chapman could always surprise him. On a little adventure in Paris he arranged to meet Chapman at Fouquets on the Champs-Elysées. When he arrived Chapman introduced him to his companion: 'Bobby, Otto. Otto, Bobby.'

Otto was Obers-Sturmbannführer Otto Skorzeny, Hitler's favourite commando, and the most colourful and famous Waffen SS commander of the Second World War. His daring at the Battle of the Bulge and missions during the Ardennes Offensive and in Hungary during Operation Panzerfaust had won him a reputation as one of the most dangerous men in Europe.

That other dangerous man of the time, Adolf Hitler, personally ordered Otto Skorzeny to rescue Mussolini, who was being held captive. Skorzeny tracked the Italian dictator halfway across Italy for a month and a half until he finally found him at the Hotel Campo, a resort high in the Gran Sasso mountains. Skorzeny took his troops up in gliders and crashed them on the steep rocky slopes surrounding the hotel. They stormed the hotel, capturing the place without a shot being fired. After finding the room where Mussolini was held prisoner, Skorzeny entered, knocked down the chair of the radio operator, destroyed the transmitting equipment and standing to attention exclaimed: 'Duke, the Führer has sent me to set you free!' Mussolini was promptly loaded onto an aircraft that landed after the assault, and flown to Vienna.

Chapman certainly had contacts.

The idea was that Otto Skorzeny and Bobby McKew would help him rob the Vatican. During his wartime escapades, Eddie Chapman had travelled to Rome and been given a tour of the Eternal City. His eyes had all but popped out as they scanned the riches on offer. He was taken to a basement where he was shown diamonds, paintings and gold. He was overwhelmed by the riches, by the possibilities. He told Bobby McKew: 'The Church have been robbing the world for two thousand years – we should rob them.'

Bobby told him: 'It's impossible – it's better protected than Fort Knox.' But Eddie was deadly serious. 'We'll all be billionaires,' he confidently predicted.

'I'd never heard the word "billionaire" until that time,' Bobby says. 'I must say it had a magical ring to it. Eddie was certainly very excited about it. And determined to do it. He made plans and set about recruiting a "crew" to raid the Vatican with him, and Otto and I were to be in on it.

'We would have been very rich men if we'd got away with it. But where would we have spent the money? Alaska? In an igloo eating lots of salmon? There are lots of Catholics everywhere in the world who would not take kindly to the robbing of the Vatican . . . but Eddie got distracted. He got involved in a huge deal in Ghana.'

Back in London, Bobby McKew found himself kicking his heels. He had become friendly with Billy Hill and helped him with the occasional situation but it was then a casual relationship. Bored and looking for adventure, in the early summer of 1953 he sailed to the Mediterranean on his friend Dennis Ives's yacht *Zura*. They found themselves in Antibes, known for sun, sea, sailing and schemes. He also met his friend from London, Michael 'Dandy Kim' Caborn-Waterfield, one-time actor, entrepreneur and well-known social figure.

Kim was aware of Bobby's abilities. 'Always well-dressed and never short of money, he was something of a mystery man. I had seen him racing with maharajas at Ascot, dining with Errol Flynn and drinking at the Astor through the small hours with the villains who controlled the London underworld. And wherever he was there were invariably beautiful girls, all of whom pulsated with an overt sexuality. Strongly built, with wavy fairish brown hair, Bobby clearly exerted a reciprocal sexual force. He was a happy extrovert, a dedicated satyr and a lot of fun at a party, and though renowned for having a short fuse he forgave as quickly as he hoped to be forgiven.

'I was walking past the Carlton terrace in Antibes when I saw Bobby taking *petit dejeuner* on the terrace with Dennis Ives. Ives looked bemused. He was somewhat older than us, a peripheral figure who was known to specialize in arbitrage and "hot" money laundering. At a glance he could have passed as a small-town estate agent but he had a villa in Le Cannet and a yacht in the harbour. He said very little but missed nothing.'

As Ives stayed quiet, the two friends caught up with each other. Kim was playing games on the Côte d'Azure, where you can lie on the sand and look at the stars, and vice versa. He had romanced Barbara Warner in New York, and in the South of France met up once again with the teenage daughter of omnipotent Hollywood mogul Jack Warner. The strongest currency on the Riviera, outbidding the dollar, the yen and most certainly the euro, is the rich man's whim. It has been that way since the Côte d'Azure became a playground for kings and princes, wet-set hedonists and international society.

The passion for possession trumps prudence every time. Since the days of Scott and Zelda Fitzgerald – Scott the novelist, Zelda the novelty – the place has been a magnet for the creative and self-destructive. Giant figures in twentieth-century art and literature – Picasso and Cole Porter, Stravinsky and Somerset Maugham, Matisse, Rudyard Kipling and Evelyn Waugh – were all awed by the magical enchantment, the magnificent 'silver clarity' of the light.

For Jack L. Warner, one of the four brothers who founded one of the original Hollywood film studios and introduced the 'talkies', his villa on the western coastline was just another accoutrement, one more proof of his power and control. In the 1950s, every movie mogul had to have his waterfront chateau.

The west side of the Cap d'Antibes has always been accepted by the cognoscenti as a richer venue than the east. It has to do with the view towards Cannes and the setting sun. This is what provided extra cachet for Warner's Villa Aujourd'hui, a dominant, gloriously white house on the S-bend of coastline above the rocks and the Lilliputian-style harbour of L'Olivette. It was designed in 1936 by the American Barry Dierks, the fashionable architect of the time. He created floor-length windows throughout so that most of the rooms looked straight out to the Cannes headland and that unique blue sea, all the way to the horizon.

Warner enjoyed showing off this prize. There were huge and often wild parties. The guests were household names: Charlie Chaplin, Marilyn Monroe, Elizabeth Taylor; Frank Sinatra and Mia Farrow spent their honeymoon at Villa Aujourd'hui. Warner, brash and arrogant, lorded over all of it. He would take up residence with his wife Anne and daughter Barbara. Later, he would use it as a getaway to be with his lover, the French singer and actress Juliette Greco.

Kim Caborn-Waterfield was in a situation Jack Warner would never understand – he was low on funds and keen to change that situation. He had bar bills to pay and wanted to ship his car back to London. He told me:

'Jack Warner was away and Barbara said she would get money – money I had loaned her in New York – from her father's safe. It was his casino winnings and she said he had promised her a percentage as she had brought him his good luck. She gave me the cash in big ten-thousand-franc notes.

'That escapade got me the reputation of a Riviera thief. The actuality of it was that I didn't even have to open the safe which earned me that dubious renown. I was charged with stealing a quarter of a million pounds in twenty-first-century money.'

Bobby McKew was also charged.

The story of that evening at the villa on 25 August 1953 changes according to who is telling it. Later, Barbara Warner offered her version to a London courtroom: 'At about 9.30 p.m., before dinner, Kim took my arm and led me inside. He said he needed more than 100,000 francs to pay his hotel bill. He asked me if I knew where the key to my father's safe was.

'He searched in my father's bureau for the keys. I did not tell him where they were. I just stayed there. He found the keys and he opened the cupboard and then the safe. Inside he found bundles of banknotes and a travelling bag. Kim took them out. I noticed he counted the bundles to a total of 2,000,000 francs. They were in 10,000-franc notes.

'He opened the bag and went into raptures about the contents. He was going to take everything, but I resisted that. I took the bag from him and he took the bundles of notes. He said he was going to take more than the 100,000 francs. He could have taken 300,000 to 400,000 francs. He then took out a handkerchief and carefully wiped the walls and the safe to remove the prints.

'He put the money in his pocket, and when we got downstairs he told another man about the contents of the safe. His exact words were: "Do you know there is a safe with a great deal of money in it?"

'The other man was agreeably surprised. He turned to me and said: "Can anybody take it?"'

The other man was presumably Bobby McKew. There was, says Bobby, much 'ducking and diving' following the villa robbery: 'The French authorities wanted me to appear in court but I refused. At the time I just pissed off and tried to stay out of trouble and out of France. That Dennis Ives had some of our money and he might have half grassed. All the time they were saying they wanted to interview me, but I've never wanted to be interviewed. I never made a statement then. I won't make one now. I never make a statement.

'Once I was on the boat scrubbing the deck and they came down looking for "Mr McKew". I looked like a tramp and said he wasn't there and they went away. I was the only person who never made a statement.

'The money? Oh, it went to some interesting places, and people. There was strict currency control at the time, so having that sort of cash in your pocket was useful.'

There was an intriguing aftermath to the Riviera robbery when Bobby McKew returned to London, reflecting the power of the then 42-year-old Billy Hill. The Duke and Duchess of Windsor were visiting, staying in the English countryside. And the Duke of Windsor had been robbed. It was something that has never been reported, but what concerned the Duke most was his missing diary; it was a five-year day-at-a-time diary which detailed his movements and meetings, his opinions of the Royal Family and of politicians. It was crackerjack material. Bobby McKew remembered:

'I was out on the Thames with Eddie Chapman and Jimmy Hunt. We were just messing about, trying this boat out, and when we came back to the dock a couple of police squad cars appeared. It was Fabian [the famed Superintendent Robert Fabian, on whose career a popular 1950s television series was based], and he wanted to know if Eddie could help with the return of the Duke's diary. It seemingly had lots of delicate material, who he was seeing, talking to, who, or possibly what, he was screwing, that sort of thing.

'They were quite willing to do a deal. No questions asked. Fabian knew Eddie very well, there was no question about that. As it turned out, Eddie couldn't help. But someone must have, for nothing was ever heard about the diary – and no one was nicked.'

This sort of approach was not unique, says Bobby McKew, even if, in the Duke of Windsor's case, it was extremely discreet. When Gordon Richards, the only jockey to be knighted, was robbed of the golden spurs presented to him by the present Queen's father, King George VI, the higher echelons of Scotland Yard were in something of a frenzy. 'One of the senior coppers was friendly with Billy. Bill had some very heavy contacts there. One day he came off the phone and said, "I've just been talking to ___ _____ and they want a favour."

'Bill got the gold spurs back for Gordon Richards. I don't know how, but I do know he never got a note of thanks from that man Richards who knew what had happened. Every time Richards' name came up Bill would mutter, "That fucking pygmy."'

By now Bobby McKew had a strong association with Billy Hill but was also close to an Indian princess whom he had met through 'Boss' Baroda. One evening the princess introduced him to her friend Shiv Kapoor, partner of fraudster Emil Savundra who, when he arrived in London from India, opened a travel agency in Victoria. He was an enterprising chap and that enterprise took Bobby McKew on the road to Morocco, or rather to the seas off Tangier where he went to work as a smuggler. It was a clever operation, much like a VAT fraud today, where goods were smuggled into Morocco and then came out, officially stamped, as genuine Moroccan-made. It gave Bobby McKew a taste for smuggling, and he began his own operations.

The whole idea of devilry on the high seas and the centre, Tangier, has a romantic ring to it. As Bobby McKew discovered, the reality was more mundane: spark plugs, nylons (the dodgy salesman's best-seller throughout Europe, particularly England), booze and cigarettes, Les Blondes for the light-coloured American tobacco. But he liked the life, the adventure. He sailed with an assortment of crews, mostly contacts from London, around from Tangier to Gibraltar, and along the Spanish coast from Marbella. In 2007 the locations have not changed, just the contraband. Bobby McKew shakes his head, recalling his innocence.

'I remember another smuggler asking me, "When are you going over to Spain?"

' "On Friday."

' "Would you take a couple of suitcases for me?"

' "What's in them?"

' "Hash."

'I thought: "How dare you!" Hash! Drugs! I was very priggish about it. I don't know how many months later I woke up at four in the morning and thought: "Oh God, what I am being such an idiot for?"

'In those days dope just didn't enter our minds. We were getting gin and Scotch out of bond at six shillings a bottle and selling it on for a couple of quid a bottle. But we were really into cigarettes, which is where the big profit was. We put them into Spain and sometimes on long hauls to Italy. We worked all around the Mediterranean. There were quite a few Brits. One smuggling boat captain was "Skip" Edwards, the brother of the comedian Jimmy Edwards who was a big radio star as Pa Glum on *Take It From Here*.

'Lots of different sorts of people love it out there.'

Bobby McKew was commuting between London and Morocco. He was socially adept, a businessman with interests abroad. He was now seeing Anna Gerber, a waterski champion and the daughter of South African multimillionaire 'Lucky' Jack Gerber. His friend Billy Hill, although he did not divorce his wife Aggie, had become enamoured of 'Gypsy' Riley, who as Phyllis Riley had left East London, taken up with 'road' people and then been recruited by Maltese pimps. Then, to all purposes, she became Mrs Billy Hill. The two couples would often go out for an evening together.

And with Billy Hill interested in the action in Morocco and financing some of the operations, they all went to Tangier. Bobby McKew already had accommodation, but Anna Gerber found a flat for Billy Hill. In 1954 it cost £4 a week and in 2007 it was still in Hill's name.

Billy Hill liked the Mediterranean too. And Tangier. 'Tricky Tangier, lovely little spot,' he called it. The city is on the North African coast at the western entrance to the Strait of Gibraltar, where the Mediterranean meets the Atlantic Ocean off Cap Spartel. For opportunists it was all about location, location, location.

The smuggling was good, regular if not spectacular business. Nonetheless, as well as the irritation of customs boats there were the hazards of French gangsters and the power of the Union Corse, the criminal organization which originated in Corsica but was now a highly corporate underworld operation run out of Marseilles. Billy Hill had connections with its leader, Marcel Francisi. That link, similar to but stronger than those he had with the American Mafia, allowed him to take out some insurance on his and Bobby McKew's enterprises. In return the Union Corse needed Hill's backup for any operation in London. Foreign travel was good for Billy Hill's mind. And, in time, very profitable.

Bobby McKew is admiring of the Union Corse. 'Much more powerful than most people ever realized – tougher than tough, more so than the Italian or American Mafia.'

Somehow Hill, whose seventeen years behind bars had left him with a lifelong penchant for prison food, especially corned beef and potatoes, connected with the world of couscous. 'I ate food I had never heard of, met people who were actually kind as well as educated, who were friendly although they were loaded with gelt,' is how he described this particular 'abroad'.

That was his publicity statement. Privately, Billy Hill imported his own food: corned beef, sides of meat, tomatoes and eggs. Bobby says, 'He used to go to a restaurant called the Nautilus in Tangier and give them the food. Then at night he'd come and order dinner and he'd pay for his own food. He was unusual.'

Hill was more than unusual. He had been involved in scores of gang fights, and cut and punched his way out of trouble. His reputation was fearsome, giving him an iron grip on his crime empire. He stood for no nonsense. At an illegal gambling club he ran in Soho a punter, Sammy Naylor, who owed Hill £200, appeared one night to gamble. Naylor wanted to win back his losses. Hill explained that he must pay off his debt first.

'You can't get blood out of stone,' objected Naylor.

Hill gave him a light slap on the face. 'Sammy, who says you're made of stone?'

The debt was paid the next day.

Hill watched over all the details, small debts, big robberies. All the people who worked with or for him, and many of the lawmen, the judiciary and the police who tangled with him, credit him as a criminal mastermind. One of twenty-one children born into a family of criminals in 1911 in Seven Dials, near Leicester Square in London, he was 'at it' from his youth. He became a house burglar in the late 1920s and moved on to specialize in smash-and-grab raids targeting furriers and jewellers in the 1930s. During the Second World War, he moved into the black market, operating in foods and petrol. He also supplied forged documents for deserting servicemen.

In the later 1940s he was charged with burgling a warehouse and fled to South Africa, where he took over illegal activities at a string of Johannesburg nightclubs. After being arrested for assault, he was extradited to Britain, where he was convicted and jailed for the warehouse robbery. It didn't deter him. Prison never had, just as it never seemed to bother 'Mad' Frankie Fraser, who appeared to have no regrets about spending much of his life in jail when I met him in July 2006. He didn't, they say, get his nickname for nothing. We went for a wander near his home in south London and past a pub called the Stroke of Luck.

Frankie, aged eighty-two, his hair styled like a Brylcreem advertisement and coal black, wearing a blue pinstripe suit, and pristine apart from one spot of blood on the collar of his freshly ironed white shirt where he'd nicked himself shaving, was in lively humour. Brighter and louder than a brass band, he bubbled down Browning Street ('after the fuckin' poet, don't you know?'). He looked over at what had once been white and brown paint, now peeling in faded shreds from the pub: 'Stroke of Luck? – fucking place has been closed down. We'll go round the corner.'

The landlord and the scattering of lunchtime customers greeted him like a returning war hero. We sat in the corner where he nursed a vodka and tonic. Yes, Billy Hill, whom he worked for most of his life, when not in jail, was a mastermind who ran London's crime scene like a chess game.

'Bill didn't know the meaning of the word fear. That's why he was special. If fear had come anywhere near him, he would already be plotting how to go around it. Or he'd get in first and wipe them out before they could have him. At certain times, he knew every cop that mattered in London. He could pick up the phone to the top men. I reckon at one time he had a hotline to the Commissioner. They knew they could trust him. There has never been another man like him before or since. If you wanted to pull a bank job, rob a post office, or make chalk drawings on the pavements of London, you had to have Bill's OK.

'I first met him when I was very young and getting a name for myself – not Bill's standards, but always in plenty of trouble in prison. Your name went around. I done a call for Bert Rogers, him and his brother. They were in Chelmsford Prison with Bill before the war, when Chelmsford Prison was a Young Penal Service institution for those around 21 to about 28. Bert Rogers knew Bill well and he introduced us to him.

'Some years later, 1947 or beginning of 1948, I was in Wandsworth Prison with Bert Rogers and who come on the exercise but Billy Hill. He had just got three years for a warehouse job. Bill didn't want to hang around that long. That's when he tapped up Jack Rose. Jack Rose had the cats [whipped by the cat-o'-nine-tails] done three times, he'd been birched for punching screws and he wasn't getting out early.

'Bill said to me: "Do you think he'd stand for it?"

'I said: "What do you mean, Bill?"

'"Well, get him to attack a screw – he's lost all his remission; I jump up and save the screw . . . Do you think he'd stand for it?"

'I said: "Provided he's going to get some dough out of it, of course he would, Bill. He'd love it."

'We approached Jack and he did love it. He got a monkey (£500), which was a lot of money in 1947. A lot of money. A day or two later, all of a sudden, Jack jumped up and shouted at a particular screw: "What do you keep looking at me for, you bastard?"

'The screw hadn't looked at him at all! But Jack goes for him, starts attacking him. Bill's rushed in there and pulled Jack off the screw and calmed it all down. For his good deed Bill got a few extra months on remission. Everybody was happy. Including the screw. What I didn't know then is that Bill had the screw in his pocket 'n' all! Bill always covered all the angles.

'I go way back to when Bill was a kid and I would put Billy above everyone else. In our life, our world, I would put him above everyone. As much as Charlie and Eddie [Richardson], which are two terrific guys, and Italian Albert, terrific guy, nevertheless, I would still put Bill up there. I haven't met another one yet.'

Once out of jail, Hill planned daring 'larks' including a

1952 post office van robbery and a spectacular bullion heist in Lincoln's Inn Fields in 1954. Ten days before the bullion job he had announced his retirement, and when the robbery took place he was giving interviews about his 'retirement' in the South of France. He was never charged.

Cat burglar George 'Taters' Chatham, who only stole the very best from the very best of people (he styled himself 'Burglar to the Gentry') found himself in deep difficulties after the post office robbery. Chatham liked to think of himself as a Raffles figure. He wore Savile Row suits, drove a drophead Mercedes, and in his long career as a gentleman thief (much of it spent in jail) stole an estimated £100 million worth of treasures.

He was on the Hill team for what was then Britain's biggest armed robbery. The gang pretended to be a film crew working near the post office depot by St Paul's Cathedral. Chatham disconnected the alarm system on the mail van and Hill's mob moved in and hijacked it. The take was £287,000. Of that, £15,000 went to Chatham – who immediately gambled it away at Billy Hill's gaming tables. Chatham then attempted to 'retrieve' his share from Hill's safe but was caught. Hill did not punish him – he would get even more money from the gambling cat burglar after his next job. It was a mature, pragmatic move.

Hill was forty-three then, a snappy dresser in his handmade suits and a fedora with the brim neatly snapped forward. His hair was carefully dyed and slicked back with Morgan's Pomade. By then he had proved himself as a fighter: now he saw himself more as a businessman, someone to gain advantage from every opportunity. He had no intention of ever going back to jail. There were escape routes mapped out for every hint of trouble. Hill was not a literate man but he was numerate. You could tell him the income and outgoings of the

Star Tavern and he would give you the percentage profit in seconds. The point was that Billy Hill was only interested in profit, and in opportunities for making it.

His passion for moneymaking was illustrated after Bobby McKew and another of Hill's henchmen, the engaging gambler, club owner and smuggler Patsy Murphy, got into trouble at a London club popular with lesbians.

'Patsy had started out doing photographs of tourists in Trafalgar Square – Bill had given him permission to do that for a few bob in return. Much like these street folk in Soho now have to pay over a backhander if they want peace,' says Bobby.

'One night we went out to the Star. Afterwards, we all went round to this lesbian club we'd heard of. Some tart asked Patsy's wife, who looked about seventeen, to dance.

'They danced, and the next thing a butch one came along and said that Patsy's wife was dancing with her girlfriend. Before we knew it, they were on the floor. I said to Patsy, "That's your old woman under there." Patsy pulled her to the top and pulled her over. The next thing mayhem broke out.

'I never knew lesbians could fight like that. There was blood everywhere and I got hit in the chin. It was a terrific bump, a Sonny Liston with a bit of Ali spin on it. I happened to be standing about a foot from the wall. I hit the wall but if I hadn't, I would have gone down.

'I remember hitting someone over the head with a bottle. Gave someone a good bash.

'But everyone was at it, all over the place; I don't think they'd had such fun for a long time. Anyway, there were bodies everywhere and we left.

'The police came but we managed to get out. About two or three days later, and it shows what Billy was like, I got the command performance. "Come round, have a cup of tea."

'I went round and he said in that quiet, drawling voice of his: "Here, what was all that commotion in that club the other night?"'

'I told him. He said that he wanted me to do him a favour. He had his dead eyes on: "Look, I'll give you a monkey and you take a monkey up to Murphy but you must promise me one thing – you don't go in there any more. Ever, ever."'

'For a monkey you could buy a car!'

'I remember going up to Murphy who lived up in Maida Vale. He shouted: "Oh, God, a monkey. We'll never go in there again."'

'We didn't, thank God.

'It wasn't until about a year or two later that we found out that the owner of the club had gone to Bill and she said, "I want that McKew and Murphy killed." Bill said: "It will cost you ten grand."'

'He got the ten grand and gave us a monkey each! That was Bill. But we got on well. That was just a little bit of business. But if I hadn't kept my word and stayed away from the club I suppose he would have had to enforce his contract.

'Ain't life grand – or nine grand, as Billy would have seen it.'

Indeed, Billy Hill considered himself a winner. He was in profit. Which was perfect.

There are hosts of stories of Hill taking money to 'sort out' problems, of everything from 'cuttings' to contract killings. There are stories of bodies being burned. How true are they?

Hill, in his memoirs, *Boss of Britain's Underworld*, suggests that all he did was stop people doing 'foolish things'. He and his team solved problems. There is one ominous note about this enterprise: the name he gave it, saying: 'During 1952 to 1953 we undertook three hundred missions on our Murder Inc. business.'

Bobby McKew remembered one 1950s gangland get-together, a show of support for a nightclub owner: 'One night at the Pigalle there was a charity evening and a row broke; the police arrived in a rush of cars. They leaped out and asked the doorman, "Who's in there?"

'He told them. There was Billy and us at one table. At the next table was Albert Dimes and his crowd. Beside him was the Twins' table. Billy Hill, Albert and the Krays. The police wouldn't come in. If they had everybody would have united, for the police were the police, so they never came in.

'Mind you, it wasn't a terrible row. It was only that fellow Tony Mellor who got killed afterwards in Soho. I think he got shot. Or maybe he had his throat cut. Can't remember.'

The nightclub 'row' at Al Burnett's club in Swallow Street had begun when Mellor, who was into girls and pornography, upset Billy Hill. Hill made no fuss, just got up and hit Mellor over the head with a big glass carafe of water, knocked him clean out and then poured the chilled water over him.

Bobby McKew said: 'He made his own rules and stuck to them. Always. He had an illegal club in Gerrard Street. He wouldn't go into it. It was a gambling club where all the waiters and all the ponces and pimps went in those days, because it was Soho. Billy wouldn't go in. On Saturday nights, late, at 2 a.m. or 3 a.m. Sunday morning, I'd drop him at home and go down and pick up the money. He didn't want to say "hello" and didn't want to talk to ponces. He just wouldn't go in.

'I knew a chap who was an actor and he did quite well; one day Billy asked me in a quiet voice if I was friendly with this actor.

'I said: "Yes."

'He said: "He's a ponce."

'I said: "Don't be silly."

'"He's a friend of Carol Reed's. I see him all the time at the clubs, at parties. His old woman's at it."

'"Oh, Billy," I said.

'A couple of weeks went by and I'm sitting in this cafe in Denman Street and suddenly Bobby Warren came in: he was the boxing promoter Frank Warren's uncle. He said that Billy wanted me. I went outside and Bill was there and said, "Come on, I want to show you something."

'We drove all the way down around Piccadilly, came up by Duke of York Street, St James's. He stopped the car and he said, "Who's that standing at the corner there hustling?"

'It was this actor's missus. I couldn't talk to him again. Bill wouldn't have stood for it: he paid the money, made the rules. In those days you had to be aware all the time that things and people were not always as they seemed.'

That other quiet and clever survivor, south London gang boss Charles Richardson, gave Hill respect. Over lunch at the Savoy in November 2006, he explained: 'Bill survived for such a long time because he was clever and careful and not greedy. He also looked after the people who worked for him. They were loyal and that's important.'

The Krays, who craved his empire, deferred to him. The brothers, although so much has been made of them, were but schoolboy thugs compared to Hill. There was no animosity between them. In a bedside interview in September 2000, when he was dying in a Norwich hospital, Reg Kray told me: 'With Bill the only clever thing to do was listen. He knew what and how to make everything work. I'd never known anyone make trouble go away as easily as him. He was a one-off, nobody ever like him. It was like he could see into the future. He was a businessman, lovely man – if you stayed in line.'

Billy Hill was a different breed, possibly because he came from an even tougher time and background. His chief opponents were from his own time and place, and his rival was Jack Spot. They had fallen out over who would control the London underworld, which led to a nasty fight between Spot and 'Italian' Albert Dimes on the corner of Frith Street and Old Compton Street on 12 August 1955. Dimes was working for Billy Hill and, rather to his surprise, came out top in the fight after he almost severed Spot's arm. From that point onwards, no one disputed Billy's ascendancy.

Spot and Dimes were arrested for assault. In September 1955, Spot was defended at the Old Bailey by the talented Rose Heilbron, the first woman to become a QC and the second to be appointed to the bench. She was supported in the Spot case by Sebag Shaw, a clever advocate and enthusiastic gambler from the same East End street as Sydney Summers. Sebag Shaw, who in his youth haunted spielers and card clubs, would go on, like his leader in the Spot case, to become a judge and to play his role in gambling history. And, inadvertently, to help Billy Hill.

4. GAME PIE, GEMS AND GREYHOUNDS

Mae West: Is poker a game of chance?
W.C. Fields: Not the way I play it.

MY LITTLE CHICKADEE, 1940

The genial John Burke is not a man, or gambler, to be flustered. He doesn't believe in luck. His investment is in odds, in numbers. He is a man whose practicality is probability. Yet his beliefs were to be tested as his London life raced ahead.

It seemed as if the world had suddenly woken up. So much was happening. And, seemingly, so quickly. John Burke had arrived in London in time for the Queen's coronation on 2 June 1953. He was there when Edmund Hillary and Tenzing Norgay conquered Mount Everest the following month.

The lust was for post-war sophistication: as the decade rolled on, London's bleak 'cafe society' with its old, dark-wood tables and bar, its net curtains and bentwood chairs, was replaced by coffee bars with horseshoe-shaped counters, jammed jukeboxes, painted metal chairs, high bar-stools, line drawings on the walls and striped curtains. At the fancily named coffee bars – the Mocamba, Moka-Ris, La Ronde, El Cubano, Negresco, Il Latino, Sphinx, Aloha and Las Vegas – top table was reserved for the whistling, steaming Gaggia espresso machine. For all that window-dressing, it was at the more blandly named Coffee Inn, an establishment in Park Lane where the discriminating customers were cared for and the ladies elegantly kissed on the hand by the Polish owner Teddy Knight, that society's various desperadoes congregated.

The grand society story of the day involved Jimmy Goldsmith. After two years of national service, on coronation night, in Paris, he fell in love with Isabel Patino, daughter of Antinor Patino, a Bolivian tin millionaire who objected to the love affair. The story goes that Patino said to Goldsmith, 'It is not the habit of our family to marry Jews.' To which Goldsmith retorted, 'It is not our habit to marry Red Indians.'

Isabel Patino was several months pregnant when the couple eloped and, after a legal battle with her father, married in Edinburgh. In May 1954, Isabel Patino died giving birth to their daughter Isabel. Her father never got over it. The events, of course, made headlines, something Jimmy Goldsmith would do for the rest of his life.

It was the heyday of soccer stars like Tom Finney and Stanley Matthews. Brylcreem cricketer Dennis Compton helped England to the Ashes at the Oval in August 1953, and Roger Bannister ran the mile in 3 minutes 59.4 seconds on 6 May 1954.

Then, in 1955, the Goons were on the radio, Teddy Boys were hanging around jukeboxes in the newfangled espresso bars and Bill Haley and the Comets were in the hit parade. More than half the decade had gone when, on 28 July 1956, Egypt's President Nasser nationalized the Suez Canal. Prime Minister Anthony Eden weeks later ordered an abortive invasion. A rising against communist repression was brutally crushed in Hungary. On 19 April 1956, Hollywood actress Grace Kelly became a Princess in Monaco. Elvis Presley pumped his pelvis in the interests of rock 'n' roll.

In the village which was London at that time, where people, places and deals appeared to be interconnected, Tommy Steele, hired by Raymond Nash, was getting £10 a week appearing at the Condor Club above the Gaggia-gushing and popular Sabrina coffee bar in Soho. Aspinall's world, and the real world, were changing.

By 1957, Harold 'You've never had it so good' Macmillan had ousted Anthony Eden from 10 Downing Street. As the months went by, the Broadway musical *My Fair Lady* would open for its first night in London, to a rapturous reception. The event, at the Drury Lane Theatre, was stellar: Ingrid Bergman, Dirk Bogarde, Terence Rattigan and John Strachey arrived at the theatre to be cheered by huge crowds. Yet the intriguing connection, to many observers, of Rex Harrison and Julie Andrews, of the odd couple, of two worlds intermingling, the East and West End of Eliza Doolittle and Professor Higgins, also brought into play a new phenomenon – the ticket touts. For the first time in London's theatreland there were black-market tickets selling for as much as £5 – almost five times their original price. Oh, what a lovely scam.

But not as good as chemmy. Aspinall was doing all he could to prove that, as far as his own life went, Harold Macmillan was accurate.

From the moment John Aspinall realized what a jackpot the Vicar's games could be, how they could be boosted both in grandeur and in cash with the right settings, accoutrements and players, he attacked the idea with the enthusiasm of one pursuing his first love. Which, at that time, it most certainly was.

There were gangland gambling spielers, but the only real rival for John Aspinall's enterprise was the Vicar. And he did not have the correct vowels or connections or the secret weapon of Lady O.'s game pie, which, like all her cooking, was by all accounts far more pleasant than she was.

Lady O. was an anomaly and a fixture at the games. And, surprise, she usually won – in her own enterprising way. At her son's chemmy evenings she'd provide encouragement to the players, often having a bet herself on the back of a young man's gamble; she would take her share of a win but happily forget to pay up if it was a losing hand. Her 'pocket money' often amounted to hundreds of pounds in an evening. She found pleasure in that system, and since her bets were small in comparison to their wagers, the other players were willing to regard it as 'tips'. Five-star 'tips', nevertheless.

Lady Annabel Goldsmith and Mark Birley, who had worked for the pioneer advertising agency J. Walter Thompson after leaving Oxford, before establishing the Hermès franchise in Jermyn Street, were among the usual suspects at the games, along with prominent players like Lucian Freud, Johnnie Holbeach, Dickie Muir, Nick Ackroyd, Richard Parkes and Gerry Albertini.

Aspinall – flush one day, broke the next – borrowed and cadged what he needed. He rented a good address in Mayfair, on Upper Brook Street, a short walk from Claridge's, and talked his way into getting free and good art for the walls and polished furnishings – the sort you'd inherit – for his punters to relax around. From Sussex and her Aga came Lady O.'s home cooking, from Paddy Kennedy's Star the potent but discounted booze.

And so the chemmy games began. Half a dozen or so went by and, as expected, with reliable players and the *cagnotte* all but winking its cheering connivance from the end of the table, they were extremely profitable. Aspinall used the profits to upgrade the surroundings constantly and tempt more and more high-stakes players. Like all good managers, he ploughed the profits back into the business. A great advantage for Aspinall, then and even more so later, was that the people attending his chemmy games were 'straight', in that their cheques would always be honoured at some point. This might have contributed to the error of judgement he was about to make.

Always dancing attendance was the man regarded as the

best 'house' player of the era: the urbane, intelligent, charming Peter West. He was the son of a Victoria Cross-winning
First World War Air Commodore (the RAF had a fly-past over
London when he died) and had 'honest' blue eyes (Aspinall
called them 'VC blue eyes') that told the world he could never
tell a lie. He was married to and divorced from the aristocratic
Davina Portman. 'Westie' lived on his wits. His father had
flown the skies over the English Channel – his son flew 'kites',
naughty cheques. He was a master of it, as were many of his
circle.

Forget credit cards and debit cards; the money-go-round
then was all about pieces of paper. John Burke told me how
the banking business worked then, something that now seems
extraordinary: 'We used blank cheques, pieces of paper on
which you just wrote the name and address of your bank and
signed it. In the old days of the gambling clubs, they were very
generally used. Also, of course, cash cheques were very much
involved then; you make a cheque payable to "cash" and the
person can go to the bank with it, and provided you know
them, the banker would pay the cash over the counter, if you
had the money to cover it.

'Peter West was a master of the system of getting cash you
never had to pay back. He explained this to me once in detail.
Apparently, every bank manager had a limit up to which he
could lend money without reference to head office. Say the
manager had a £5,000 limit; Peter discovered this. He would
then go in to the bank manager and get to know him and have
a chat, and open an account. Peter had superb manners and
was always beautifully dressed, and there was always a reference in conversation to his father being the Air Attaché at the
Embassy in Paris, and his father's VC, and all that sort of
thing. He'd been married to a very rich girl.

'Having established himself with the bank, he would open
an account with an agreed overdraft limit. Peter would use the

account, and the overdraft would go up slowly and eventually get up to about £4,000, and then he would stop using the account and nothing much would happen for a while, and he would get the odd polite letter from the bank suggesting he pay it off or that sort of thing. Perhaps, after a while, slightly ruder letters.

'By this time it was more than likely he was living somewhere else. What did the bank manager do? He has now got this debt which he realizes is a probably a bad debt, and if he goes to head office and tells them what has happened, he'll be in trouble himself. The manager is probably going to retire in a couple of years anyway, and he didn't want aggravation, so he would do what was simplest for him. He would sweep the debt under the carpet. With the big turnover of the bank, it would get covered up some way or other. He would keep it showing in the balance of debts or whatever. Eventually he would retire.'

But 'Westie' wasn't the only master at this. Aubrey Wallace was a skillful practioner too.

'Aubrey was rather naughty, but charming,' says John Burke. 'Aubrey and I once fancied the same horse in the Cambridgeshire Handicap and both had a good bet on it; we were flying together from Heathrow to Limerick on the afternoon of the race, which was on the BBC. The next thing I knew, it was coming through the Aer Lingus broadcast system. Aubrey had had a word with the captain.

'He always liked to "have a word". He was particularly good with bank managers.'

Once, when he needed a new bank account, Aubrey made an appointment to see a West End branch manager. He arrived armed with a cheque for £1,000 that he had got from a friend, and he chatted up the manager in marvellous style. The manager opened the account on the spot.

A couple of glasses of Tio Pepe later (it was a civilized

era), Aubrey was given a chequebook – twenty-five cheques – having lodged his cheque for £1,000. John Burke explained, 'Aubrey tended to treat chequebooks in a rather cavalier fashion and he soon got writing and paid one or two trades-men's bills; looked after a couple of bookmakers; gave a couple of dinner parties; paid by cheque. He cashed cheques and generally behaved in the way men tended to do in those happier, more casual far-off days.

'There was one major snag. The cheque for £1,000 which Aubrey had lodged was a dud. It bounced. That meant, of course, that Aubrey at no time really had any money in his account, and his cheques, as they came into the bank, also bounced and were sent back "refer to drawer". Aubrey went through the entire chequebook, and every single cheque came back. They all bounced. Zero cheques paid. It was quite a performance, and surely worthy of mention in the *Guinness Book of Records*.'

Wallace was certainly a legend in his own chequebooks; he had been nicknamed 'Educated Aub, the Downside Dude' by East End bookmaker Eddie Fleischer, but now he needed a new name under which to operate. John Burke and Richard Parkes suggested Major Jamieson; it had the right sort of sound, and rank ('Captain' was too golf-club secretary, 'Colonel' too old), to impress potential landlords and bank managers. And it did, oh, it did.

There were several variations, in these supposedly 'casual' times, of financial endeavour.

'Kiting was a very important activity in those days,' said John Burke. 'Other than "Westie", the greatest exponent of kiting I ever came across was Ian Maxwell-Scott. It was a marvellous activity – if you had the nerve.

'Kiting is very simple. If you cash a cheque on Tuesday evening at the pub/restaurant, they would lodge it on Wednesday and it will get to your bank on Friday. You have two and a half days to put in the money to cover it. Of course, if you cash a cheque on, say, Friday, after the bank closed, it would be lodged on the Monday and see your bank on the Wednesday, so you got five days to clear it. Ian would write cheques like that. When the two days were up he would have written other cheques; on the next day he would have to cash cheques and put in the cash to cover the cheques which were the first to be done.

'He was well known in the pubs all around Belgravia, and he'd go in and start off in the morning having found out from the bank how much was needed. The first call in the morning for all of us was always to the bank, and, for most of us, to Martin's Bank in Sloane Street.'

A moment from Sloane Square, Martin's Bank at 153 Sloane Street, is, alas, no more. Forget the call centres so popular with today's banks. The only numbers Martin's Bank knew in Bombay belonged to maharajas. Through their doors some of the era's most talented exponents of these extra-special social and financial skills had wandered confidently – including Leslie Price, who deposited his chemmy cheques there and issued winning payout cheques. He signed all the paperwork 'the Vicar', which the bank found quite acceptable.

Maxwell-Scott, when he knew the exact jeopardy of his finances after his morning phone call, would go on his rounds, as John Burke recalls. 'Ian would raise enough cash to cover the day's cheques. The next day he'd repeat the performance to cover the cheques two days previously. If he were lucky at the races or the tables he'd clear the thing off, and start again.

'The staff at Martin's Bank were very pleasant. I was there one day when Ian Maxwell-Scott arrived, and it was quite late. Banks shut at 3.00 p.m. in those days. It must have been about a quarter to three and he arrived with a bundle of cash he'd achieved at some of the local pubs. He was in high spirits.

'The cashier, Jim Gore – a clever, marvellous man – produced all the cheques he had that were to be paid by 3 p.m. Ian didn't have enough cash to cover all of them. One or two had to be dropped. Had to go RD – refer to drawer. But Ian had a system – he would chose the right ones to have the RD on. There might be some cheque to the bookmaker and he would say "I've to pay him." On the other hand there might be some cheque for laundry and he would say "Oh well, so what." And so on. He'd get to the end of the pile of cheques and there were two or three that were not going to be paid.

'At this point the manager came in – he'd been out for quite an alcoholic lunch – and Gore explained about the bunch of cheques and that Maxwell-Scott was putting in cash to cover all these cheques. The manager said, "Well done, well done." Then he noticed a couple of other cheques and asked, "What are these?"

'Ian, rather shamefaced, said, "Well, you see, those are the nasties."

'There was a tremendous roar of laughter and we all went off to a drinking club where Ian cashed another cheque. But not before Ian told the bank staff to "have a bit each way on Blue Nile in the 4.30".'

Ian Maxwell-Scott, Aspinall's close and trusted confidant, was still an important friend but began to fade from the scene. Aspinall had 'dropped' people like Aubrey Wallace, as they did not fit with the image he was trying to acquire. Many of those he left behind were remarkably like him, eager to make money and make their way. Maybe he didn't like the mirror image they presented.

Maxwell-Scott was a different matter altogether. He had become involved with and married Susan Clark, the daughter

of legal titan Sir Andrew Clark. As Susan Maxwell-Scott she
was much admired as a strong-minded supportive woman,
and as a gambler. After their wedding at a Catholic church in
Chelsea, in the tradition of the day, congratulatory telegrams
were read out. One was from Lady O. She expressed fulsome
wishes for their happiness and future. And, she added, the
bridegroom still owed her 'a pony' she had loaned him.

Soon afterwards Lady O.'s mailbag began to feature
strange cheques from odd places around the world, made out
from the 'Dodder Bank'. One was signed 'Aly Khan but
Maxwell can't'. Another was signed 'Inspector Rogers'. It was
the work of Paddy Kennedy and his Australian film-maker
friend 'Bluey' Hill. Lady O., it seems, was oblivious to the
prank and kept going on about 'Ian's pony'.

Aspinall did not attend his friend's wedding. No explanation has ever been given, but there was word that he had a
good tip at a race meeting the same day. Whatever went on
around it, the marriage of Ian and Susan Maxwell-Scott was a
long and glorious union. Both were devoted to each other and
to gambling – and they were loyal, always, to their friends.

Susan Maxwell-Scott's family, especially her father, were
not so keen on her choice of husband. 'They didn't like Ian's
lifestyle and they were particularly uncomfortable with his
association with John Aspinall. Also, he was a Catholic,' said
John Burke, who retains fond memories of the couple as
people he knew well and really liked. 'That's why Ian wasn't
around in the early games. It was only later that he rejoined
the team, as it were. Dominick Elwes wasn't involved, either.
He was only ever there to laugh at John's jokes and take free
food and drink. John was left to his own devices, which was
not always a good thing.'

Tipping his hat to the glory Regency days of William
Crockford, Aspinall created an aristocratic atmosphere at his
chemmy games; no longer did the gamblers feel they were

men behaving badly. Aspinall laughed with them, not at them. He entertained them with his stories. And the stories about Aspinall's chemmy parties were getting around in 1955, especially from Ludgate Circus to the Strand, along Fleet Street. As a result, Aspinall received a serious knock – and a lesson.

The *Sunday People*, then arguably Fleet Street's premier muckraker (and, apparently, the Billy Hill house journal because of the work of crime journalist Duncan Webb, who exhaustively detailed his exploits), had somehow got wind of one of the Aspinall high-flying gambling evenings. It was at the Grosvenor House Hotel, where Aspinall was staying, and with the gentlemen gamblers turned up the gentlemen of the press. It was a big story and big headlines, and bad luck for Aspinall who had to stop the games for some months. It taught him a lesson – to keep the venues and all that went with the games a secret, and not to let journalists anywhere near the premises.

In spite of the publicity, the resilient Aspinall managed to retain his extraordinary circle of friends. It appeared that he could talk himself out of anything. 'John,' said John Burke, 'could switch topics and tales to suit every punter. He was masterful with the words. When he was in the room or at the table no one was going to be bored. He saw to that.'

Lady Annabel Goldsmith said in an interview with *The Times* in 2000: 'I will never forget the first time I clapped eyes on "Aspers". It was 1954, I was 19 and married to my first husband, Mark Birley. We were supposed to go out for dinner, but he started to tell a story . . . It lasted two hours. "Aspers" was the most incredible raconteur.' In 2006, Mark Birley gave John Burke and myself lunch at his Mark's Club in London. He said: 'It was fun with "Burkie" and the crowd when it all began. The world will never see such people again, they were an extravagant and extraordinary mixture.'

And one of the most colourful, then or at any time, was Nancy Gillespie, girl-about-Mayfair. She moved in similar circles to John Burke and John Aspinall and knew everybody. It was a tremendous asset, for she was also 'Ephraim Hardcastle', one of a team of reporters on the *Sunday Express* gossip column. Today, she is as alert and amusing as the young girl from the Scottish mining village of Patna, Ayrshire, who entranced 1950s London society, European and Arabian royalty and Hollywood movie stars. And her employer, Lord Beaverbrook.

She also impressed John Aspinall. It wasn't mutual, although she happily recalled one evening out with him. 'Greyhound racing was not the sport I'd expected to be popular with that crowd. "The dogs" were supposed by Mayfair to be for the common people. So I was rather surprised when John Aspinall invited me to go with him to the White City. Ian Maxwell-Scott was in the party, and Gerry Albertini. All top-drawer chaps.

'But it seemed that they were not snobbish about greyhound racing. Or any form of racing. Or any form of gambling, for that matter. We did rather well at the White City meeting. And we were just about to leave when Aspinall called out to the other two, "A tenner for the winner. Once round the circuit."

'Before I realized what was happening, Ian and Gerry were over the rails and haring around as if they were greyhounds themselves! Thousands of spectators making for the turnstiles stopped to watch the fun. Some bookmakers even started to make bets on the result. Ian romped home first – he was a lean, lanky man – with Gerry a length behind. Ian got his tenner immediately.

'John Aspinall was a wonderful talker. When he began to have games in private houses he would get people to lend him things – he could talk them into giving him everything from antique lamps to big cheques. When I was having a fling with Gerry (Albertini), he was always after something.

'I knew them all, but I couldn't write about the games. I went to lots of games, but never to Aspinall's or the ones he ran with John Burke. Two more different men you couldn't meet. John Burke is a kind person. The worst man I ever met was John Aspinall. He was a rotten man. And his mother – Lady Osborne. Lady bloody O. She was a bitch. Lady Macbeth was an angel next to her. But Aspinall could turn on the charm like a tap. It was the cold tap for me, but not for many others.'

His magic certainly worked with Jane Gordon-Hastings, who would become one of Aspinall's grandest assets in those early days: a hostess with, according to every eyewitness, the mostest. Aspinall met Jane Gordon-Hastings in 1955, and, much to his friends' surprise, married her eight months later. He was twenty-nine, and she was twenty. The wedding took place in February 1956 at Caxton Hall, in London, the two-night 'honeymoon' at the Connaught Hotel and the Dorchester wedding reception paid for by a £500 wedding-gift cheque from Gerry Albertini. The groom was all but penniless, but the event was billed as 'the wedding of the year'.

As with almost everything Aspinall touched or talked about, Jane Gordon-Hastings was not quite what he said she was. But then, neither was the man who introduced her to her future husband. Aspinall created much myth about the early romance, and how he first saw the fresh-faced Scottish beauty at a fashion show one afternoon at Fortnum & Mason's in Piccadilly.

What, most people who really knew Aspinall ask, would he be doing at a fashion show on a weekday afternoon? It was not possible – nothing could keep Aspinall from the races. It seems more likely that he was at the track or at Sydney Summers' Jermyn Street establishment. In his later life,

Aspinall, the great raconteur who could talk his way out of trouble and into anywhere, conjured the images he believed his social advancement required in a world of serious snobbery.

Indeed, John Burke was first introduced in 1955 to the lovely lady, at a poker game at the Mayfair Hotel where Aspinall was staying. Aspinall, the organizer of the game, also saw her, but was holding a hand of aces and queens which, for him, added up to far more important figures.

The future Mr and Mrs Aspinall properly connected at the White City greyhound track where Bobby Buchanan-Michaelson had taken her on a 'date'. 'I knew where she worked and she came over after work for a drink and that's how it all happened,' he told me in September 2006, at his home in Chelsea. 'It's so difficult looking back on fifty, sixty years ago. "Aspers" is dead, Jane Hastings is dead – everybody I seem to know is dead.'

Bobby Buchanan-Michaelson, known as 'Buck Mick', was another of the colourful characters who flourished in those freewheeling days, with considerable entrepreneurial skills. Starting out on his commercial and social career as plain Bobby Michaels, he had decided to add some class to his name by making it Michaelson. Then – the brainwave – he incorporated a famous Scotch whisky into his moniker. He became Bobby Buchanan-Michaelson.

It was enough to intrigue the Queen. Or, rather, as she was then, the Princess Elizabeth. He took her dancing, reportedly to the Casanova Club, which was run by the Hungarian Rico Dajou, who had the disquieting habit of always telling visitors, 'Oh, you just missed Princess Margaret,' or claiming that one duke or another had just left. He believed this to be good for business, and it was. Bobby Buchanan-Michaelson says now that he can't recall where they went. It was 'somewhere near Claridge's'.

The people whom today we'd think of as 'spooks', however, were not so keen on Bobby B-M. Although, given his humour and panache, it was probably one of the most amusing nights the Queen ever enjoyed, when Bobby requested a second date, the Palace had done some checking up and said 'no'.

So he moved on, and later met Jane Hastings from the Scottish highlands. Naomi Jane Hastings was from Tomintoul, a small village near Aviemore. She made what was only pocket money as a beater on shoots in the area; her life was remote and very different from that of the social gadabouts of London. Yet she was special, and a Londoner on a shoot encouraged her to travel south and try modelling.

'She just had that look that could capture kings and emperors,' said Nancy Gillespie. 'She had imperial looks – and that, of course, is what Aspinall went for.'

Bobby Buchanan-Michaelson had told Jane Hastings how he had 'elevated' his name. He suggested that he'd already fabricated himself into the whisky market; she should go for the gin. And his great friend was Dougie (adopted surname) Gordon.

She became Jane Gordon-Hastings, a name that perfectly suited her looks and personality: tall, elegant and possessed of inherent good taste and good manners. It didn't help her confidence; she was still that young girl from a Cairngorms village. Marriage did, though. She seemed to mature with it.

John Burke was awed by Mrs Aspinall. 'To say that Jane was beautiful is an understatement – she was stunning!' As a gambling promoter who aimed to make his fortune from the higher echelons of society, Aspinall instinctively understood what an asset a glamorous hostess would be. It was never apparent that she understood that.

Early in their marriage they were invited to Highclere Castle, the home of the Earl of Carnarvon. 'Porchy' Carnarvon, whose mother was a Rothschild and whose father had

Right.
The Wild Bunch:
Hollywood legend
William Holden shows
gambler Ray Ryan
how far to set his
sights in Kenya.

Below.
The debonair
safecracker
Eddie Chapman (right)
outside court with
Wilfred MacCartney
in 1946.

Left. The Maharaja of Baroda, and a female friend. Eddie Chapman considered 'Boss' the nicest foreign person he knew.

Right. Dressed to kill: the suede shoes, the trilby, the double-breasted suit and ever present cigarette, Billy Hill in full gangster chic.

Right.
Bobby McKew
and bandleader
Paul Adams (left)
relaxing in Tangiers.

Below.
Billy Hill in
holiday mode, as
he and Gypsy Riley
soak up the sun
in Tangiers.

Above. Nancy Gillespie (right) on the town in 1954 with Michael Heseltine and Lord and Lady Docker.

Left. Claus von Bülow, pictured in 1985, after being acquitted of the attempted murder of his wife. He was often at the chemmy games in the early days.

'Burkie' – John Burke in 1958.

Not a man to be crossed: the young and very determined James Goldsmith.

Always happy to oblige,
the great friend and middleman
Peter West in 1961.

The man with
no luck: the tragic
Dominic Elwes and
his runaway bride the
heiress Tessa Kennedy,
in Havana, February
1958.

Today a successful publisher, this is Mark Sykes dressed for a touch of cold weather in the Swingin' Sixties.

The keepers of many secrets: happy-go-lucky Ian Maxwell-Scott and wife Susan, still keeping her hat on events, in the summer of 1976.

John Aspinall, wife Jane and capuchin monkey Dead Loss at
93 Eaton Place, in 1958.

discovered the tomb of Tutankhamun, was entranced (as so many men were) by the extraordinarily attractive Mrs Aspinall. Aspinall believed that Carnarvon could advance his standing; this invitation was the first move into the highest echelons of society and created great excitement.

By then Aspinall had his black Rolls-Royce and Jim, the driver. Jane Aspinall, as enthusiastic as her husband about the Highclere excursion, packed four trunks of clothes, giving her a dozen changes of outfit. Aspinall's twin ambitions were to make money and to move up the social ladder. The weekend in Gloucestershire would pay social though not financial dividends, as Carnarvon was never a gambler. In time, though, he would become useful in that area too.

Jane Aspinall was also the ideal hostess for Aspinall's high-class gaming parties. Aspinall cast her in that role, and, no matter what the circumstances, did not waiver. 'When John Aspinall made up his mind about something, nothing in the world would make him change it,' said Bobby Buchanan-Michaelson.

John Burke was fond of the future Mrs Aspinall. 'They seemed to be happy in the beginning but, like his cards, you could never really read what was in John's mind. He was an illusionist.'

The grand magician did not explain to his beautiful wife, who quickly became a Mayfair favourite and known as 'the Spirit of Park Lane', that she was entering a superficial sphere which for all its glamorous froth had a hard, cynical core. It was a Jekyll and Hyde environment where decency had nothing to do with social status, either earned or inherited. Aspinall cynically encouraged her to flirt with his punters like Sunny Blandford, the Marquis of Blandford (in 2007 the Duke of Marlborough), and other high-stakes players. It must have been difficult for her to accept that while flirting with the rich heir to a stately pile was a highly praiseworthy activity in her husband's eyes, dalliance with a young man she liked, but who was not a commercial asset to the chemmy games, was an unforgivable sin.

An encounter with an exotic woman and her lover saw Aspinall again making headlines in August 1956. In 1943, John Burke and Bobby McKew's drinking pal at the Star, 'Boss', the Maharaja of Baroda, Sir Pratap Sinh Gaikwad, had married an extraordinary beauty called Sita Devi, who became his second maharani. By the time Aspinall's chemmy games were becoming more and more popular, the couple were divorced, which was no surprise to anybody given Boss's proclivity for young and statuesque girls. Yet it had been Boss who had brought divorce proceedings, citing Neville Clark, the former racing manager of the Maharani of Baroda, as co-respondent.

Sita Devi had an extraordinary reputation. When Bobby McKew attended the 1957 wedding of the Maharaja's son, she, as the queen, was present: 'She wore a suite of jewellery. It was all the good stuff, the crown jewels. As was traditional, the happy couple went off on elephants to parade among the crowds. Before the elephants returned, Sita was off, on her way home to Monte Carlo. So was the jewellery.'

Which was where for many years one of the most priceless Indian treasures, the pearl carpet once owned by the Maharaja of Baroda, which ranks with the Mughal Peacock Throne as a symbol of India, was rumoured to be. Sita Devi supposedly kept the pearl carpet, the 'Moonstone' of its time. It's impossible to estimate its worth. Bobby McKew believes it to be in the palace of an oil-rich nation, but he is at great pains to point out that he does not know for sure.

Bobby McKew would often be seen on the town with Boss

and saw at first hand how much he enjoyed the company of the most attractive and desirable women. 'I don't know where Boss found the girls, but they were always marvellous. I must say, I looked very good in such company. Too good, as it turned out. This prominent businessman, a very rich man who ran a huge car franchise, and I won't embarrass him by giving his name, approached me and asked, "Bobby, where do you get the girls for the Maharaja? I'd like to meet them very much."

'He thought I was a ponce! I was furious but I didn't show it. I said the girls all came from a good contact, a Wilhelmina Hill. I gave him the phone number, Bayswater 7338, and told him to call. I said, "If a man answers, don't worry about it. He's the caretaker."

'So this guy starts ringing Billy Hill and asking about the girls. About a week later, he came up to me and apologized. He said he knew who he had been telephoning. He never asked about girls again.'

But this well-connected businessman did meet the exotic Sita Devi. It was at a dinner party, and the two of them talked about Aspinall's chemmy games. Sita Devi was intrigued, but rather than attending one of the games herself, she sent Neville Clark.

Sita Devi could not have foreseen that entering Aspinall's orbit, even indirectly, was to result in her name being splashed over the newspapers again. It seems that Aspinall took against Neville Clark and at their next encounter provoked an argument that provided the press with a delightful tale of high society scandal. 'Film Stars See Row in Mayfair Night Club' ran the headline in the *Daily Mail*.

It was on 8 August 1956, and the magnums of champagne were exploding at London's most fashionable nightclub, Les Ambassadeurs (£7 a year subscription). Situated off Park

Lane, it was run by the clever former boxer and Polish immigrant John Mills. He was on a winner that evening, hosting the post-premiere party of *The Iron Petticoat*, a British-financed romantic comedy starring Bob Hope and Katharine Hepburn.

The film's stars were absent but there was still much glamour, with Hollywood actor Robert Mitchum at one table and the British star, the elegant Laurence Harvey, with his actress wife Margaret Leighton, at another. Across the room sat Sharman Douglas, daughter of the former US Ambassador. Next to her was the legendary bandleader Jack Hylton. All around them were the socially keen and accepted.

At one table was Nancy Gillespie, in her 'Ephraim Hardcastle' role, with Peter West. They spotted Neville Clark and the Maharani of Baroda enjoying themselves at a central table with another couple.

John and Jane Aspinall were at home at their rented flat in Upper Brook Street, entertaining Mark Birley and Lady Annabel. It was to there that Peter West telephoned and gave Aspinall the news about the presence of Neville Clark and the Maharani.

Both couples walked down to Les Ambassadeurs. Aspinall went over to Neville Clark and the Maharani: they needed to talk. 'After dinner,' said Clark.

Aspinall joined Mark Birley and the others at the bar. As the orchestra played softly, Aspinall stood there working himself up. He approached the table again. It was 10.45 p.m. They had to talk, he said – immediately.

'You bother me,' said Clark. And Aspinall did. He went berserk, grabbed Clark's hair and pulled him off his chair. The table's contents went crashing to the floor. Guests looked around at the sound of smashing glass. A couple of punches were exchanged and the two men rolled on the floor.

The Maharani shouted that she was pregnant. That was the cue for hip-led Robert Mitchum, certified movie tough guy, to move in. He took a couple of punches at Aspinall. At which point Jane Aspinall entered the fray, armed with her handbag. Fists and handbags flew.

It was a few moments of mayhem. There were gasps and a couple of screams from nearby tables and then the head waiter, William, and a couple of others moved in and separated Aspinall and Clark.

Intriguingly, the society crowd and movie stars were loath to talk about the incident. As he left Les Ambassadeurs that night, Robert Mitchum said, 'Fight? I heard a glass fall. It was all over in a flash. I wish there'd been more to it.'

Laurence Harvey was equally reticent: 'I was eating sole when I heard the din. It wasn't much. Then I heard something smash to the ground. I got on with my sole. It was delicious.'

Nancy Gillespie recalled: 'It all got calmed down quite quickly, champagne on the management, that sort of thing. They had quite a set-to. Aspinall put on a brave face – his crowd all thought it was a "lark", made for an entertaining evening.'

In spite of the titillating headlines, business continued as usual for Aspinall until, in 1957, John Burke 'joined the firm'. The close racing friends partnered up in a lucrative endeavour, Sky Masterson and Nathan Detroit to the gentry, with Aspinall as the owner and chairman of 'the Firm' and John Burke as the finance director.

For them, this was an exciting page-turning period, for not only was there the glory of the gambling, the naughty glamour of the parties that ran in tandem with the gaming; for these young men there was also the devilment of flouting the law of the land. 'Ian Maxwell-Scott wasn't around and John knew he needed someone he could trust to "manage" the games: look after the money, pay out and get in the cheques,' John Burke remembered. 'It was detail he didn't want to bother with. He wanted the grand scheme of things. I, as "Burkie", became the financial director of the operation. John was the chairman and managing director. I learned to be a croupier and from then on John never employed professional croupiers, either he crouped himself or I did.

'Our private chemmy parties attracted a financially solid, honourable clientele. They were men of value, who paid their debts and could afford to wait for payment themselves. Aspinall once got into a difficult situation when a loser's cheque bounced and he couldn't afford to pay the winners from that evening's party. It could have been the end for him, but it wasn't. The players to whom Aspinall owed money were important and reliable men. A few grand floating around between friends was not a problem for them. It could be shrugged off, and was, as fast as they would enjoy a plate of scrambled eggs, a touch of smoked salmon and wild mushrooms. Aspinall was lucky.

'You have to understand the sort of people involved – they don't exist any more. To someone like James Goldsmith, his winnings, a few thousands pounds – enormous amount in those days – was still nothing to him. He'd rather wait for his money, or not have it at all, than fall out with friends.

'John was also close to Richard Parkes and Gerry Albertini and they bailed him out – in their terms it cost them little. It was money they would themselves have casually lost at chemmy.'

I brought along Steve O'Flaherty to our games, which was a very popular move – he would have been the richest player in the early days. The games were not attended by many rich aristocrats or men of national importance. It's easy to understand why. Would a government minister, or a steward of the

Jockey Club, or a prominent merchant banker, or the chairman of a large public company risk the glare of media publicity were he to face in open court this charge of "frequenting a common gaming house"?

'Nonetheless, our profit was impressive. There was the *cagnotte*, the losers paid their debts: we couldn't lose. There was no point in "bent" games with the stakes on our table. It was profit, profit, profit and no tax to pay.'

5. THROUGH THE LOOKING GLASS

Most of our people have never had it so good. Go around the country, go to the industrial towns, go to the farms, and you will see a state of prosperity such as we have never had in my lifetime, nor indeed ever in the history of this country. What is worrying some of us is, 'Is it too good to be true?' or perhaps I should say, 'Is it too good to last?'

HAROLD 'SUPERMAC' MACMILLAN, JULY 20 1957

With his enticing dark-haired wife as a siren at the card evenings, in 1957 John Aspinall was back in very serious moneymaking business and John Burke found himself almost constantly whistling the song 'The Man who Broke the Bank in Monte Carlo'.

The chemmy games, following the caution brought on by the bad luck of an exotic cheque and the press invasion, returned to a reliable routine. The 5 per cent charge, or *cagnotte*, raked off by Aspinall and 'Burkie' on the bank's winning bets provided steady, tax-free income, as much as £3,000 to £4,000 on a good evening.

John Burke explained: 'In France, chemmy, from the point of view of the proprietor, was a brilliant game. It is a one-against-one game and probably takes about thirty seconds, and the outcome is that there is one winner and one loser. The winner, if the bank wins the coup, pays the 5 per cent tax on what he wins, and so you can imagine the profits rolling in.

For us there was only one possible snag. In France, gambling was legal, and if you lost money you could be sued. Gambling debts had to be honoured, legally honoured, whereas in England of course they weren't.

'If you lost money gambling and told the other person to get lost, there was nothing that they could do about it. Even if they were given a cheque, the person who wrote it could plead the Gaming Act and dishonour it. There was no legal redress, which made it none too attractive in England, unless you were dealing with people who would actually pay. And that was our secret weapon. Our players played and paid.'

Towards the end of 1956, John and Jane Aspinall had moved into 93 Eaton Place. Their landlord, the Old Harrovian property developer Douglas Wilson, accepted from them a good rent of £50 a week. They were joined by Bob, the butler, and, later, a capuchin monkey called 'Dead Loss'. For a time, Aspinall kept a bear in a cage at the back of the flat; one winter he took the bear to St Moritz in a trailer behind his chauffeur-driven Rolls. 'It got him noticed,' said John Burke.

Within a couple of years, the animals had all but taken over at Eaton Place. There was Tara, a tigress; and two Himalayan bears, Esay and Ayesha. The Aspinalls' friends were wary of visiting, the neighbours fretful for their safety. Aspinall knew he needed somewhere in the country. After a wonderful, lucky bet at the Newmarket races, he was able to buy Howletts, an eighteenth-century Palladian house set in thirty-nine acres of parkland, near Canterbury in Kent. He founded his first zoo there in 1958 and from then on met its huge and seemingly always rising maintenance costs.

'In fact, "Aspers" far preferred animals to humans; he regarded them as equals, loved them like his friends,' Lady Annabel Goldsmith told *The Times* after Aspinall's death on 29 June 2000.

As it turned out, the monkey, the first member of what

became Aspinall's part-famous and part-notorious wild animal collection, was to be less trouble in the early years than another new friend.

To escape press attention after the debacle at Les Ambassadeurs, Aspinall had taken his wife to the South of France. There, in the casinos, they had met the American Eddie Gilbert, a rather mysterious entrepreneur labelled 'The Boy Wonder of Wall Street' by *Time* magazine.

Gilbert was aggressive and arrogant, and laughed at John Aspinall's stories. A long association of mutual hero-worship began, one that would have long-lasting and remarkable repercussions. The American, even if he did not quite 'belong', became one of the set, someone who was promoted and helped by Aspinall as introductions were made during chemmy evenings at 93 Eaton Place. John Burke had rented a flat (for £60 a week) at 60 Eaton Place from the Egyptian Madame Zulificar. He told her the extra large, elegant drawing room was ideal for his needs, for his nocturnal work table which happily seated nine.

They used other venues apart from the Eaton Place apartments to keep the gambling evenings 'nomadic' and so somewhat within the 1854 Gaming Act. John Burke says that, despite supposedly 'authoritative' reports, they had no 'arrangement' with the Mayfair police.

In this way, a steady business built up, around which an eclectic bunch of those given to risk and chance gathered. Mark Sykes shakes his head at the memories. 'I look back and I'm astonished at what went on. You forget the unbelievable change in lives and the way we lived in forty and fifty years. It was an insane but marvellous time, never been anything like it.'

The pace of life in London, though still snail-like compared with the supermotion of the twenty-first century, was gathering an uneasy momentum, a stretching of the muscles. Almost everyone wanted action, a chance at the jackpot, the bullseye. At Eaton Place, normally at number 93, chemmy for the smart set was quietly fashionable: the gambling was very hush-hush; the atmosphere always convivial. There were girls willing to thrill and be thrilled, the best food – caviar and French pâté and that day's seafood specialities – plus fine wine, and, of course, there was the gambling. Since it was illegal, there was the delicious frisson of risk.

Lucian Freud; Claus von Bülow; Mark Birley and his good friend Geoffrey Keating; Clive Graham; Yorkshire landowner Henry Vyner; Kosoro Ghasghai, a Persian prince who flew from Munich – where he lived in a penthouse hotel suite – for the games; the well-off avant-garde as well as renowned gamblers like Stephen O'Flaherty; all became regulars. It was rare to see the players' spouses at the games, but Janet Mercedes Bryce, who would later marry the Duke of Edinburgh's cousin David Mountbatten, Marquess of Milford Haven, attended on 17 November 1960. Why not? It was fun.

The beautiful debutante Theresa Follet used to drive John Bingham, the future Lord Lucan, to the games in her second-hand green Ford Popular. She talked at her home in Switzerland in December 2006 about her gambling evenings: 'He was not a boyfriend. He lived with his mother in St John's Wood High Street and I lived with my mother in St John's Wood. I had a car and he didn't, so I used to take him. I used to go and pick him up from some awful Victorian building.

'I found him an extremely nice person and a good friend. I went with him many times to the games when it was all highly illegal. I enjoyed it. I like gambling but I didn't have the big money to gamble, I just did even-money things but it meant I could play through the evening at Aspinall's parties. If I won I put a little bit more on, but I had to be careful. One evening I was the only winner in our group, I've no idea how, but I remember everyone being cross that I was the winner and everybody else lost. Including John Bingham, who I don't remember being a very good gambler.

'I think it probably was considered very racy for me to go gambling, but it was good fun. There was good champagne and food and it made for a lovely evening. It was a very small circle in those days. A lot of my friends at that time wouldn't have dreamed of going to Aspinall's. They would rather have died.'

The champagne and the deb delights – equally bubbly – were sideshows, more for hangers-on than the real gamblers. Mark Sykes, who would later run his own games in partnership with Peter Scaramanga, shrewdly pointed out: 'The reason why people gamble is for utter escape from reality. More than sex, more than booze, more than heroin, it is a complete, utter escape from reality. It takes over. Gambling is as addictive as any drug.

'Playing all night was normal, but the concentration on the gambling was go great it was as though the players had snoozed the hours away. They'd thought of nothing but the gambling. All their other senses were resting. That's why you'd often see at eight o'clock or nine o'clock in the morning, after whole nights of gambling, people as fresh as though they'd all slept all night. That's why.

'Many people would go straight to their office. There were lots of City folk – stockbrokers were making huge amounts of money in those days. All crooks, of course. But they gambled and they paid up.'

So Aspinall and Burke were on to something which, in their world, supposedly did not exist – a sure thing. And, of course, it didn't. Well, not exactly. Or, more precisely, not yet.

John Burke, who has seen more millions won and lost than most, has thought much about the motivation of gamblers: 'Is it excitement, greed, sheer pleasure, showing-off or masochism? Gambling is generally asexual. I have seen several masochistic gamblers. Class, the English obsession, is part of the equation. The English upper classes have a strong gambling tradition and the working class enjoy their punting. It is only in some sections of the middle or lower-middle class where there is a puritanical disapproval of gambling, a feeling I believe to be stronger in America than in the UK.

'Of course, as Damon Runyon so wisely said, "All life is six to five against."'

Off Sloane Square, it was difficult to calculate the odds. The cavalcade of con men passing through the doors of Martin's Bank on Sloane Street was not an unusual sight during the summer of 1957, a time of regular and impressive takings for Aspinall and Burke. Yet, despite appearances, the bank did not have such clientele exclusively.

The discreet charm of the confidence man was in the air; it perfumed post-war society. One early afternoon Nancy Gillespie was walking towards Martin's Bank when a familiar, smiling face appeared. It was the Ceylon-born Charles De Silva, dressed at his sharpest. They chatted amicably for a few minutes and then said goodbye, agreeing to have a drink later. De Silva walked down the steps from the bank to a dark-blue Rolls-Royce, where an equally immaculate chauffeur (both hired for the day) held the passenger door open. The Rolls drove him off at a purr.

As she entered the bank the manager came over and after greeting her said, 'I see you know the Maharaja?'

'Charles was a genius,' recalls Nancy Gillespie, of one of the great con men of the era. 'Mind you, the manager's approach was tricky. On one hand I didn't want to grass on Charlie, but I didn't want to claim a great friendship either. Because, whatever Charlie was doing there, it was unlikely to be for the good of the shareholders of Martin's Bank.

'I said, "Oh, I met him a drinks party at the French Embassy."

'He seemed genuinely pleased at that. Certainly, they cashed my cheque without any trouble, and my solvency wasn't always a guaranteed sort of thing.'

De Silva was a swindler of the highest order. He worked, mostly, on 'commission'; he'd put deals together, everything from 'establishing' chinchilla farms in Ceylon to selling a (young) women's reform home on the outskirts of London to Huntington Hartford, then one of the world's richest men; Hartford had so much money he could, and usually did, buy anything he wanted.

Hartford spent his time with heiresses – Doris Duke and Barbara Hutton; and movie stars – Marilyn Monroe ('too pushy, like a high-class hooker', he told *Vanity Fair* magazine in December 2004) and Lana Turner ('way past her prime', in the same interview). The second of his four wives was Marjorie Steele, an aspiring actress. When they married she was 18 years old. Charles De Silva always did his homework. Bobby McKew relates the story:

'Charlie had got himself into the good graces of the governor of this girls' reform school. Then he arranged to have Huntington Hartford come along for tea. He told him there was an "investment opportunity", but not to mention to the old bird running the place anything about buying it. Anyhow, they turn up there and have tea and buns.

'Charlie could see that Hartford needed encouragement and he wandered over to the window, which he had previously found looked out over a tennis court. There were these attractive birds in their tennis skirts skipping around the place. "Oh, do have a look at the property," Charlie said to his man.

'Huntington Hartford took a look, finished his tea, left the governor's office and before they got to the car Charlie had a cheque for a great big deposit on the place. Charlie sold him the reform school – it was astonishing.'

De Silva was so good at his game that he was entertained at 10 Downing Street by Dorothy Macmillan, wife of Prime Minister Harold Macmillan. In those aspiring post-war days it wasn't six; but arguably three, degrees of separation. Dorothy Macmillan was sleeping with Lord 'Bob' Boothby, who was sleeping with the same boys as Ronnie Kray, possibly a ménage too far. Too rich, certainly, for the always cautious Billy Hill, who detested a fuss.

Once, when Bobby McKew had treated himself to a new sports car, the two were driving from London to Maidenhead, to a club which Hill owned and McKew ran. The driver was showing off his car:

'Bobby, why are you going over the speed limit? It just gives them a chance to pull you over and then they'll want to search your flat. Are we in a hurry?'

Charlie De Silva always was. He never met a person who wasn't a 'mark'. There is a story about the dinner where De Silva met the prime minister's wife. It was a charity affair, and he told Mrs Macmillan, 'My mother died of cancer. May I give you a cheque for the charity?'

'You must come and have tea one afternoon,' she said. He followed through and took a guest, a rich Chinese businessman to whom he later sold the Ark Royal after talking at some length about 'my friend the prime minister'.

But Charles De Silva could not fool Billy Hill. He tried, and tripped up, as so many did, by being a little too greedy – the mistake of almost all of history's players of the confidence trick.

De Silva and Hill set out to swindle a couple of chinchilla breeders in Yorkshire. They were told that the government in Ceylon (now Sri Lanka) was willing to invest £200,000 in chinchilla farms. They, in turn, would hand over cash to De Silva for investment in shipping contracts and other aspects of the hustle, such as moving surplus US Forces cameras from Germany to Switzerland.

It all went wrong. De Silva then involved Billy Hill in a paint-buying scheme – and was found out. Somewhere, £80,000, which Billy Hill believed belonged to him, was missing. Correctly, he blamed De Silva. De Silva said he had given the money to his friend Mark Sykes, and about three weeks later there was an interesting encounter over the matter.

Mark Sykes was enjoying a midmorning cup of coffee outside the Carlton Hotel in Cannes when he saw Billy Hill get out of a cab with Gypsy and go into the hotel. Sykes wondered at the chance of it but did not run over and say 'hello'. Billy Hill didn't like surprises. Instead, Mark Sykes allowed Hill half an hour to settle in and then telephoned from a coin box.

'Could I please speak to Mr Hill?'

'Who is calling, sir?'

'Mark Sykes.'

'Hello.'

'Oh, Mr Hill. I just happened to be in town and saw you going through the door of the Carlton Hotel. I rang on the chance you were staying there.'

'Oh.' A pause. 'You'd better come round.'

Billy gave Mark a warm welcome. His voice stayed at an even level, but gradually his guest realized that something was seriously wrong.

'I'm told you have some money for me.'

'Money?'

'I'm told by Charlie De Silva that you've got eighty grand for me.'

'What!'

Mark explained that he knew nothing about it. Hill did not

seem surprised. This had happened before with Charlie De Silva.

'I thought if you did have it, it was unlikely you'd be phoning me from a call box and coming over,' Hill said. He was playing games.

Mark Sykes said: 'He had a sort of macabre sense of humour, Bill. You'd never at first sight take him for what he was. He had flat, black hair in an old-fashioned way. You would think he was probably a bookmaker or a garage owner, someone like that. With me and the De Silva thing he knew the score from the start, but took his time in sorting it out. I stayed for lunch and then we went to the casino with Gypsy.

'She was a character. She wore a ring, a sort of diamond-as-big-as-the-Ritz affair. Enormous. Her hands looked like jewellery boxes. There was an argument and she cuffed some chap and the man's ear came adrift. She cut his ear off. It was colourful. It was all colourful.'

'She was a tough one,' said Frankie Fraser, 'but I think that's why Bill liked her.'

Billy Hill and Gypsy's home in Moscow Road was an expensive flat, filled with the best of everything. There were chandeliers in every room – even the loo.

'Bill had the money to spend and bought the best of everything. The problem was, nothing matched,' said Bobby McKew. 'It was a nightmare of place, like the aftermath of one of those dreadful television makeovers that go wrong. Carpeting on the toilet seat, that sort of thing. Billy and Gypsy thought it was smarter than Buckingham Palace.'

One of the great haunts of the 1950s was the Milroy Club, which sat almost next door to the Hamilton Bridge Club on Park Lane. The ground floor was a splendid reception, bar and dining room, with dancing on the first floor. In charge of

the music was the bandleader Paul Adam, who was Princess
Margaret's favourite. She would send on requests ahead of her
arrival. The band played, as it were, by royal command.

Adam was a charming man, a diplomat with his crowd,
and would always play special sequences of music to announce
the arrival of a regular. Generally, he was known to be discreet.
One evening he and Bobby McKew were driving off from the
Milroy and stopped in at Moscow Road.

'We walked in and sat down and I watched Paul's face
light up in amazement. He eyed the walls, the decor of flocked
wallpaper and all the terrible, terrible rest.

'He looked over at Bill and said, "I've never seen anything
like . . ."

'I grabbed his arm and pressed on it ever so tightly. He
smiled just as tightly and managed, ". . . like a place like this."

'Billy said to Gypsy: "See, darlin', Paul likes it and he
knows all about decorations."

'I got Paul out of there as fast as I could.'

Billy Hill was not a gadabout. He could sit in Moscow
Road and ponder for two, three and four weeks at a time,
rarely stepping outside his front door. He liked his associates
to visit him at his home, which was a four-minute walk or so
from Bayswater Tube.

One afternoon Bobby McKew was driving his E-type
Jaguar to Moscow Road: 'I saw Peter West rushing into the
Underground. I was parking the car, and then there he was
again, rushing out carrying a couple of bags. I thought he'd
done a robbery! When I got to Billy's flat I told him what I'd
seen, and he said in his slow drawl:

'"Yeah, he's got a deal going with these stations. He's
buying sixpences off them."

'Well, work that out.

'In those days you paid cash for the Tube, and there was a
lot of change around. Peter West toured the Underground

twice a week and bought up the sprats [sixpences], giving them the equivalent money. He didn't cheat. If there was £500 of sixpences he handed that amount of money over. The point was that the silver in the coins was worth *more* than £500. It was so profitable, it was worth all that trouble – it was worth between 10 and 20 per cent more, melted down. And there was nothing illegal about it – although I don't suppose you were meant to melt down the Queen's currency.

'Bill said to me: "He's collecting for me." He knew all about it.

'Peter West was a very pleasant fellow. He was best friends with Jimmy Goldsmith and he used to go out with birds for Jimmy, one bird in particular. She went to hotels with Peter and people thought she was screwing him. But no, she was screwing Goldsmith.

'That arrangement, or others like it, went on for years, until Jimmy Goldsmith died. Not much was as it seemed.'

6. THE LONG LEGS OF THE LAW

When in doubt, have a man come through the door with a gun in his hand.

RAYMOND CHANDLER, 1952

The private chemmy parties attracted a financially solid crowd, but many rich aristocrats and men of national importance still remained shy. It was, as John Burke remarked, too dangerous for any high-profile person to risk the publicity were he to find himself in court.

'The thing was to be careful, not to draw attention to ourselves,' said John Burke. 'We had a very successful business going on and it appeared it would go on for ever. There was no reason to think otherwise.'

Happenstance intervened – spectacularly.

During one gambling evening, John Aspinall and John Burke were discussing the need to move the chemmy games around to prevent the police deciding they were involved in a 'habitual' gambling operation. John Burke recalled:

'We decided we couldn't stay in the same place all the time because it was too dangerous. At this point, what we were doing was clearly one hundred per cent illegal, there was no doubt about that. It was done very quietly, all kept very secret, but we had to be even more careful. It was a moneymaker and we didn't want to spoil it. We talked about getting another flat.'

One player, a young man about town, said that his aunt wanted to let a flat in Hyde Park Street, Hyde Park Square. There was one great problem with that: 1 Hyde Park Street was to the north, at the 'wrong' end of the park. But the flat had a grand reception room for gambling and an equally generously sized kitchen for catering. Suitability triumphed over snobbery even with Aspinall, to whom Burke had to explain the advantages.

John Burke did the paperwork for a three-month lease which, for reasons of discretion, was taken in the name of Lady Mary Grace Osborne.

'We went ahead there from 5 December 1957, in just the same way we operated in Eaton Place. I have notes of the *cagnotte* at the games that month and they ranged from £1,100 to £3,000 and £4,300.'

The original, historic account books also show that in that first month Prince Kosoro Ghasghai won £1,854 on 12 December, won another £5,935 on 17 December and lost exactly £9,000 on 19 December. The fanciful Aspinall amused dinner-party guests by telling the story that the prince went everywhere with an armed manservant who stood behind him at the chemmy table to prevent his being assassinated.

The prince missed the excitement on 10 January 1958. That was when an event occurred which was considered unremarkable at the time, but which would change the face of gambling in Britain and rapidly turn London into the gambling capital of the world.

As we know, John Aspinall and John Burke had no arrangement with the Mayfair police. The gambling had gone on; most people were aware of it; but by going 'door to door' (hosting 'floating' games at different addresses), it had stayed safe from interference by the law.

As the Sixties came closer, the ancient gambling laws were regarded as out of touch and contravening them was not a serious crime: nearly half a century on from 'The Night They Raided Hyde Park Square', a suitable analogy might be the smoking, if not the distribution, of marijuana.

The Paddington police were, perhaps, not as sophisticated as their Mayfair counterparts. The 'gambling den' in Hyde Park Square had supposedly been 'observed', to use the police term, for some time. In fact, the chemmy evening of 10 January 1958 was, because of the Christmas holidays, only the fifth game at Hyde Park Square.

It was another pleasant evening. Lady O.'s game pie was as perfect as ever, the champagne chilled, the conversation warm. Just before 11 p.m. the players sat down at the green-cloth-covered gaming table subdivided by chalk marks into units of ten. At number ten sat John Aspinall, as the croupier. In front of him was a wooden box with seventy-seven units in it. Aspinall broke the seal on the required six packs of cards and shuffled them in preparation for the next shoe. Players were sitting at all the marked positions, and most had chips in front of them.

Unknown to the gamblers, one of Paddington's finest, Inspector Samuel Herbert, had shinned up a drainpipe and was now, as he later said in court, 'hanging by his eyebrows' from the edge of the fire escape. Inelegantly perched there, he peered through chinks in the red velvet curtains. He watched the cards being dealt. He saw the chips slide across the table, even if he was not close enough to catch the glint in the players' eyes.

Inspector Herbert breathlessly left his observation post and scrambled down the drainpipe from the fire escape. Waiting in the rain for him was the man in charge, Chief Superintendent Richard Rogers. With this eyewitness account, the Gaming Act of 1845 (not the later 1854 one) allowed the police team to raid the flat and proceed with their inquiries. At 12.45 a.m., Chief Superintendent Rogers blew, as it were, the whistle. He knocked heavily on the door of 1 Hyde Park Street.

Accounts of the evening are legendary and varied. Which waiter was it? Was it Bert Payne or Bob Richardson who opened the door in white tie and tails to find Chief Superintendent Rogers, Inspector Herbert and their uniformed team calling? The truth was far more prosaic. It was a rather flustered washing-up lad who performed that chore, and the police duly marched in. Bob and Bert, both in their smart waiters' gear, rushed over to try and prevent the intrusion but the detectives could not be stopped. They were determined to make their arrests.

There was a cry of 'Hello, hello, hello, what have we here?' as Aspinall barked at Chief Superintendent Rogers, 'What right have you to come breaking in here and searching people?'

'You are breaking the law, sir. This is a common gaming house.'

'I dispute that. These people are all intimate friends of mine and have been invited here.'

Lady O. piped up, 'Anybody would think we were a crowd of criminals. Why don't you catch some real criminals; there are plenty!'

Her intervention allowed the alert John Burke to bundle off with the *cagnotte* and hurriedly stow it in a corner of the room.

'Well done, Burkie,' John Aspinall said with a grin, as Chief Superintendent Rogers asked him and the other players, 'What game were you playing?'

'You know what it is,' replied Aspinall.

'What is going on?'

'My guests are just having a spot of after-dinner fun.'

'What is the bank worth, and the chips?'

Aspinall initially refused to answer the policeman. He paused for a few moments and then said, 'The bank is worth £500.'

Jane Aspinall looked a detective constable straight in the eye when asked her profession, and stated, 'Housewife'.

The startled guests watched and listened in silence. Man about town Lord Timothy Willoughby D'Eresby, Michael Alachouzos and Dougie Gordon shrugged with mild amusement. Bill and Bridget Mond also thought it all hugely amusing.

Lady O. was horrified at it all. She watched her son stand by the chemmy table as Superintendent Rogers, still in his raincoat, formally charged him with 'common gaming house' offences. Next, the policeman charged John Burke. Then it was Lady O.'s turn. Seeming to swell to twice her normal size, she boomed at Superintendent Rogers, 'This is absurd. All these people are friends of ours. And none of them is common. Young man, there was nothing common here until you walked in.' Or at least, that was the after-dinner story Aspinall loved to tell.

But common or not, London's good, great and not-so-great were marched out to Black Marias and driven the short distance to Paddington Green nick. John Burke recalls it all with some whimsy:

'It was all quite civilized. The police are awful snobs, so they treated these people with the right accents in a very nice way, cups of tea and that sort of thing. Of course, half of them were pissed and found it all a great joke. It wasn't a joke for John and me, of course, for it looked like the end of an especially good way of making a living. God's revenge for going to the wrong side of the park. But the police were polite enough, it had the flavour of an Ealing comedy that evening.'

Theresa Follet was there with John Bingham and somewhat alarmed. 'My mother nearly had a heart attack, for my uncle [Sir Alvery Gascoigne] was an ambassador in the Foreign Office and she was terrified it was going to come out. Yet Johnnie and I were the only ones they didn't mention in the *Evening Standard* the next day.'

Mark Birley said that he recalled being bundled off to

Paddington police station. Peter West gave his name as 'Peter Wales' and claimed that he lived at the Ritz.

Nancy Gillespie, banned from the games as a member of the much feared press, nevertheless caught up with events. She said: 'John thought it was very funny. Peter West and Lady Jane Willoughby were at the game when the police arrived, and got arrested. The next night, the two of them went to Le Club. It was past closing time but, of course, they ordered a drink. The next thing the police ran in, and they got arrested again! For drinking after hours. It was quite something to be arrested twice in forty-eight hours.'

Officially, Aspinall, Burke and Lady O. were charged with keeping a common gaming house, while the others were charged with simply being on the premises, 'frequenting a common gaming house'.

But farcical as it may all appear so many years later, the events were absolutely crucial to the future of the UK's millions of gamblers. They were vital in other matters, too, but overall, the Big Casino landscape of twenty-first-century Britain began when the Paddington police raided that spacious rented flat which had the temerity to be on the wrong side of the Park.

And all because John Aspinall and John Burke were bloody-minded.

7. LOADSAMONEY

Your pony, Pony.

SYDNEY SUMMERS, 1958

The Hyde Park Street affair could have been over without much fuss. The three accused of running a 'common gaming house': Lady O., her son and John Burke, could have pleaded guilty at a magistrates' court. Aspinall and Burke, both 31, were accused of using the flat for unlawful gaming; Lady O., as the tenant, for permitting them to do that. The fine would have been something around £100.

'We would then have had to decide whether to continue giving chemmy games while being extremely cautious and security-conscious, as a second offence would probably jeopardize the whole operation, or whether to abandon the scheme,' said John Burke. 'This latter option was clearly one to avoid if possible. It portended the unpleasant possibility of having to work for a living.'

The other option was to fight the charges when they appeared at Bow Street Magistrates' Court.

Aspinall and Burke sought the advice of Sydney Summers, who had, as we know, marvellous police contacts. It was part of the gambling business, a small piece of profit-sharing as it were. He gave Burke and Aspinall a secret weapon in their little bit of difficulty with the law. Publicly, their big gun was a brilliant advocate called Gilbert Beyfus, who would, after an initial hearing at Bow Street, defend them before a judge and jury at the London Sessions on 17, 18 and 19 March 1958 – as it turned out, some of the most memorable dates in the history of gaming. For John Burke, for gamblers worldwide, it was to turn out to be some St Patrick's Day.

Clever as Beyfus was, he was aided by the scheming of his clients and the connections of Sydney Summers, who arranged for Aspinall and Burke to meet a senior police officer who, he felt, might be able to help. How right he was.

The policeman was nicknamed 'Pony', which referred to the gambling sum of £25 that he was prepared to accept for meeting and perhaps giving advice to a 'client'. A 'result' would, of course, call for a larger contribution, possibly a posse of ponies.

John Burke drove Aspinall's black Rolls-Royce (Aspinall never learned to drive) to Sydney Summers' flat in Barons Keep for their important rendezvous. They arrived before the policeman, a tall middle-aged man, who blustered in shortly after them. First, there were the formalities: Summers extended in his nicotine-stained fingers five crisp £5 notes (they were the largest banknotes at the time), and said without a smile, 'That horse you had a tenner on, Pony, won at five to two. Here are your winnings.'

Later, when they were all more familiar with each other, Summers abandoned the charade and at the start of a meeting would hand over £25 with, 'Your pony, Pony.'

John Burke connected well with 'Pony', who was an intelligent man with charm and a sense of humour. He officially earned around £1,750 per annum; nevertheless, his sons all went to public school, at a cost then running at around £600 a year for each schoolboy. Pony, it seemed, had ways of earning lots of ponies.

The chief inspector, always smiling, always happy, was not involved in the case of *Regina* v. *Aspinall, Burke & Osborne* himself, but he was sufficiently high ranking to have access to all the police papers related to it. He supplied the inside story of the prosecution; of their plans, legal tactics and witnesses. Burke and Aspinall then formally passed on the information to Beyfus, quite properly and with no hint of where it had come from, in the presence of their well-known and equally innocent solicitor, Eric Leigh-Howard.

Beyfus used the inside knowledge with deadly skill. Because few people in court, including the jury, had any knowledge of *chemin de fer*, the police had to put an expert witness on the stand to explain how the game was played. This was a Frenchman, Mr Maurice Pomerand, who after working as a croupier in Paris and Monte Carlo for fifteen years now lived in Jermyn Street in the West End and worked at the very proper Crockford's Club.

Across Court No. 4 from Beyfus, his adversary was Mr Sebag Shaw, an eminent QC, and the man who had valiantly but vainly defended Ruth Ellis, who on 13 July 1955 became the last woman hanged in Britain. He helped defend Jack Spot in the same year.

On 18 March 1958, prosecution counsel Mr Sebag Shaw called his expert to the witness box. He adjusted his wig with one hand, and with the other handed Mr Pomerand a wooden card shoe containing cards, telling him, 'I want to play, as though we were at the table.'

It caught the court's interest, and peering over the public gallery was David Mountbatten, Marquess of Milford Haven, who watched Sebag Shaw hitch his gown over his shoulders and say, 'Imagine yourself to be the banker. You are now going to deal the cards. What happens?'

'I put a certain stake, say £100, in the middle of the table, and the croupier announces what the bank is.'

Mr Pomerand then dealt out four cards from the shoe and

neatly placed them on the edge of the witness box. Sebag Shaw got a king of diamonds and a five of spades. Mr Pomerand had served himself a queen of hearts and a six of clubs. Mr Shaw gave his witness a look which was taken as a question.

'If we were gamblers you would take another card . . . and perhaps I would also.'

'Let's be gamblers, then,' replied the QC.

There was a shuffle of bodies in the courtroom, people peering for a look, as Mr Pomerand flicked a card from the shoe. Jane Aspinall's white flowerpot hat almost fell off. He held up the cards for everyone to see. A seven of spades for Sebag Shaw, a queen of diamonds for himself. The player: two. The bank: six. Wildly, with a big smile, Mr Pomerand threw his arms in the air and gleefully shouted, 'I win.'

He didn't. Officially, he was the 'catering manager' of Crockford's Club. Beyfus, however, with Pony Moore's inside information, knew that Mr Pomerand ran the poker room at Crockford's Club.

Crockford's was the bridge club and home to MPs and Conservative Cabinet ministers, where membership had the benefit of agreeably priced food and drinks. John Burke often played bridge there, sometimes with Selwyn Lloyd, Eden's Foreign Secretary during the Suez crisis and Harold Macmillan's Chancellor for two years from 1960. Sadly, despite the eminence of its members, it was not financially viable for Crockford's to maintain its high standards on the revenue derived from bridge players. To remedy this shortfall, Crockfords, through Mr Pomerand, ran a poker room open seven days a week with a table charge for all players. This was illegal.

Whether Crockfords enjoyed an unofficial licence to break the law because of its elite membership or whether it had a deal with the local police, has never been disclosed. In either case, they could not refuse a police request to supply an expert witness for the prosecution in the case of *Regina v. Aspinall, Burke & Osborne*. So, when Gilbert Beyfus cross-examined the unfortunate Maurice Pomerand, in charge of a non-stop illegal gaming operation, it was excruciatingly embarrassing for the gentlemen of Crockford's Committee Room.

John Burke sat in court listening to all the evidence. 'It was a tricky case from the point of view that in order to convict us the prosecution would have to prove that there was profit. There's nothing illegal about friends sitting down and playing cards with you, but if somebody is taking money out of it or a *cagnotte* on every pot, as they do in France, that is another matter. There were some lovely arguments about the Gaming Acts.

'But what really turned the case was that the prosecution needed their expert witness. They were describing *chemin de fer* to the judge. I don't know if he understood it, but the jury certainly didn't. Pomerand had worked in one of the big casinos in Monte Carlo and knew the game inside out.

'Beyfus was brilliant. He wanted to know Pomerand's occupation at that exact moment and exactly where he worked and what he did. The man did not commit perjury. So you had this expert witness in a prosecution admitting he was running an illegal gambling operation at Crockford's!'

After four hours of discussion about the gaming laws (even Henry VIII got a mention), and with the jury absent, Beyfus QC told the court, 'Every single club in St James's with a bridge table is a common gaming house, although the police prefer not to prosecute. In my submission the prosecution have failed to prove that in this case it was a common gaming house. There is no evidence of any illegality at all. If there were, there is no evidence that my clients are guilty of the particular charges that are made against them.

'Our gaming laws are a complete jungle and it is always difficult to draw a straight and easy path through them.'

Sebag Shaw, who shared the same roots as Sydney Summers, was himself a gambling man. His heart did not appear to be in this particular prosecution. Possibly, he thought that the 1854 Gaming Act was inappropriate for the time, for a changing London. He certainly did not press his case aggressively. If he had called the players present that evening to give evidence, and they had told the truth, he surely would have won the case. He decided, for his own reasons, not to do that.

Which allowed Beyfus and his junior counsel, Billy Rees-Davies – a former MP who had lost an arm in the Second World War and was known as 'the one-armed bandit' – after the long legal submissions, to persuade Frank Cassel, the deputy chairman of the London Sessions, to shut down the prosecution with: 'I do not think there was sufficient evidence of unlawful gaming and that is the end of the matter.'

The dismissal of the charges was a virtual acknowledgement that private gambling would be sanctioned. It was a cork-popping moment. There is a grand photograph of a quietly smiling John Burke and a super-confident John Aspinall, rolled umbrella in hand and having a Count of Monte Cristo moment, striding triumphantly out of court. And others of Aspinall and his wife driving off.

They went on to Aspinall's flat at 93 Eaton Place for a celebration. There, Lady O. held court in the olive-green-wallpapered dining room and said without a trace of irony, 'It's a poor thing if you can't have a private party in a private flat without the police coming.'

John Burke recalls Aspinall being asked what odds he would have given on the outcome of the case and him saying in a rather foolhardy way: 'It was a bit of a certainty.' Without

Pony's help, John Burke reckoned the odds against them winning were a 'double carpet', 33–1.

Best, thought John Burke, simply to enjoy the moment. He was certainly going to. He had a goblet of champagne with Gilbert Beyfus and a long talk with Jane Aspinall, who had to keep excusing herself to be presented with bunches and bunches of congratulatory flowers. One punter arrived with a dozen deep-red roses.

John Burke did not stay for more champagne and Lady O.'s reputedly remarkable curry. He had to leave. He had a dinner date at the Brompton Grill with the increasingly popular elegant model Sandra Paul, now a novelist and Mrs Michael Howard, one-time First Lady of the Conservative Party.

Pony was the recipient of £1,000, what is technically known as 'a drink' – and a 'long one' at that. It must have sweetened his retirement. John was sorry to learn some years later, from Sydney Summers, that Pony had died.

Supermodels, champagne, carte blanche; Burke and Aspinall were in open season. The failure to prosecute them resulted in a bonanza.

Newspaper editorials thundered on about the anomalies of the gaming laws. The *Sunday Dispatch*, on 23 March 1958, asked: 'Why are the odds so uneven?' Their leading article said:

'The whole ragbag of our betting, gaming, and lottery laws is chaotic to the point of nonsense. Legislation still in force includes an Act of Henry VIII which was passed to prevent Henry's gambling citizens from being "distracted from the practice of archery". Now is the time to introduce legislation that will clear up the mess. Mr Aspinall's victory cannot fail to inspire the gambling classes to breathe new life into the business. When the law's an ass – and when it is proved to be an ass in public – the time has come for action.'

How true.

The legal triumph was to herald the cry of '*Banco!*' and '*Suivi!*' and the sudden movement of many more thick chips, monetary and aristocratic, around the smart set. Belgravia boomed, as did the profits for John Aspinall and his financial director. The chemmy began again only six days after the case, on 25 March 1958, at 93 Eaton Place, with a *cagnotte* of £1,295. For Aspinall and Burke the purpose was to make their mark, and it was a small game with Gerry Albertini, Richard Parkes and Henry Vyner as the biggest players.

It was now accepted that it was legal to have *chemin de fer* parties. Word was going around that there would be no more police raids, no more fuss and that at any moment Macmillan's government would – as they did – announce new gaming laws.

Others would also benefit, as the Vicar and his many converts held their own gambling evenings. John Burke said: 'One of the instant effects of the case was that every young man in Chelsea who had a flat started a chemmy game and invited his friends to play. There were hosts of chemmy games all over London and other parts of the country. Most of them failed as they ran into one major snag: unless the losers paid it was no good. There was no way you could make them pay. We aimed for the top. The only people we had were people who actually paid.'

Impressive players entered this new, tacitly legal, world of chemmy. Aspinall and Burke hosted games all over London, including one long evening at Pelham Cottage, the family home of Mark Birley. After the case, to be invited to one of their floating society *chemin de fer* games was an honour; it meant you were 'in'. The invitation cards had a gloss of importance about them. They were delivered by hand and with no RSVP; more got delivered to Whites than anywhere else. The venue was handwritten at the last moment to keep the games safe from newspaper intrusion – like today's rave parties, that knowledge enhancing the edgy credibility of the enterprise. And like the raves, they were an endorsement of someone's social acceptability. And wealth – only those with money to lose were invited.

Out of the woodwork, or rather out of Debrett's, Britain and Ireland's stately homes, and the City, came the gamblers. They were hugely wealthy, and the stakes went higher and higher at the lavish and exclusive gaming evenings. Whereas the *cagnotte* had previously been £2,000, £3,000 or £4,000 in an evening, the takings were soon regularly in double figures. Aspinall and Burke were sitting on a gold mine. The figures tell the story. John Burke's records of the games in early April 1958, a couple of weeks after the case, show the 'purses' steadily spiralling upwards. At a game on 23 April 1958 the *cagnotte* was £9,529. That same evening, John Pelham, Lord Worsley and later the Earl of Yarborough, an enthusiastic, even reckless gambler, appeared for the first time. He lost £28,044.

The men now playing knew each other socially. Many were members of Whites. Others were respected figures in the City and there were the smart racecourse owners. But there was an enormous snobbery: 'No jockeys, footballers, book-makers or such like.'

Lord Boothby ('for his assignations with Lady Dorothy, Boothby used to call ahead to Number Ten and say he was arriving to "fix the boiler",' said John Burke) was another jovial new face. He had reason to be even happier: he won £2,160 on 23 April. That evening was also good to Henry Vyner, who won £6,000. Then there was Major Billy Straker-Smith, a director of the Warburg bank, who went home with

£1,323. And for every winning bank, Aspinall and Burke took their tax-free percentage . . .

Another winner that evening was Claus von Bülow, the agreeable man about town who then worked with John Paul Getty. The affable von Bülow was a great friend to the gamblers. He said at his home in Chelsea on 26 September 2006: 'John held one of the first games at my flat because they had to move the games around and that was within the law. Then he had a dance there for Eddie Gilbert, but that had nothing to do with the gambling parties. He staged a ball at my flat and it was an event which attracted a great deal of publicity.'

Of course, the ball, written up as the event of 1959, was a massive and expensive – £15,000 – exercise in public relations. There were fine wines, a lavish dinner, an orchestra and 'minders' to make sure that no one who wasn't wanted came in. The departing coup was the revealing of a huge pack of playing cards. As they left, each guest watched as Aspinall cut the cards and dealt them one. It was the contact for the next chemmy evening.

Claus von Bülow's Belgrave Square flat, despite not being a regular venue, played a pivotal role: it was there that the Duke of Devonshire first appeared at a game. With him was the respected horse-breeder the Honourable Monica Sheriff. John Burke recalled, 'We were told she was his aunt – certainly her treatment of Andrew Devonshire had moments of P.G. Wodehouse, of Aunt Agatha:

' "Go *banco*, Andrew.

' "Now, *suivi* . . . bad luck.

' "*Suivi* again . . . bad luck again! Burkie, another two grand for the Duke!" '

Aspinall could operate in any environment; he was wonderful at working the room. The regular Eaton Place waiters,

Bob and Bert, circulated with the the beluga, foie gras, vintage Cristal and Delamain cognac, and the players would gamble, gamble, gamble. John Burke recalls, 'We were very much still with Martin's Bank in Sloane Street – Tim Holland Martin came to the games – and our cheques were blank cheques which we used to supply to the customers. The customer's name didn't appear on it. It just needed a signature, and often just one name, like Faversham, Derby, Suffolk, Devonshire, whatever.

'One of the Martin's cashiers asked me: "Why don't people use their Christian name as well?"

'He didn't quite understand titles. A great many people who played with us banked with Hoare's, which seemed to be the popular bank for gamblers. Often some punter would have a couple of losing *suivis* and then say, with cheerful laughter: "Quinny Hoare [a bank partner] won't like this." Then they'd play on, true gamblers.'

With John Burke in control behind the scenes, Aspinall was the circus ringmaster of the show: he'd '*banco*' and '*suivi*' with his lunatic punters, calling out 'Napoleon' for a natural nine, or any one of his marshals for a natural eight; his favourite was Marshal Ney, just as Ney was to the Emperor. Aspinall would always turn his 'Napoleon' over with a wonderful flourish. There was something of P.T. Barnum, as well as something of the night, about him.

But the cavalier gambling was an act. Aspinall might lose £1,000 for the house, but so what? It was simply the catalyst to get others betting and so boosting that ever-greedy *cagnotte*. 'John Aspinall was a fine actor in the Tony Blair mould of acting. He emoted. Separating fools from their money is, of course, an essential part of the gambling promoter's trade,' points out John Burke.

'The General' arrived on 7 May 1958 for his first game.

The Sandhurst-educated, socially well-connected General J. E. Spencer Smith had a senior post with NATO in Germany. He was deep in John Le Carré country; the cold war was at its most delicate, but still he flew to London for the chemmy. It used to make the organizers shudder at the thought of the press discovering this particular soldier's tactics.

John Burke liked the General: 'It used to be a standing joke that when the Russians were going to invade, they'd pick a night we had a chemmy game. The General would be absent from his post and his mind would be on much more important things than defending Western Europe from Bolshevism. It would be on the cards.

'Jerry Spencer Smith always said when he was given a card, irrespective of whether it was a good card, bad card or indifferent card: "Quelle jolie carte."'

It was certainly a jolly evening later that month when the big breakthrough happened and the cash began to pour in, like an endless waterfall. With chemmy the rage, they got a multimillion-pound endorsement; after the Derby Dinner on 29 May 1958, a couple of the top people's top people announced they could take a crowd to a card game where the champagne and fun would be flowing. And into Burke and Aspinall's chemmy game walked a history of bulging bank balances led by the Queen's friend, the horse-trainer Bernard van Cutsem, who also became godfather to John Burke's daughter.

'It was a bonanza from then on,' recalls John Burke. 'Not only were these people with money, they were people willing to lose money – and pay up. It was cashier's cheques all round; a wonderful time.'

The 'A' team turned out for the game: names like Derby and Devonshire and Faversham. John Burke said: 'The Derby Club Dinner was a very smart affair at White's, a grand event, and they all came on from it and from the clubs, many pissed members from White's looking for more fun. They were there on the recommendation of my good friend Bernard van Cutsem, who also introduced Andrew Devonshire, whose horses he trained.

'Ackroyd (stockbroking), Gerry Albertini, Jocelyn Hambro [head of the Hambro's Bank] and Major Billy Straker-Smith, Bingham [Lord Lucan], Major Nicoll Collin, Peter Lloyd (property), Dickie Muir and John Ambler, two big, rich gamblers, Tim Willoughby [Lord Timothy Willoughby D'Eresby] – he won £30 – and Colonel Bill Stirling who won ten grand that night. Billy Straker-Smith had a good win and Lord Worsley won a bit.

'But the king of the gamblers, John, the Earl of Derby, lost £24,500. John Derby's young brother, the Hon. Richard Stanley MP, who was a junior minister for Macmillan, appeared for the first time at that game.

'The *cagnotte* that night was £19,401, and as the records show, the house players were, on balance, winners. In 2007 money this might be presented as a tax-free half million pounds' earnings for one night's work.

'Of course the takings weren't always as much as that. Jane Aspinall, playing for the house, lost £700, Peter West lost £1,100; on the plus side Lady O. won £1,800, I won £200, so the house players showed a tiny profit; yet, generally speaking, house players showed a loss, especially when Aspers played himself.

'By being intelligent, and understanding gambling and gambling psychology, John recognized the advantage of displaying himself as an open, free-betting generous gambler, rather than as a calculating promoter. This usually meant losing, but he was only giving back a small part of the profit, and might be described as the sprat to catch the mackerel.

'It is rather ironic to discover from the books that the

person who brought this flock of potential golden-egg-laying geese to our door was my friend Bernard van Cutsem. He was one of the big losers of the evening. He dropped £19,700. As Oscar Wilde said, "No good turn ever goes unpunished."'

8. MASTERMIND

Ah, Mr Hill, murdered anyone recently?

JACK GERBER

By the late 1950s, Billy Hill was extremely comfortable and satisfied, an established, savvy criminal player, yet still aspiring to even more lucrative endeavours. He saw opportunities everywhere. His reputation was now so entrenched in the national psyche that he even 'appeared' in the movies. In John Boulting's 1959 film *Carlton-Browne of the FO*, a vehicle for Terry-Thomas and Peter Sellers, Ian Bannen appears, strangely cast, as the king of some obscure and mythical European nation. The king takes a date to a nightclub, where it's pointed out that he is not wearing the requisite black tie. The management want him ejected, until a waiter pipes up: 'He's royalty.'

'I don't care if he's Billy Hill,' says the manager. There's a pause, and then: 'Don't take a cheque.'

Hill, of course, dealt in cash – usually other people's. Bobby McKew was still flitting between Tangier and London, and avoiding France, where there remained difficulties following on from the robbery of Jack Warner's safe. Now aged 33, McKew had an eclectic collection of contacts, many from his now fixed association with Billy Hill; others from his film company days and many now socially far grander.

In April 1958, he had married Anna Gerber. The quiet
ceremony was at Hampstead register office. His brother-in-
law was Robin Gerber, who had gone to Eton with John
Bingham; his father-in-law was 'Lucky' Jack Gerber, a multimillionaire and an enthusiastic racehorse owner and gambler.
They would often go to the racetrack together. Jack Gerber
knew horses and would bet heavily, often winning at good
odds. He would not bet against Bobby McKew, whom he
believed had 'an edge'. Which, in a sense, he always had, for
McKew would not bet on anything unless he knew he would
win.

Socially, Jack Gerber was a jovial character, though not a
man of great tact. One day at the races, he and his son-in-law
encountered Billy Hill and some of his associates, including
Hill's now ever-present 'minder' George Walker, brother of
the useful heavyweight Billy Walker. Bobby McKew and Hill
were talking when a jovial Jack Gerber appeared, and with a
smile said, 'Ah, Mr Hill, murdered anyone recently?'

It was a freeze-frame moment broken by Bobby McKew
turning to Hill and asking: 'Had any winners, Bill?' Hill smiled
and said, 'Not been my lucky day.' He turned and walked off.
He never mentioned the incident.

There were other tricky encounters, one with Ronnie Kray
in Tangier. Ronnie enjoyed visits there, for Tangier offered
lots of chances to indulge his particular sexual tastes. Bobby
McKew remembers: 'Ronnie, of course, was the other way.
He settled in happily in Tangier.

'Once we were having lunch and there were eight or ten
people around the table. A ladyfriend of mine was there, and
she leaned over and tapped Ronnie on the tummy:

'"Ronnie, if you put on any more weight, the next time we
go out I'm not going to introduce you to any of these good-
looking young boys."

'I could feel the sweat running down the back of my neck. But give Ronnie his due. The woman was a *lady*, and he looked over at me and in his quiet voice simpered, "Bobby, tell her to leave me alone."

'Once when he was with us, I said, "Oh, for fuck's sake," in front of a woman, and he went all peculiar. "I don't like you using language like that in front of a lady."

'Ronnie was very like that. With "ladies" he would always lean over and light their cigarettes. Or get up and help them to or from the dinner table. He was very well mannered. Of course, as we know, not to everybody.'

Bobby McKew's circle of acquaintances was growing constantly. At the time he was the director of a West End steel company. His associate, Shiv Kapoor, had been involved with a huge fraud involving the Costa Rican government, a massive and later missing shipment of coffee, and Emil Savundra. Kapoor had gone to jail; Savundra had escaped; but landed in more trouble and a longish term in a Belgian prison for another fraud.

The Ceylon-born Emil Savundra had just arrived in Britain, and kept in touch with Bobby McKew. A remarkable series of coincidences would follow, perhaps not so surprising, since London was a village, and people in certain circles knew, or knew of, each other.

At this time, John Burke was asked by Aspinall to give money – £3,000 in cash – to Tom Corbally, who was familiar with gambling clubs and with the American Embassy in Grosvenor Square. Corbally was a friend of society osteopath Stephen Ward, whose patients included Winston Churchill, and he was linked to several intelligence agencies in Washington and Moscow.

'I have no idea what the money was for. John's story was that he had foolishly joined a poker game, but had soon realized that it was not a game in which he would be allowed to win anything. He had wisely left the table, promising to pay what he had already lost. I've read of Corbally's CIA connections. On much better authority, I've been told that he had stronger Mafia ones.'

Yet it was not an organization but one man, the cool-headed Billy Hill, who still ruled the London underworld. He took much interest in the Aspinall and Burke court case; an intelligent man, a thinker, he believed that the law would change and that he could use it, rather than break it. Meanwhile, following the case, he took an interest in the host of de facto legal games all over the city. John Burke got lucky at one run by Hill's associate, Patsy Murphy:

'Patsy, who was then at the top echelon of the gangster world, and a good friend of Paddy Kennedy, frequently ran a Saturday night chemmy game at a flat in Eaton Place near to me. I had an open invitation to these games, but I did not attend because I'd been told by Sydney Summers that Murphy's game, like many others, was not always dependent on chance. Skill sometimes replaced luck, and a lot of games around London at that time were bent.

'But one Saturday night, on my way home, probably not totally sober, I decided to call in at Patsy's flat and found a game in full swing. Paddy Kennedy was playing sitting opposite the croupier, at number five, and the shoe was getting nearer to him, about two places away. Seeing me, Kennedy exclaimed: "Here, Burkie, take my seat. I can't win at this fucking game!"

'He then got up and checked how much money he owed, said goodbye and went out into the night. I accepted Paddy's invitation and sat down in his vacated place. I called "*banco*" to the player on my left. Won the bet, left the money in for my own bank, and this then started a winning run. I left the maximum allowed in the game in the middle every time, and kept on winning. I do not remember how many coups I won, but eventually, when the bank lost, the croupier pushed over about £3,000 in chips to me.

I played on for a couple of shoes, lost some of my winnings and went home with a cheque for about two grand plus in my pocket. This was a pleasant profit.

'When I told Sydney Summers the story I found out what had really happened. Patsy Murphy, who liked Paddy, was owed quite a lot of money by him, gambling losses. So he and his croupier had constructed a "sandwich" – fixed some of the cards in the shoe. It allowed a long run of winning banks to arrive at the number five seat where Paddy Kennedy was sitting. Of course, there was nothing they could do about it when Paddy decided to give up his seat to myself. Patsy Murphy's behaviour was beyond reproach. He did not show the slightest sign of any annoyance or disappointment.

'Another fair-sized chemmy game run in that period was organized by a very personable young man called David Patrick. He and his wife Primrose had a pleasant flat just off Lower Sloane Street, and had a good clientele of punters. It was a very curious game because it was strictly in two halves. From 10 p.m. to midnight, the game was run as a benefit for different parties, namely David Patrick and two Cypriot characters who were bridge players from the Hamilton Club. One was known to most of us as "Crooked Deeds". The fourth person, and the most important, was Louis the Rat, on loan from the Vicar. Louis's skill saw these four profit on the evening, taking the other players to the cleaners in a small way, which was clever. It was lambs to the slaughter, fleecing all the way. Later, the Cypriots and Louis left, and an English croupier took over; by now more and more players were arriving and the game continued probably until breakfast time.

'Now, the only occasion where the game ceased to be totally honest was if anyone was lucky enough, or should I say foolish enough, to win too much money. I went in there once and left with a cheque for £1,900, serious money in those days, and alas, I discovered it was too big an amount to win. I think I still have the bounced cheque somewhere.'

There was, of course, no legal redress. The story emphasizes the value of Aspinall and Burke's players. They had an extraordinary situation. And, possibly because of the status of most of their players, they were not victims of outside influence.

David Patrick was not so lucky. His friend David Pritchett, a tea-broker who returned from India in the 1950s to a career in the City, also ran what was regarded as the only totally honest chemmy game of that era ('I had no private income') and talked to me over lunch in Knightsbridge in August 2006:

'David Patrick was quite a mate of mine. He died young, because one of his games was raided, not by the police, but by a mob. Gangsters came at him. He got set on and was hit across the back with a crowbar. That didn't do his kidneys any good – it damaged them permanently. He died two years later of kidney failure. He was killed, murdered really.

'I suppose David had been asked for protection money and he hadn't paid it. I often wondered if it was a subsidiary mob of Billy Hill's. He and David certainly had dealings. David was partnered up with Jimmy Mellon and Dennis Hamilton, who'd been married to Diana Dors. Hamilton didn't appear at the games, but he was a sinister figure in the background.

'I was running a private game once a week for about

twenty people. I took 5 per cent *cagnotte*, so it was technically illegal. My games were quite small, banks were £10 up to £100. No more than that. Yet people like Billy Rees-Davies, the MP, and David Milford Haven came. It was fun, and you could make some money.

'The first games I gave were in a flat next door to Esmeralda's Barn. I used to wonder why between shoes everybody would dash out. Then I discovered that if you stood on the seat of the lavatory and looked through the window, you could see these girls changing for the cabaret. My punters weren't all true gambling addicts.

'But the money did sometimes get serious. I had a partner, Alan Elliott, and sometimes I would give my games in his great big flat at 26 Belgrave Square. Our arrangement was that I was responsible for my punters and Alan was responsible for his punters. We would take it in turns to take and pay out the cheques.

'I had a punter who was a friend of mine who I unfortunately introduced to David Patrick, and he bounced cheques with him as well as me. When this debt was run up and it didn't look as though it was going to be paid, there was quite a spat between my punter and Hamilton, who wanted his money. He said he was going to get it. He threatened to bring in Billy Hill.

'I went round with David Patrick to Hamilton's to plead with him to drop all the naughty business. Mellon was also there. They seemed to agree they were being too heavy-handed about it.

'Hamilton was a very nasty piece of work. When I got in there, there was this rather sad little girl present. He ordered her: "Go into the bedroom," and he followed her. He was in the bedroom screwing this girl when the telephone rang, and it was Billy Hill for Hamilton. David Patrick took the call and he said: "Mr Hill, sorry to have bothered you, there's been a mistake, a mix-up." I will never forget that.

'It was an intriguing time. If I wasn't giving a game I'd go to others. A wonderful woman, Mrs Emerson Potter, was one of my rivals, but I was very fond of her. She came off her deathbed and gave a game on the night she knew I was giving a game, and, of course, she got the punters. Naughty old girl. She was a widow of a soldier from the First World War and had terrific style and no question of any ill manners – no swearing at her table, or anything like that. When she died all she had were her poker chips, and she left them to me.

'Characters! Tony Psycopolos was a very anglicized Greek. He had been in the Navy in the war and he was a magnificent boxer. He had been to St Paul's public school. Although he was at least twenty stone, when he went out for a meal he would order a main course twice, if not three times. Yet when you watched him dance, he was straight across the floor of the Milroy. Princess Margaret would stare at him. He was sophisticated.

'He had a mistress in those days. Of course, he was foreign. One Guy Fawkes night he was with her in the upstairs bar of the Star and Paddy came up and said: "Get that whore out of here." Tony told Paddy: "You say that again and I'll knock you down the stairs."

'Of course Paddy said it again. Tony knocked him down the stairs. Paddy came up again and Tony knocked him down again. Paddy took him to court. Tony got knocked down for knocking him down the second time. He had a right to knock him down the first time but not the second time.

'On 5 November for the next two or three years, we'd go round to the Star in Tony's large Jaguar with a lot of rockets and fireworks and blow up the place.

'I went to games run by Mark Sykes and Peter Scaramanga but I never went to the Vicar's card parties.

'I was in the illegal gambling business at the same time as Aspinall,' said Mark Sykes, 'but at a smaller level. I like to think we were more charming than Aspinall. He behaved very badly towards his first wife Jane: it is embarrassing to even think about it. I used to get quite a lot of his leavers, his cast-offs. It was a huge business.'

And there were also other sources of 'income', as John Burke recalls. One involved, in this so-circular world, his acquaintance Patsy Murphy. 'There was a burglary at 93 Eaton Place, and Jane's jewellery was stolen. John had been generous in buying his new and beautiful wife jewellery. Of course, he bought most of it from Mr Money, who was a terrific fence. Jane's jewellery was, as they say in the trade, "bent gear" or "dodgy gear". It had been valued for insurance purposes by Armour Winston in Burlington Arcade, who had no idea it wasn't straight. The theft was no tragedy, because they weren't family heirlooms or anything like that, and they were well insured and John stood to collect about ten grand from the insurance company.

'I was in the Star having a drink and Patsy Murphy came to me and said: "John, tell your friend if he wants his jewellery back I know where it is and I'll get it for him. It won't cost him more than two grand, perhaps a bit less."

'I relayed the news back to John, and he was not pleased at all. He said: "Tell them to keep the bloody jewellery." The last thing he wanted was to get it back. He got his ten thousand pounds and the jewellery was never heard of again.'

That wasn't the only time that Aspinall bought jewellery from Mr Money. Bobby McKew had also bought his wife a splendid diamond necklace from Mr Money – made of fake stones from South Africa. He said, 'It cost me £200 and the only way you could tell the stones were not real was because they were so shiny. Anna knew they were not genuine, of course. One evening she met Lady O. at a Mayfair drinks party and Lady O. gushed about the diamonds. She had exactly the same sort. She told Anna, "You must have a wonderful and rich husband. My son John bought me mine, and I know they cost him an absolute fortune." Anna simply smiled and agreed.'

It was a small, if complex, world, full of intriguing people, gambling dens and nightclubs, with social mixtures not seen since, where it seemed most people were welcome to the party. John Burke's good friends included the extremely well-connected Barbara Langrishe and John Aspinall's half-sister Jenny Osborne, later Jenny Little, whose husband Anthony formed the designer wallpaper company Osborne & Little with her brother Sir Peter Osborne, father of the 2007 Conservative shadow chancellor, George Osborne.

For many, social life revolved around clubs, which were popular in the afternoons and when the pubs closed in the evening. 'Oh, yes, there were many, many places to go,' said Mark Sykes. 'The Maisonette was the melting pot, very much so; other than that there were pubs, restaurants, nightclubs.'

'Indeed,' said John Burke, 'there were always places to be, drinking clubs to go to. On an afternoon at the Colony Room in Soho you'd have Muriel Belcher glaring at her customers, and most days they included Francis Bacon and Frank Auerbach. I'd see Lucian Freud there. He'd work all night and would relax there.

'Drinking clubs were popular because the pub, by law, had to shut at 3 p.m. In theory, people who entered the clubs had to be members, and the clubs were supposed to keep proper books and membership details and all that sort of thing. The Maisonette was easily the best of them, run by Ruby Lloyd and her friend and partner Jock Campbell Muir, who was a most delightful character and a friend of mine. He was also a regular player in David Pritchett's chemmy games.

'Ruby was quite class conscious and loved having people of higher social status: nothing pleased her more than to look around and see titles, gentry idling the afternoon away in her club. She had one great advantage: one of her very close friends was Wally Virgo, who was the Commander of Scotland Yard's Serious Crime Squad. With such a friend, Ruby was not troubled by the local police, who would turn a blind eye to any minor infringements of the drinking laws; sometimes she didn't close on time, and on one or two occasions we played cards there all night. That was obviously against the law. The other great advantage that it brought on was that no would-be gangsters or hoodlums tried to have a go at her for protection money. People didn't want to fall foul of the Commander of the Serious Crime Squad.

'Ruby was quite a tough businesslady – she had to be, in that profession – and she didn't cash cheques foolishly like the barman at White's. The only known instance of her catching a large bouncer was one from Eric Steiner, the famous Swedish con man. He was hugely persuasive and talked her into exchanging a monkey for one of his pieces of paper, something she regretted bitterly for a long time. Were Ruby with us today she still wouldn't have forgiven Steiner.'

Steiner, the son of a Swedish clergyman and one-time manager of tennis champion Björn Borg, would later go into the gambling business with Mark Sykes: 'Eric Steiner was a very funny character. He was an absolutely brilliant table tennis player. Brilliant, and very funny. He died in Marbella. I saw him in 1996 about five years or so before he died. He was one of the first people into heavy facelifts and plastic surgery. He looked about 45 when he was 80.'

John Burke said, 'Eric Steiner was very popular in London in the 1950s. People all over the city knew him. When he went to the Milroy, Paul Adam and the band would strike up the appropriate tune, and somebody would sing, "Nothing can be finer than to wake up with Eric Steiner in the morning."'

Or with a showgirl from Murray's Cabaret Club in Beak Street. A short walk up Regent Street from Piccadilly Circus, it was one of the first of London's fashionable nightclubs. The showgirls stood bare-breasted and motionless on the stage (as required by law), and the cleavage-endowed or uplifted host-esses sought 'scalps' in the form of fruit cups. Every sale meant a 'tip'. Princess Margaret, queen of the royal gadabouts, went there, as did Princess Muna (Toni Gardiner), who took many Arabs to the club. King Hussein was a regular. It was where Christine Keeler met Mandy Rice-Davies and Stephen Ward, and the seeds of the Profumo affair were sown.

'I'd be at all these places for the newspaper,' said Nancy Gillespie. 'It was lots of fun, with the gamblers and the characters. You never knew when you'd open a door and walk into a headline.'

Or, in her case, romance. She'd found that in 1956 when she met Gary Cooper by a Riviera swimming pool. 'We started to chat, when a woman at the other side of the pool realized that her husband was engaged in picking me up. Mrs Cooper jumped to her feet, a pair of binoculars to her eyes. "Gosh, I'd better nip off," Gary said out of the corner of his mouth. "Give me your telephone number, will you – please?"

'I knew I shouldn't, but I was dazzled and flattered and thrilled at the thought of Gary Cooper wanting to date me. I gave him the number of my flat in Lowndes Square. Gary swam off. And I only half believed that I would ever hear from him again. At that very moment I was a guest of my old friend the Maharaja of Baroda at his chateau near Cannes. If I was good enough for him and his friends, why not Gary Cooper?

'A few days later I flew home to London. I still had not heard from Gary again. Then, one night, as I was getting ready for bed, I got a personal call from Cannes. "Come and see me, honey," said the unmistakable drawl. "I need you. Get an air ticket right away. I'll be waiting for you."

'I ought to have turned haughty and said "No". But, of course, I did nothing of the sort. I said "Yes" – and a couple of days later I began my one crazy week of fun with Gary Cooper.

'He had packed his wife off back to the United States, so the coast was reasonably clear. Not entirely clear, because Gary was scared of his fans finding out. So I did not stay at his hotel. I was booked in at another hotel three miles away. I occupied the bridal suite. Gary gave me the money – £20 a night. The manager was most surprised that Nancy Gillespie, the "bride" from London, had no bridegroom with her. He became quite suspicious when he found that I hardly ever used my suite, except to sleep there. And I was a very late bird all that week. I used the suite mainly as a dressing room.

'Every morning I changed into a bikini and went to join Gary on the beach. Every night I changed into evening clothes and met Gary at his hotel or at a restaurant. It was our beach outings that I enjoyed most. We would find some remote stretch of sand and sunbathe. And Gary would whisper all sorts of nonsense into my ear.

'At night we went on fantastic binges – well away from the areas favoured by tourists. And the back of Gary's Bentley Continental was stacked with empties. Usually we covered up the bottles with a travelling rug. It would never do for the fans to have spotted them. But one night, as the Bentley pulled up

outside Gary's hotel, the pressure of the bottles in the back
forced the door open. The whole lot shot out onto the
pavement! It was terribly embarrassing for Gary. He whispered to me, "Gee, kid, I hope there are no newspaper people
around."

'Those weren't the only bottles that Gary carried around.
He was a hopeless hypochondriac, and he never travelled
without a large case that contained bottles of medicine, boxes
of pills, lotions and ointments to cope with every emergency.
He was always talking about illness and forever showing his
suspicion of food that was offered to him. One day we had a
perfectly delicious lobster for lunch at an expensive restaurant
in Monte Carlo. I thought the meal was wonderful. Gary
thought it was horrid. He carried out every possible test on his
lobster. He sniffed and he peered and he chewed experimental
morsels before every mouthful.

'That night we had a date with Prince Rainier and Princess
Grace, his *High Noon* co-star. They were throwing a party at
the Sporting Club of Monte Carlo. Before it, Gary was sick. I
am sure he had imagined himself into being ill. He recovered
before the party. But when we arrived at the Club, Gary was
still thinking of his sickness.

'Flunkeys bowed us to the regal presence.

'"Glad to see you, Mr Cooper. How are you?" said Prince
Rainier.

'"Not so good, your Highness," replied Gary. "I've been
throwing up all day all over your kingdom."

'It was unforgivable, of course. And Prince Rainer did not
try to hide his annoyance. I loved every dyed hair on Gary's
head, but he just did not appreciate how this could shock. He
flew back to London with me – and there we parted. He had
to return to America.'

Nancy was moping around London when she met the man

whose title would put her on a par with Princess Grace – though, sadly, without the money. It was an encounter which would bring her even closer to the gamblers of London.

'I was dining alone, and rather miserably, at a Polish restaurant in Soho. I knew the proprietor, who came to my table. "Miss Gillespie, may I introduce to you an old friend of mine, Prince George Sapieha?"

'I looked up at the tall, handsome figure by his side. Somehow I managed to smile. I gave him permission to sit with me at my table. There was charm in every word he spoke. I was grateful for his company. We agreed to meet the next evening. He took me to dinner. When the time came for him to see me home I knew I was in love.

This was something different. Or so I imagined. Never before had I felt so stricken with helplessness. Every touch, every gesture, every word told me this was the man I would marry. George told me he loved me too. And within a month we were making arrangements to marry.

'But George's parents disapproved. He was not quite 21. I was five years older. So we decided to elope. Without a word to anybody, we packed two suitcases and went to Scotland. At Glasgow we gave notice at the register office. Then for three weeks we hid at a small hotel.

'On the eve of the ceremony, I could contain myself no longer. I phoned my best friend, Sarah Rothschild, the daughter of Lord Rothschild, and straight away she caught the night train from London to Glasgow in time for the ceremony. I had never been happier. I was in love with the most wonderful man in the world. I was now Her Serene Highness Princess Sapieha. I was a member of one of the most noble families in the world. George's ancestors included a Tsar of Russia, a cardinal, and an ambassador to the Court of St James. Their vast estates spread throughout Poland to the Lithuanian border. Then the Germans invaded in 1939, and George's family became refugees.

'George himself was almost penniless. He had nothing apart from the few pounds a week he was earning as an advertising representative. By that time I was expecting a child. I had to get some money from somewhere. So I decided on the easiest way of making a living I knew – gambling.'

From then on she witnessed the action at illegal games all over the capital, but not at Eaton Place or at any of the accommodations (like interior decorator David Hicks' apartments) taken for the evening by John Aspinall. She was very close to John Burke but, as a journalist and, worse, provider of high and low society gossip to 'Ephraim Hardcastle', there was no way that she could attend his games.

The press were the enemy. John Burke: 'In Dublin I had been very friendly with Paddy Campbell, who was a writer and also heir to his father Lord Glenavy, the then Governor of the Bank of Ireland. Paddy was now living in London and writing for the *Sunday Times*. He told me he enjoyed a flutter and, therefore, would like to come to some of our games. Having discussed this request with John, with some embarrassment – I had to say no. It was not that we did not trust him implicitly, but that some of the players, knowing that Paddy worked in Fleet Street, might be worried by seeing him at the chemmy table; such was our anti-publicity phobia.'

Still, while John Burke and John Aspinall attracted the top end of the money, Nancy Gillespie had other contacts: 'Some of the Society people who ran private gambling parties were my friends. I knew that they would willingly pay if I brought along clients to their parties. For this service I was never actually paid in cash. I was usually given a certain amount of credit at the tables. Once it was as much as £100 for introducing two millionaires and an industrial magnate on the same night.

'Sometimes I hired out my own flat in Lowndes Square for chemmy parties. That was worth £60 a night to me. But mostly it was at other people's houses that I did my gambling.

'On occasion I could afford to risk as much as £2,450 on the turn of a card or a spin of the wheel. My winnings were tax free. So I was in clover. And I might have gone on being a gambling agent and hostess if it hadn't been for a couple of nasty experiences. I do like my gambling to be above board. And I struck a couple of rigged games in one of the most fashionable homes of Mayfair.

'At one of them I saw an Old Etonian, with a terribly upper-class background, take a dear old millionaire for a £2,000 ride. From the start the millionaire forced the pace. His winnings rocketed. Inside two hours he was £500 to the good. The others seemed almost happy at the millionaire's run of luck. Then I became suspicious. I noticed a girl standing behind the lucky winner. She was looking at the cards he held in his hand. First she raised her right hand and touched her nose with two fingers. Then she touched her hips with her left hand. Glancing to my right, I saw her signals were being received by another player.

'It was the end of the millionaire's winning streak. From then on he began to lose heavily. First one pretty girl, then another, would sidle up to his side with a word of sympathy. They then would take it in turns to stand behind him to continue the tic-tac. He had obviously been specially invited to be "skinned".

'The riggers were my friends. But how I hated them at that moment! I wanted to cry out a word of warning but I knew that I dare not. I was forced to sit in silence and watch helplessly. Like a sportsman, the victim wrote a cheque for that amount and handed it over to his principal opponent. With a cheerful goodnight, he put on his coat and left.

'I confronted my friends, and the truth came out. Several people at the party openly admitted the game had been rigged. My Old Etonian friend had agreed to split his "winnings" 50–50 with his helpers. But then the rumpus started. The millionaire's opponent, who was a little drunk, refused to hand over the cheque. He yelled: "I did all the dirty work – now I'm sticking to the profits."

'One of his opponents sprang forward to snatch the cheque. In the scuffle which followed, it fluttered to the floor in two pieces. There was a ghastly silence. Calamity – cheques from gaming parties were bank expressed. That meant that the winners asked their banks to rush the cheques though for immediate payment – before the losers changed their minds. Here was a case where the loser had to be asked for his cheque again!

'The task was delegated to a young blade, who called on the millionaire next morning. After a sociable drink or two, he gave the millionaire some highly suspect answers to some pointed questions. So he was told to get out – without a penny.

'Sometimes real tragedy followed gambling parties where I was a guest. Johnny Levy, son of the proprietor of a fleet of taxis, sat opposite me one night. He was, I knew, in the middle of a losing streak. At this party, too, he kept on losing. By the end of the evening he was £500 down, bringing his total losses for the month to several thousands. He was ruined. He went home that night and gassed himself. It would have been easy for him to have welshed, but back then doing that was looked on in some circles as worse than death.

'It was horrid. A reminder, if I'm not being too Calvinistic, that retribution exists. Yet such things happened and the gambling went on – even more so. The stakes got higher. In every sense.'

Which is why some of the most famous names in the world

wanted to be playing chemmy. With the threat of prosecution gone, in 1958 they all but paraded along a remarkable rainbow to what had become the most socially acceptable, upmarket games in town. John Aspinall and John Burke simply held out the pot of gold for their punters to fill, in a series of spectacular days and nights of feverish chemmy.

9. LA DOLCE VITA

Who Dares Wins.

SAS MOTTO

Of all the fearless, fanatical gamblers who provided style, dignity and impeccable good manners to Aspinall and Burke's upmarket private chemmy games, John Burke singles out one man as a giant. Indeed, he sounds like someone from the pages of John Buchan.

Funded by ancestral wealth, Scottish landowner Colonel William Stirling was larger than life. He had two younger brothers. Peter Stirling was a diplomat, working mostly in the Middle East. David Stirling was the famous 'Phantom Major' of the Second World War; the founder of the Long Range Desert Groups which became the SAS Regiment. Churchill called him 'the bravest man I have ever known'. He was promoted to the rank of Colonel after the war.

John Burke said: 'He was a charming, modest man. Once, before I knew him well, I introduced him to some other player whom he did not know as "Colonel Stirling"; afterwards he told me gently: "I am not Colonel now, Burkie, I am David." He was always a gentleman. He never wanted to make a fuss – and he was arguably one of the greatest heroes of the twentieth century. Fascinating, all those Stirlings were.

'It's strange, because I watch television and I see Colonel Bill Stirling's granddaughter Rachael, from his son Archie's marriage to Diana Rigg, and I can see the similarities. His like is not to be seen today in any of London's pseudo-smart gambling clubs. A proud bunch, the Stirlings – every reason to be.'

Colonel Bill Stirling was very special. The gambling duo had rented a house in Ascot for Royal Ascot week in 1959. At about eleven o'clock on the morning of 19 June, the all-night chemmy game finally came to a halt. The financial records tell an amazing story. The dubious Eddie Gilbert won £60,000, which was fortunate for all concerned; had he lost an amount like that, the chances of his paying it, even had he wished to do so, would have been rather worse than negligible. Gilbert was a sinking ship who got lucky that night. Most of the players did well.

Bill Stirling was the biggest loser. He lost £174,500, which is more than £4 million in 2007 values. Four million pounds gone – on one night of chemmy. Stirling went into the drawing room of the house, and John Burke joined him with his account book. Stirling signed an IOU in the account book, which John Burke still has. When he had signed off on the money, the Colonel waved to a waiter and quietly asked for a plate of scrambled eggs. There was no sign of distress, and he ate his eggs quite quickly. He had to be off – he had a busy day.

That afternoon at Ascot, in the royal enclosure, Bill Stirling did not appear to recall the loss. He went about the racing as if all was as it should be. He cleared his debt in a few weeks, and his big loss did not divert him from the chemmy tables – or his own rules.

The multi-Oscar-winning Sam Spiegel was an extraordinary character: he began life as a penniless refugee, became a specialist in 'kiting' cheques and went on to produce some of the most renowned films of the twentieth century: *On the Waterfront, The African Queen* and *The Bridge on the River*

Kwai. His financial dealings were often questioned, and writer-director Billy Wilder described him as 'a modern-day Robin Hood, who steals from the rich and steals from the poor'.

Spiegel turned up at the home of Lord Timothy Willoughby D'Erersby, who had given his house over for the gamblers to host a chemmy evening. Tim Willoughby was a genuinely well liked and trusted man about town, heir to Astor money and the vast Ancaster estates, and was soon to play an important role in the lives of John Aspinall and John Burke. Sam Spiegel was then very much in the public eye. He was currently in London to work on *Lawrence of Arabia* with director David Lean, and was gambling on an unknown actor called Peter O'Toole in the title role.

There had been a lot of coverage of the film in the newspapers, but Bill Stirling was not a reader of the popular press, the red tops of the day. The fortunes of film personalities were not something to trouble or intrigue him. He was probably one of the few people in the country who knew nothing of Sam Spiegel.

At that time John Burke had his shoes made by Fosters of Jermyn Street; Sam Spiegel was also a patron. One of their designs was a comfortable dark-blue suede shoe. At Tim Willoughby's, John Burke was wearing these shoes with a dark suit. He admits it was bad taste, maybe rather vulgar: gentlemen wore black shoes with laces in the evening. Then came the Elvis moment. Spiegel arrived wearing identical shoes. He, however, was dressed in a dinner jacket, so suede shoes were definitely 'not on'; wearing them was a sartorial solecism.

Suddenly, between chemmy shoes, Bill Stirling took John Burke aside and, indicating Spiegel, asked: 'Burkie, who is that Yid wearing blue suede shoes?' John Burke hastily shuffled his feet under a chair as he explained Spiegel's status in the world of film, a world light years away from the Stirling family.

Spiegel was a sensible chemmy player, if anyone can be

described that way. Sometimes he won, sometimes he lost; never vast amounts either way – merely plus or minus a few thousand. He did employ a strategy, however, that, while not affecting his winnings, nullified his losses. He wisely did not stay at the table all night, and when he left, if he were a winner he would leave with a cheque payable to himself in his pocket, while if a loser he would agree the sum with John Burke and then ask him to go to his office later that day to collect it.

Waiting at the Spiegel office in Dover Street would be a cheque payable to John Burke: 'This was quite normal; many gamblers did not wish their bank managers to see the name Aspinall on large cheques. Yet, while Spiegel's winnings were paid to him personally, his losing cheques were always drawn on a production or film company; successful financiers are ever loath to waste their own money. It's interesting to think, historically speaking, that *Lawrence of Arabia* may have paid John Burke several thousand pounds. Possibly tens of thousands. I can't recall it all.'

For the promoters, one of the most important games, the smartest and, they hoped, the most financially rewarding of their season, was the private game staged during Derby week. In 1959 it was on Thursday in John Burke's flat at 60 Eaton Place, in the drawing room, which was ideal for their nocturnal activities. It was a jovial scene, and most of the gambling was going well.

But outside, danger was lurking. News of the game had reached Fleet Street, and the street outside the front door was alive with newspaper reporters, scenting a front-page scoop. The threat of police action had been replaced by an even more deadly and destructive force. Aspinall and Burke did not alert or alarm their players. They prayed that the press would get fed up and leave. But at breakfast they were still there. The resourceful waiter Bob Richardson carried out a reconnaissance of the basement. He discovered that it was possible to gain access, through a window, to a small back courtyard, and from there onto a low flat roof from which it was feasible to get down into a side street. On that Friday morning in June 1959, this route was used by some notable escapees, among whom were the Earl of Derby, his brother the Hon. Richard Stanley, the Duke of Devonshire and Bernard Van Cutsem, who remarked, 'Colditz would have been child's play to Bob.'

Yet not all the players could use Bob's *Great Escape* route. As always, needs must. Lady O. was anxious to go home, and Bob ensured that she was carried out to a waiting van in a laundry basket. When the game eventually ended at lunchtime, the press had decamped. John Burke points out that the pubs had opened.

Super-punter Lord Derby, having lost tens of thousands of pounds, shinned down a drainpipe to escape the press; later that day the very English, pink-faced John Derby looked immaculate in his morning coat and top hat as he chatted to the Queen at Epsom (the Derby was then run on Wednesday and the Oaks on Friday).

Stamina was an essential for the smart-set gambler in the late 1950s. It appears that waiter Bob Richardson had smarts with his stamina. While it is not essential for play to begin that all nine players' seats at the chemmy table be filled, it looks better for the promoter if they are. In those (for Burke and Aspinall) halcyon days, house players played an important role. There were two types: the obvious 'house' player, as in John Aspinall himself, John Burke, Lady O. or Jane Aspinall – or people who were supposedly independent and gambling with their own money.

It was important, if two or three big players arrived early, to fill up the table and keep the action at a high pitch. As more real punters arrived, the house players would drop out.

Yet, towards the end of the night – which could be midmorning and sometimes later – important (as in rich and foolish) players like Lord Derby would want to play on. This happened at Tim Willoughby's house, with Peter West, the ultimate charming house player, betting £1,000 at a time with Derby and Devonshire until the game ended at 2 p.m. the next day. It is understandable how a character like Peter West could confuse fantasy and reality. Moments after the game was over, he had to check on his account at Martin's Bank. He was £50 short, and looked at his friends. John Aspinall, John Burke and Peter West had £10 between them. Bob the waiter, who as usual had enjoyed lavish tips from the gamblers, loaned West the £50 he needed.

'Let me give you a cheque for £60 for that very kind thing you are doing for me,' West said to Bob.

Bob was not a risk-taker: 'No, better if you give me cash at the next game.'

The chemmy gamblers were an extraordinary collection of people. Edward John Stanley, MC, 18th Earl of Derby, had plenty of stamina and was the leader of the pack. John Derby might have been the reincarnation of some legendary eighteenth- or nineteenth-century aristocratic English gambler. One of Derby's ancestors, when heir to the earldom, was offered the throne of Greece, but replied that he preferred to be king of Lancashire.

Indeed, the chemmy-playing Derby owned lots of Liverpool and much of Lancashire. He was a slightly masochistic gambler and had the same penchant in sexual matters, liking to be beaten with shoelaces tied together by a particular lady he knew from Les Ambassadeurs. He was recklessly fearless at the gaming table (one chemmy game lasted for thirty hours), completely honourable and always courteous – but a lunatic gambler nevertheless. John Burke recalled, 'John Derby was a crazy gambler in that he would double up more and more when losing, a disastrous gambling strategy. One night at 93 Eaton Place, playing against house players after everyone had gone home, Derby was losing £300,000.

'John Aspinall thought that this was too much, and he feared – wrongly, as subsequent events were to prove – that when his lordship sobered up next day he would refuse to pay and never return. Therefore in the last shoe it was artificially ensured that Derby won back half of his losses. This decision was a calculated commercial one, in no way quixotic.'

Of course, if you could allow a punter to win you could also make him lose; you could control the play.

The wealth that was squandered in those long evenings and nights remains astonishing, even to those who enjoy gambling. Before his death, Colonel Bill Stirling in 1975 sold thousand of acres; the family home, Keir House and some extraordinary works of art. Archie Stirling told the clan's website in February 2006 that it was not just 'foolish expenditure' which caused this, but also an 'inability to understand cash flow'.

Aspinall and Burke understood cash flow. They seemingly couldn't lose. Yet, for Aspinall, there never seemed to be enough money coming in. His expenses were enormous. Aspinall, a strange, amoral mix, an apparent emotional wasteland, did not appear to understand how to apply the brake. At times John Burke was uneasy about Aspinall's flexible morality. There is the nagging passage in Brian Masters' 1988 biography, *The Passion of John Aspinall*, on which Aspinall cooperated, where the author suggests that the court case discouraged the punters, when in fact it brought more and more powerful players to the games. At the same time, he writes: 'There was never any suggestion that he was less than scrupulously honest, never a hint of suspicion that he would permit cheating; indeed, this was one of the firmest rocks upon which his success so far had been founded as gambling promoters were, on the whole, a thoroughly reprobate lot without a moral between them. One of the reasons the aristocracy went to Aspinall was that they knew they could trust him.'

'Win or Lose, We'll Have More Booze' was the rallying cry of Major Billy Straker-Smith, late of the Brigade of Guards; the banker was the epitome of an English gentleman and had a passion for the game of cricket. As the long gambling nights went on, fuelled by the liquid ministrations of the waiters Bob and Bert, the gallant major would describe each coup of the chemmy game in cricketing parlance. 'Knocked that one into the crowd for six', he would cry, when some lucky punter turned over a nine, while the smaller 'natural' eight was 'stroked it through the covers for four'. When the *banco* caller narrowly beat the bank, he'd offer: 'stole a quick single', or 'nicked one through the slips'. If the coup went the other way, in the bank's favour, it was a case of being 'caught behind the wicket' or, sometimes, 'run out'.

Major Straker-Smith occasionally expressed himself in language that some might consider rude. John Burke says he always did so in a good-humoured fashion, never with even a hint of anger or bad sportsmanship. His great cry, having lost a coup, was 'Fuck my tits, we're cattled!'

Four members of the Macmillan government were regular players at the games: Churchill's son-in-law Christopher Soames, the Duke of Devonshire, Richard Stanley and Bob Boothby. One night in David Pelham's flat, three of them were at the table. At 8 a.m. two of that trio, the Duke and Stanley, were sober and sensible – they were expected at 10 Downing Street to meet the prime minister at 10 a.m. The third minister, Lord Boothby, was exuberant and not totally sober, clearly enjoying himself. When his Cabinet colleagues tried to induce him to come away with them, he banged the table and shouted: 'Fuck the Cabinet. Fuck Macmillan. I want to play chemmy – *Banco!*'

'It was a strange thing, the language,' said John Burke. 'Nancy Mitford had brought out her book about what was "U" and "non-U". There were words that were unbelievably, terribly "non-U", like "toilet" and "pardon". These were words which a lady or gentleman could never use. Quite acceptable to say "fuck", of course.

'One night Lord Stanley of Aldernay was playing, and his wife Kitty, who didn't often come to the games, was there. Ed Stanley was cursing like the best of them. "Oh, darling, watch what you're saying," said his wife.

'He turned on her: "I'll stop saying fuck . . ." – there was a pause – "if you stop saying pardon."'

One great exception to the press ban at the games was Clive Graham, the racing correspondent 'Scout' of the *Daily Express* in its heyday. He and his wife were well known socially, but Mrs Graham was sometimes protected from knowledge of her husband's gambling. One evening when Clive Graham was playing, Bob the waiter went outside to get a breath of fresh air and saw, coming along the pavement, Mrs Graham with her two little dogs.

'I see you've got a game in John's flat. Can I come in and have a drink?'

Bob, unaware of the instructions to keep her in the dark about her husband's gambling, invited her in. Graham recognized her voice and dived under the table. Mrs Graham went into the game, where one seat was vacant, and Bob poured a drink for her. She would have simply had her drink and gone home none the wiser, if it hadn't been for the dogs. They sniffed around and, as is the way with dogs, they sniffed out their owner. They ran under the table barking, and Clive Graham was flushed out of his hiding place. 'I don't think there were any serious consequences,' says John Burke. 'Mrs Graham had a good sense of humour.'

Not all that happened was amusing. One chemmy evening at 93 Eaton Place, Billy Straker-Smith was a heavy loser: he got up from the table having lost £50,000 and having behaved impeccably throughout the game. Although it was nowhere near the biggest loss that a player had suffered at Aspinall and Burke's tables, it was still the equivalent of around £1 million in 2007 money. It was a great deal to lose in a friendly card game, especially for someone who honourably intended to pay up without much delay.

Straker-Smith was a rich man, but he was not in the same financial league as some of the other players like Devonshire and Derby who had won from him. He put on a brave face, but behind that iron facade he must have been feeling sick. As Straker-Smith was about to leave, having agreed his account with John Burke, 'Aspers' went over and put his hand on his shoulder. Aspinall adopted the most genuine manner he could muster. He nodded at his victim, smiled charmingly, rubbed Straker-Smith's shoulder and then said sympathetically, 'Hard luck, Billy. You played a great game.'

The gallant major drew himself up to his full height, shoulders back, head erect, took a firm grip on his perfectly rolled umbrella and replied in his military voice, 'Yes, John, straight back to the bowler, straight back to the bowler.'

Billy Straker-Smith, soldier and gentleman, then stepped firmly out into the Belgravia dawn.

It was also at dawn that one of the most phenomenal chemmy encounters to take place at 93 Eaton Place finally concluded. In 1960, European playboy Gianni Agnelli was the uncrowned king of Italy. Lord Derby was royalty at the chemmy tables. What luck it seemed that they were both staying in London on 28 June 1960. It was an opportunity, a gift, for John Aspinall, who a year earlier had met the Fiat heir at a Monte Carlo casino.

This fabulously wealthy legendary lover of the good life was on Aspinall's list of the 'Top Ten Most Wanted Gamblers'. Agnelli – suave, sophisticated, a picture of good taste and breeding (his mother was a Bourbon princess) – was regarded as one of the richest men in the world. In 2000, three years before his death at the age of 81, his family fortune was estimated at $5 billion. He was a superb catch for the gambling promoters.

Aspinall and John Burke quickly arranged to have a game that evening at Aspinall's flat. Lady Annabel Birley was recruited to socially impress the Italian. The wine was chosen more carefully than ever, the food presented more lavishly. Extra flowers had been bought. Aspinall wanted the perfect ambience.

Agnelli, who had chased around the world with his friend Prince Rainier of Monaco, dated Rita Hayworth and Anita Ekberg, and escorted Jackie Kennedy Onassis, both before and after President JFK's assassination, now turned his charms on John Burke's Italian girlfriend and future wife, the great beauty Liliana Livon.The two Italians chatted amicably between the chemmy shoes and then the Earl of Derby arrived and the action really got started.

The game was organized so quickly that Aspinall could not contact other big players. The 'A' team was absent. At the table were Michael Alachouzos, Henry Vyner, Peter (Lord) St Just, an American businessman called Ted Bassett and, for the house, Peter West and John Burke.

Aspinall was the croupier. He took the job in order to avoid being caught in a betting crossfire between Derby and Agnelli, where he might have been forced for reasons of prestige to bet large amounts foolishly.

The game had got under way after dinner and a few hours later it had reached, at least for the hosts, a truly happy state, better than they could ever have hoped for. The limit on an opening bank was £10,000 – a large white chip and an astonishing amount of money at the time, the equivalent of more than a quarter of a million pounds at 2007 values.

Agnelli was losing £200,000, and announced that he was not going to play on. That meant a huge payout. There were two big winners, Derby and the house. John Derby was a consistent loser in the games and was, at that time, heavily 'on the books' – that is, owing vast sums to Aspinall. He would therefore collect only part of his winnings. Agnelli, of course, would pay his losses in full and probably quite promptly.

The winners were desperately trying to appear cool. They had won an absolute fortune. How could they spend it? What wishful thinking.

Lord Derby, tall, thin, bespectacled and unprepossessing in looks but not attitude, had other ideas. He wanted the game to continue, and, after much cajoling, he eventually persuaded Agnelli, albeit reluctantly, to sit down again at the table.

In the middle of the shoe, Agnelli opened a bank with a £5,000 blue chip. Derby instantly called '*banco.*' He wanted action. He'd take the bet, all of the £5,000.

The Italian – tanned, neat – stretched out his arm, revealing his watch worn over his shirt-cuff, and picked up his cards. Agnelli's luck was about to change.

Derby lost, an eight to a four. The bank was now £10,000. Derby promptly called, in his thin voice, '*Suivi.*' And lost.

Now, there was £20,000 in the bank. Without a moment's hesitation, the agitated Derby called out again, '*Suivi.*'

The bank was at double the evening's limit. Everyone at the table saw that Agnelli was anxious. Any sane person would be. It was the equivalent in 2007 of about half a million pounds sterling resting on the turn of a card – a gamble played and over quicker than any adrenaline rush.

Agnelli, through either pride or foolishness, accepted the challenge. He dealt the four cards from the shoe. He had a natural nine, Derby a seven. As the hosts watched despairingly, the inevitable happened. With four £10,000 white chips sitting in the centre of the table – say, £1 million pounds – his Lordship eagerly spoke the dreaded word. He squeaked, 'Suivi.'

This time Agnelli not only demurred, he insisted that he would garage £20,000, leaving £20,000 – still double the limit – to be won or lost in the next coup. Derby argued with Agnelli, a Renaissance man often called 'Prince' in Italy. He pleaded with him not to garage, but the banker was adamant.

It was at this point that John Derby turned to John Burke and asked: 'Tell me, Burkie, who is that foreign chap? He won't have a decent punt.'

Agnelli might have been the richest man in Europe, but to Lord Derby, who was unlikely ever to have travelled in a Fiat, he was simply a foreigner who had made his fortune in trade. Yet the tradesman was the victor.

Derby lost another £20,000. And also the next coup. It was only on his next coup that this particular run of Agnelli's luck stopped. But the game did not. When luck, that fickle thing, turned on him, Derby hit a losing streak. When, because of Derby's obstinacy, the cash situation had turned turtle on the hosts, Aspinall decided to play himself and John Burke became the croupier. It didn't help.

Aspinall lost £20,000, twenty long ones. So, to the hosts' discomfort, did Michael Alachouzos. Alachouzos was playing on the books, so his loss did not help the cashflow. Gianni Agnelli was no longer £200,000 in the red as the game went on; indeed, he was close to profit.

Arguably, if Agnelli had accepted the £40,000 coup with Derby, it could have gone on and on, up to £80,000 and so ad infinitum. When, later, it was John Derby's bank, Agnelli would be morally bound to *banco* any amount, however large, that Derby chose to open for, and to continue in the same vein as his opponent. The situation could have got to the point where the entire Fiat empire was wagered against the vast Stanley estates, including much of Liverpool. All on the turn of a card in a chemmy game.

The end result was that Derby retained a fraction of his earlier winnings, and instead of paying out £200,000, the Italian tycoon left 93 Eaton Place with a cheque for £22,400. John Burke was philosophical: 'His sense of relief must have contrasted vividly with our sense of gloom. For us to have collected £200,000 – £5 million or so in today's money – would truly have ranked as a very pleasant outcome of a friendly card game! As they say: "Win some, lose some."'

Liliana told John Burke that although Agnelli put on a superb, gentlemanly, unemotional facade, he had confided in her that he was genuinely nervous. He had played in Europe's major casinos and gambled for heavy amounts of money: but he had never before encountered anybody like John Derby.

Aspinall and Burke did not run the Agnelli evening in their normal manner: there was no *cagnotte*. They saw the evening as an introduction for Agnelli to their games, and hoped that he would enjoy himself and become a regular player – after all he was only a short private-jet ride away in Turin.

But Agnelli never returned to the London chemmy tables. Perhaps he had nightmares in which the Earl of Derby, in his slight voice, kept calling: '*Suivi.*'

10. MAKING A MINT

To be alive at all involves some risk.

PRIME MINISTER HAROLD MACMILLAN, 1956

For many, of course, including John Aspinall and John Burke, the Earl of Derby was a dream. Aspinall certainly regarded him as something of a private bank, a branch of Martin's, maybe, and he didn't like anyone else making or trying to make a withdrawal there.

At this time an intriguing man called Peter Scott was making many unauthorized withdrawals. Not Scott of the Antarctic, but the one known to regulars of the Star as 'Scott of the Drainpipe'. In 1958 he had officially, in underworld circles, taken over from George Chatham as king of the cat burglars. An eloquent character from Northern Ireland, he was, like Chatham, an inveterate gambler. Maybe it was something to do with heights.

John Burke recalls being at the Star one summer evening when Scott arrived driving a convertible chocolate-brown Bentley. 'In that Belfast accent of his he announced: "Sophia Loren has given me a little present." Of course, he'd robbed the poor girl.'

Or rather, rich girl. Scott knew his targets. The Italian actress was in London filming *The Millionairess*, and trying to keep her distance from her co-star, Peter Sellers. She was staying in the Norwegian Barn at the Edgewarebury Country

Club. Scott, with a stolen Jaguar and an expensively acquired green Metropolitan Police press card, drove into the area and was told where Loren's rooms were. He was in and out before you could say 'Mamma mia!' and departed with a briefcase packed with cash and jewels, valued for insurance purposes at £200,000.

Scott had a drink with his friends at the Star and told John Burke that he was looking forward to the Goodwood Races. Unfortunately for him, Sophia Loren appeared on television and put a gypsy curse on whoever had stolen from her. The cat burglar – who once described himself as 'only a dishonest window cleaner' – lost the lot at Goodwood. Not long afterwards, a well-known bookmaker was seen driving around in a very nice open-top Bentley.

The times were changing for all gamblers. The ill-fated prosecution of Aspinall, Lady O. and John Burke had persuaded the government to tackle the laws on gambling. On 16 November 1959, Home Secretary Rab Butler introduced the Betting and Gaming Bill to the House of Commons. The Lords got it six months later. There were lobbyists both for and against the changes to the law, representing all kinds of interests, including those of slum landlord Peter Rachman. He was a keen gambler and owned clubs with Raymond Nash where illegal games were played. Rachman always aspired to attend John Aspinall's games, but was never allowed.

'There's no way we could have had Rachman at our games,' explains John Burke. 'Yes, OK, there was some snobbery, but it was a matter of business. We had the Duke of Devonshire and the Earl of Derby playing with us, and the press were always a fear. Imagine Rachman at the table with people who'd been on television earlier in the evening meeting the Queen? It wasn't logical.'

Yet it was to Peter Rachman. Up to his early death, aged 42, in November 1962, he never gave up trying to join the games. Raymond Nash told me in Marbella in May 2006 that Rachman had asked him to approach John Burke. 'Peter wanted the best of everything. It was because of his background. We were very close. When he was told by the doctor that he had a heart condition which could kill him, he told me and he said: "What do you think I should do?" I said: "Have the best time of your life. Enjoy every second and do the best for yourself, because you have enough money. Anything you want you should buy, you can have."

What Rachman wanted was the beautiful sixteen-year-old Christine Keeler, then a showgirl at Murray's Club. Nash observed: 'Peter had always had an eye for her. He would undress her with his eyes as she walked by. She became his girlfriend and he bought her everything: high fashion, furs, nightgowns and jewels.'

As well as Raymond Nash, one of Rachman's aides was another East Ender, Tommy Yeardye, the co-founder of the Vidal Sassoon empire. In the twenty-first century he was chairman of the Jimmy Choo shoe company. His daughter Tamara Mellon, glossy magazine favourite and friend of Goldsmith's daughter Jemima Khan and Hugh Grant, was president in 2007.

Yeardye was amiable and well liked and also tried to help get Rachman into the Aspinall and Burke chemmy games, but to no avail.

When Yeardye died in April 2004, newspaper obituaries wondered at the source of his fortune, and the *Guardian* reported: 'The origins of Yeardye's enormous wealth have never been fully explained.' The old stories surfaced again; that he stole from his former fiancée, Diana Dors, that he'd worked with the Krays. Yet Yeardye was indeed loaded. Bobby McKew, in October 2006, offered the real and more prosaic story:

'I knew Tommy well. He asked me around for drinks not long before he died. He was an Irishman. He was adopted and Yeardye was not his real name. His money? He worked for Peter Rachman, like Raymond did. After the war there were houses all over London going for very little money, properties in Bayswater which would be in the millions today. Rachman bought them up in other people's names. He got about ten houses in Tommy's name, and then Tommy pissed off to America. By the time he came back the prices of the houses had soared, and he built on it from there. I don't think he gave Mrs Rachman any of the money after her husband died.'

And Mrs Rachman wasn't familiar with Bryanston Mews, the lavish apartment her husband had bought for his girl-friends after the death of Diana Dors' former husband, Dennis Hamilton.

Hamilton had supplied girls and sex orgies at the grand house he shared with Diana Dors in Maidenhead. He took films and recorded – on a system linked to loudspeakers – familiar names in unfamiliar positions. Rachman went for the high-stakes gambling sessions – and the anonymous sex. He never talked to his sexual partners there.

A relentless voyeur, Dennis Hamilton had a two-way mirror at the house; it was installed in the ceiling. Guests were diverted to watch the action. After his marriage to the tragic Diana Dors ended Hamilton moved the ornate mirror to Bryanston Mews. He died not long afterwards from complications brought on by venereal disease – the Al Capone curse.

Rachman got the flat, and the mirror. Christine Keeler lived there with the model Sherry Danton, who became Raymond Nash's girlfriend. Later, when Christine Keeler had left Rachman, her friend from Murray's, Mandy Rice-Davies, moved in. Rachman gave her £80 a week and bought her an Arab stallion. Mandy enjoyed the good life, and her taste would be indulged by Bobby McKew's business acquaintance, Emil Savundra.

Nash, who in 2007 was 75 and married to a Korean princess, was the only man that Rachman allowed at the flat. Together they owned the Condor Club, where Michael Caine and Terence Stamp would become regulars, but Rachman was very much the silent partner. Rock star Marty Wilde, earning £1 a night plus a bowl of spaghetti, was talent-spotted there by the all-powerful entertainment agent of the day, Larry Parnes.

Raymond Nash said: 'Peter was very good friends with Diana Dors and Dennis Hamilton, and went to their house a lot. He liked the fucking there. When Peter started spending all his time fucking and gambling, he more or less gave me the Condor Club.

'Aspinall's sister Jenny Osborne worked for me at the Condor. She worked there for quite a long time. She was one of my trusted cashiers and waitresses.

'I was the one who gave Tommy Steele a job. We had cabaret at the Condor. I paid him £10 or £20 a week. I can't remember exactly, but I gave Matt Monro the same deal. Later, the Rolling Stones worked for me for a little while. The Beatles? They wanted six hundred a week. I said they would never make it. I said that nobody was worth that much in the world!

'The club was a huge success. And my property business was booming. I used to buy twenty properties at a time. I had nearly as many properties as Peter at that time. He was my Godfather, he was the guy who taught me how to borrow 110 per cent from banks, and buy and buy. He was a very kind and gentle man, contrary to what everybody thought – that he was ill-treating tenants and all that. But his reputation was terrible. After Peter died, my lawyers said I should make a statement. I distanced myself from him because his name had become so bad. So many things happened.

'I was running chemmy games. By then they were only semi-illegal but they were quite low class. I used to hire apartments for the games. I started that at a very low level, almost playing on the floor! But people took to it – they loved it. It was chemmy, chemmy, chemmy. Instant gratification. Win or lose, it was over in seconds.

'We had tables where fifty people could go around it. The croupiers were in the centre, and they played with actual coins. We were just one of many games around town – some people got very smart and started importing chemmy tables from Caro in Paris. But people lost money on other tables just as easily.'

Nash and Rachman wanted the new gaming legislation to favour their plans for chemmy games in a string of nightclubs they hoped to open. Raymond Nash told me: 'Peter Rachman and I employed Billy Rees-Davies – we called him the one-armed bandit – to put through the Gaming Act. As a lawyer and an MP, he cleverly talked it up in the Commons. We also used the Labour MP Tom Driberg, who was a fairly nasty queer; people were always trying to beat him up and he didn't always like it. But he did the job for us.'

The new law didn't help Aspinall and Burke, because now the *cagnotte* was banned – whoever won a coup or a hand of cards had, by law, to receive all the winnings. And if the games were held in a club and the players were members, there could only be a set table charge, plus, perhaps, a membership fee. So the incredible profits to be made from taking 5 per cent of every winning bank, tens of thousands of pounds at a time, were over – by Act of Parliament on 29 July 1960, one month after the Agnelli–Derby encounter.

The carousel chemmy games were no longer such a sure

thing; all over London entrepreneurs looked at the odds, and there were strong advantages in opening clubs. One of the first to open, in 1961, was Les Ambassadeurs, where John Mills moved the nightclub, the Garrison, to the basement, and started government-approved gaming. It was there that Derby gambled away a huge sum in just one evening. Much has been written about that event, but John Burke played in the early stages of the game: 'I won a couple of thousand pounds and a little later Mariani, who was then the *chef de partie* in Les Ambassadeurs, said to me, "You look tired, Mr Burke, perhaps you ought to go home." He was giving me a hint that something odd was going to happen later on. Which it did, of course. John Derby lost £165,000.

'John Aspinall was absolutely furious when he heard about this, because by now he believed he was the senior partner in raiding the Stanley fortune. And now somebody else comes along stealing his money, more or less! He felt that John Mills had set the whole thing up.

'We both knew Mills quite well in the old days, because he ran the Milroy where we all went. I don't personally believe that Mills did set this game up. Although it was certainly a crooked game. There was a character there who posed as a rich Greek shipowner, yet none of the upper-class Greek shipowners who I knew had any knowledge of him. It was said that he was a big-time casino crook and he had one or two of Mills' croupiers bent, and they set up a game and the Greek guy was the big winner – he took all this money from Derby.

'I knew John Mills fairly well and liked him. By this time, he was successful and quite rich, and earlier he had made the Milroy a huge success, and the Les A. gambling club was doing extremely well. He had no need for stunts like that. Whatever the truth, naturally, he was an enemy of John Aspinall for ever more.'

Aspinall also fell out with Michael Alachouzos over the same subject – John Derby's money. Alachouzos was Greek – his family were sponge harvesters and merchants, but he was born in the Eastern Mediterranean, in Italian territory, and interned as an enemy alien on the Isle of Man during the Second World War. When the conflict ended, he was befriended by the Marquess of Milford Haven. Liberty ships had been mass produced during the war for badly needed transport, but afterwards they were sold off at cut prices. Through his contact with Milford Haven, Alachouzos bought a Liberty ship very cheaply. He called it the *Medina Princess* – 'Earl of Medina' was one of the Milford Haven titles.

It was a lucky move, because on the outbreak of the Korean War cargo shipping rates soared, and Alachouzos made money. He married an Englishwoman, Josie, and set up home with her – and with June, his mistress, the divorced second wife of Randolph Churchill. It was that rare thing, a happy *ménage à trois*.

A keen social climber, Alachouzos benefited from June's former social position. He was friendly with Aspinall and John Burke, as Burke explained: 'He came to all the private games; sometimes he played for himself and sometimes it was special arrangements. In fact, he became more or less one of the family. He had a great deal of charm and was undoubtedly an intelligent man. The real Greek shipowners who played in the games, people like John Goulandris, regarded Michael with amusement, but they did not dislike him.

'He got on extraordinarily well with the English toffs, especially with John Derby, who took a real shine to him and referred to him as "that splendid Greek". Sometimes Derby invited him to White's to play bridge. Once he invited him to Knowsley, the family seat. Alachouzos used our parties, and in turn, he was an asset to us, which was a happy two-way deal.'

Above. John Aspinall with the most important woman in his life, his mother Lady O., and his first wife, Jane, outside the flat in Eaton Place.

Right. John Burke strides triumphantly out of court with John Aspinall, equipped with his trademark brolly, following their landmark legal victory.

Overleaf.
Pages from John Burke's account book, showing the money won and lost at a single game of chemmy on 29 May 1958.

29-5-'58

W.

████████████	420
Ackroyd	102
█████████	1,023
Ambler	4,885
Brigham	450
Cundell	150
Chips	95
Gordon	761
Lloyd	1,070
Lady O.	1,870
Muir	5,840
W. Stirling	10,625
Worsley	1,400
Willoghby	30
Strober - Smith	12,235
████████████	230
J.B.	226
	41,412

L.

Jone	700
Collin	6,490
Derly	24,500
Hombro	3,750
Aspen	700
Man - Karpan	1,200
Stanly	3,373
Van Cutson	19,700
West	400
	60,813
	41,412
	19,401

Left. They'd never had such a good day out: the legendary gambler the Duke of Devonshire, with the duchess and Prime Minister Harold Macmillan.

Below. Reckless gambler Lord Derby, seen here with Princess Margaret in July 1954.

Above.
The Clermont Club.

Right.
The Star Tavern
in Belgravia.

Above, left. The nightclub maestro: the always impeccable Mark Birley dressed to charm in February 1965.

Above, right. Fraudster Emil Savundra reveals his attitude to the law and 'the peasants'.

Left. They seek him here, they seek him there. A man for all conspiracies, the missing Lord 'Lucky' Lucan, photographed here at his wedding.

Right. Bobby McKew with his friend Richard Harris at the opening night of *Camelot.*

Below. Bobby McKew with Eddie Chapman (right) and producer Dermot Harris (left).

You can almost hear them calling '*suivi*' – chemmy at the
River Club, London 1962.

Alachouzos was ambitious. In early 1961, he invited Derby to invest £1 million in creating a fleet of cargo ships. He would organize further financial backing from the City. His approach to Derby was made without the knowledge of Aspinall or John Burke, who said: 'When Derby came to John to ask his advice before committing himself, Aspers was absolutely, totally furious. He didn't explode in front of Derby. He persuaded him not to do it and then he confronted Michael Alachouzos and vented his wrath in no uncertain terms. He was absolutely red faced with fury. He saw Derby as his pigeon and his alone. The idea of another operator, who had actually met his Lordship through him, trying to hone in on the Stanley fortune, was an unforgivable transgression. A diabolical liberty. John and Michael fell out totally.'

Alachouzos also fell out of favour with the insurance companies. The *Medina Princess* had been a great success, but by 1961 she was a liability. On one voyage she encountered extremely rough weather, and, but for the skill and dedication of her English captain, might have gone down. John Burke was with his friend when this was going on: 'I remember Alachouzos pacing up and down in his Mayfair drawing room muttering: "Why doesn't the bloody fool abandon ship?" The *Medina Princess* carried plenty of insurance. Not too long afterwards, with a more compliant master, the ship went down in East African waters; where, although there was no danger of the crew not being rescued, there were no modern facilities for refloating the vessel.'

Insurance companies, wise to the effects of the long and serious slump in shipping rates, were cynical about such events. Alachouzos's insurers refused to pay out. He sued. His barrister was the eminent QC, Sir Andrew Clark, Ian Maxwell-Scott's father-in-law. Sir Andrew lived up to his reputation, and the insurance company coughed up.

Meanwhile, John Burke and other friends of John Aspinall

witnessed Aspinall's keen and rather startling social and financial promotion of Eddie Gilbert, which they viewed with some suspicion. Aspinall, although he would drop and cut people on a whim or at any imagined slight, could also be extraordinarily generous, loyal and kind, as he was to Eddie Gilbert. Gilbert was supposed to have financed him and kept him going in difficult times, but in fact it was the other way around. Aspinall treated Gilbert like a debutante, introducing him into London society whenever he could, as in his grand party at Claus von Bülow's Belgrave Square home. He did everything in his power to help his American friend.

He suggested to several people that they should invest in Gilbert's company, the Empire Millwork Corporation, which in turn invested in several American businesses. One person he approached, naturally, was John Derby. In a letter to Aspinall from the family seat at Knowsley, Derby wrote that the investment 'does look rather a good thing'. This is followed, from Stanley House, Newmarket, by another undated letter revealing he has invested £20,000 with Gilbert.

Aspinall himself invested seven times more than Derby's £20,000 in his friend Eddie Gilbert's stock dealings. However, just as the real social ritual had done in 1958, Gilbert's debutante season was about to end for ever. Reality would soon catch up with him.

The consequences of the robbery of Jack Warner's safe finally caught up with Bobby McKew in the summer of 1959, and landed him in Tangier's Kasbah jail.

The Moroccan and French authorities then played ping-pong with him, as legal arguments over his extradition were also bounced around. He was moved to another prison in the Moroccan capital, Rabat, and then, finally, on 22 November, he was flown to Toulouse. From there he was driven on to Aix-en-Provence, where eighteen months earlier an appeal court had added two years to his three-year prison sentence. His next stop was Les Baumettes prison in Marseilles, that colourful city which was then, and is still, the headquarters of the Union Corse.

At Les Baumettes, Bobby McKew was given library duties, which improved his mind and his prospects: 'I'd go through with the books and that way I met the other prisoners. They were mostly French, so there wasn't much conversation. But one guy, André Marcel, spoke English, and we used to have long talks on Saturdays. We got on well. He was a bright boy. He knew a lot of people.'

It was the summer of 1961 before he was moved from Marseilles to Fresnes prison, about ten miles from Paris, where he was reunited with 'Dandy Kim' Caborn-Waterfield. In 1960, after much British legal wrangling and the Home Secretary getting involved, 'Dandy Kim' was extradited and jailed in France for five to seven years. Kim's prison life began in solitary confinement in cell 140. Then events took over. Jack Warner's lawyer was informed about sensitive documents that had disappeared along with the cash from the safe in the Villa Aujourd'hui. So politically explosive were the documents that pressure was applied at the highest level and bargaining began for the freedom of Prisoner No. 6544.

With just twelve months of his sentence served, Kim was freed and the order for him to repay the 'stolen' money was rescinded. Jack Warner had told Maitre Suzanne Blum, the most highly regarded lawyer in France and Kim's prosecutor, that he had been advised of delicate matters he had been unaware of when he made his accusations of theft. Blum's most famous clients were the Duke and Duchess of Windsor. In 1960, Dandy Kim was freed on his undertaking that he reveal nothing of what he found in the safe until the twenty-first century. He was still keeping silent when he spoke to me in 2007, saying merely: 'I was happy to make that pledge. I was thirty years old with a life to live – and God, how I wanted to live it!'

The arrangement did not give 'Dandy Kim' and Bobby McKew much time to catch up because, of course, it benefited them both. French lawyers had told Bobby McKew's friends that if he paid over the cost of his extradition from North Africa – £1,100 – he was all but on his way home to the new gambling capital of London, having served half his sentence. His wife was living in South Africa and not immediately contactable, so to speed up the process, Paddy Kennedy raised the money at the Star from John Burke and several of Bobby McKew's other friends (all of whom he later repaid in full).

'There was no fuss, and I didn't want any. I went to see the governor of the prison and said I did not want any publicity, my picture in the newspapers. Kim was doing prison interviews and such before he was released, but that wasn't for me. They agreed that if I did just that, kept quiet, they would take me to Paris by ambulance and I could then fly to London. The problem was, the ambulance took me to a hospital, there was a paperwork mix-up, and I ended up in a padded cell. They thought I was some lunatic! It took hours to sort it out, but I was finally on my way.

'At Heathrow nobody noticed me. The press knew I was flying in, but maybe they were looking for someone with a broken nose or something. I got back with no fuss, which was perfect.

'I was glad to be out of jail, back in London. I didn't want any more nonsense. The prisons weren't health farms. Morocco was just very primitive. There were no beds or bunks there; you slept on a mattress on the floor. When you could sleep. There were always a dozen of you or so in a room with one little pisshole. It wasn't the Ritz.

'Les Baumettes in Marseilles had a reputation as the toughest prison in Europe. They still had the guillotine, and in the first few months I was there they guillotined eight men. The stricter prisons are the best prisons. The rules are there and that's the end of it. You get into a routine and you get on with it.'

Which is what he did on his return to London. He now linked up on a more formal basis with Billy Hill. After the Aspinall and Burke court victory, Billy Hill had continued to run gambling dens (spielers), but now he began his own gambling evenings. He operated around London and had one high-rollers game in Eaton Square. He also ran a betting– gambling den near Smithfield Market with Lady's O.'s one-time bookie Charlie Matthews. Hill's wife Aggie had a club in Gerrard Street, Le Cabinet, and he ran games in the basement there.

With the new Gaming Act in force, gambling in clubs was now legal, and Billy Hill took every opportunity to make money. He was 'interested' in other clubs and casinos, but he also started his own. He opened a club at 3 Green Street in Mayfair, and also the Wentworth Country Club at Virginia Water in Surrey. Bobby McKew was the manager there. Bobby was not a gambler, but luck had nothing to do with the profits he made at that grand-sounding country club.

The enterprising pair had some help from their French friends, their connections from the Union Corse – something that gave them an edge. Bobby McKew said, 'They had vast experience in gambling, and their croupiers were the most reliable in the business. They did what was wanted without ever a word. Talk about *omertà*!

'When new people came to London they got an introduction to Billy, because in those days you didn't do anything in London without Billy. We were out with the top guy from the Union Corse and he rather liked me. He'd asked me where I was in prison in France and asked, "Did you ever meet André Marcel?"

'I said: "Yes, I knew him very well."

'He said: "Really. How?"

'"Well, he spoke English." I explained about the books and the library, and then suddenly he leaned over and kissed me on each cheek.

'The result was one night he turned around, he took me out and said: "How you doing? How many girls have you got?"

'I said, "One."

'"No, how many working for you?"

'So I said, "None."

'He said, "I'll give you a job. Come work for me and I'll start you out with pretty girls."

'It wasn't a tempting thought. Billy would have lost it over something like that.'

There was another more tempting prospect. Emil Savundra.

Michael Marion Emil Anacletus Pierre Savundranayagam was a giant fraudster, but was flawed by his own pomposity and self-regard. In Ceylon – Sri Lanka – he had learned the ropes with strange arms deals and stranger shipping movements. He was jailed in Belgium over a cargo of rice for which he was paid, but which never found its way to Antwerp. Then he turned up in Ghana, around the time Eddie Chapman was there, as some sort of 'economic adviser' to the poor. Apparently his advice was not appreciated, for he was deported. He moved on to India, China and, with Shiv Kapoor, the coffee bean swindle in Costa Rica. By the time he got to London, Bobby McKew was back, and he introduced his old acquaintance to Stephen Ward, who was also close to John Burke's friend, David Milford Haven.

As a portrait painter, Ward had sketched, amongst others, the Duke of Edinburgh, Princess Margaret, Princess Alexandra and the Duke and Duchess of Windsor, as well as Christine Keeler who, with Mandy Rice-Davies, had lived with him at times at 17 Wimpole Mews, London W1.

It was an introduction that was to have spectacular repercussions. The sex-mad Savundra was 'the Indian doctor' who had sex at £20 a time with Mandy Rice-Davies at Wimpole Mews. When Ward went on trial at the Old Bailey on 22 July 1963 for living off immoral earnings, Rice-Davies testified that she had taken money from Savundra after sex. It was a tipping point of the case against Ward, the Establishment's scapegoat for the Profumo affair, who was found guilty but committed suicide before he could be sentenced.

Still, Savundra will arguably always be more infamous as a fraudster and for the disastrous crash of his Fire, Auto & Marine Insurance Company (FAM). In the early Sixties, car insurance was a booming business, with more cars and improved roads, including motorways. By law, all drivers need minimum insurance, but even that expense was too high for many. Cleverly, Savundra offered low, low policies which, in reality, were worthless. He did not have the resources to meet the claims. But thousands of new drivers wanted to drive, and the little pieces of paper from FAM allowed them to do that. They did not realize or want to know about possible consequences. It was another of those gold mines dug from people's aspirations and dreams.

As a printer, Bobby McKew did a great deal of work for Savundra, and McKew made some investments in the business. Initially, they had a reasonable relationship, but as business boomed: 'The money went to Savundra's head. He was running a Rolls-Royce and a Hillman, and spending more than ten grand a year at Harrods. He had a house in Hampstead, was gambling, into offshore yacht racing and was screwing everything he could.

'At the same time he was holier than thou. He was a good Catholic. He gave ten per cent of what he stole to the Church. When he was in jail in Belgium, the Catholic Church put so much pressure on the Belgian government that they released him. He looked after the Church; they looked after him. He originally started off doing the money for a cardinal who became the Pope. I don't remember, but you're talking about whoever was the Pope forty-five years ago.

'He took me out to dinner at the Savoy and told me he was having three red cardinals to dinner later in the week. He was all airs and graces by then. He said to me: "I don't think you should come along, Bobby." Because I'd been in prison he didn't want me getting any redemption, I suppose. No, he turned into an awful snob. He didn't want anyone reminding him he was a jailbird too.

'I was doing a great deal of print work for him at the Dulwich Press and it was profitable. But he'd ask me to do special jobs, including Mass cards; they're a piece of paper like a bookmark, with a prayer on it and a picture of Christ. I fell out with him when the money went completely to his head, so when he asked me to do 240 Mass cards I made special arrangements. When the cards were delivered he went into shock. Where the picture of Christ should have been was something completely different. It was a photo graph of me. They said I gave Emil his first heart attack.'

Heart attacks were a Savundra speciality. He sold his FAM shares in 1966, and the company rapidly collapsed, leaving its clients uninsured. Around 400,000 motorists were left with worthless insurance policies. There were nearly 50,000 unpaid claims. Savundra fled to Switzerland, but a year later he inexplicably returned to Britain to be quizzed by David Frost, in his finest hour, on live television.

The audience was packed with widows who had lost their husbands in car accidents and received not one penny in compensation. When he was quizzed by the widows, Savundra replied: 'I am not going to cross swords with the peasants.' It was a few words too many.

Then, after Savundra stated that he felt no moral responsibility, Frost looked at the camera, apologized, and marched out in anger and disbelief. Savundra was taken by stretcher from the television studios. He had the symptoms of a heart attack. He got eight years in jail, spent in a prison hospital, and died in 1976.

11. CLICKETY-CLICK!

The scent and smoke and sweat of a casino are nauseating at three in the morning.

THE FIRST LINE OF IAN FLEMING'S *CASINO ROYALE*, 1953

By spearheading the change in the law, John Aspinall and John Burke had in fact sent society off in a new direction. Their court case was of monumental importance, both social and financial. The Gaming Act had ushered in the start of Britain's gaming bonanza, estimated in 2007 to have an annual turnover of £70 billion. It was suddenly open season for bingo halls and clubs. For the first time, betting shops were seen in Britain, and within a year of the law being changed, several thousand had opened. It is difficult nowadays, when it seems you can bet on the time of day, to imagine the colossal change in attitude and the monsoon of cash involved. 'Having a bet' was no longer a naughty, side-street indulgence. It was legal. There was no government health warning. The general view that gambling was bad had been countered by the fact that the government had made it so much easier to gratify the habit.

With hindsight, it seems little thought was given to the other vices which gather where luck and chance can be the difference between fortune and ruin. The government, with its post-war mindset, did not seem to anticipate that the criminal fraternity would recognize the possibilities offered by the change in the law. Perhaps it was felt that the British would not be corrupted like their American cousins in Las Vegas, where money-laundering and prostitution were part of the package.

After the success of gambling at Les Ambassadeurs, other clubs, including Crockford's, began lavish gaming house operations. The attraction of the around-the-town chemmy games was swiftly fading, and with the *cagnotte* outlawed, Aspinall found his income swiftly diminishing while his outgoings remained vast. Extremely reluctantly, Aspinall and Burke realized that they had to expand their premises and their horizons; their own and their friends' apartments were no longer able to provide the frills, the upmarket dining and wining, to accompany the gambling. More importantly, there was the law to consider, and the competition. Aspinall told John Burke that he would open his own club. It was the only answer. But it had to be top of the tree, the market leader, a venue where millions could happily be lost in the most stylish surroundings. He outlined his plans to create Europe's grandest gambling den.

'It was a difficult decision,' said John Burke, 'because at those rather more informal games the rules were easier – we set them. With a more formal set-up, there had to be more regulation. Or appear to be.'

As early as the winter of 1960, he and Aspinall had talked about opening a club. There was some interest in Crockford's in Carlton House Terrace, which was said to be for sale, but nothing came of that. The two gamblers sat back as Les Ambassadeurs and then Crockford's itself went legitimate with gambling.

They organized a few chemmy evenings, but nothing to cover Aspinall's spiralling costs. 'We were a little bit late at the starting gate,' said John Burke. 'We hesitated. I think it was because it couldn't possibly be the same bonanza that we'd had since the court case.'

Aspinall finally decided to take the plunge and open his own club, and John Burke found himself looking forward to it with much anticipation. He, understandably, felt that there were good omens. In 1961, he had married Liliana Livon at the Catholic church on St Stephen's Green in Dublin. In September 1962, his sister Edith Carroll's horse 'Arctic Storm' won the Champion Stakes at Newmarket and his daughter Daniela was born. It was a happy time. He was also successfully investing through Rudolf Wolff, the most prestigious commodities broker in London, using his contacts and his talent for mathematics to play the market. And in only a few weeks, his and John Aspinall's greatest adventure would begin.

They were both determined that they still had to attract aristocratic gamblers, not just for their titles (although that helped business), but because they honoured their cheques. That meant luxury and location, location, location. It was Aspinall who discovered what he regarded as the perfect venue, in the bullseye of Mayfair.

It was a town house at 44 Berkeley Square, created in 1742 by William Kent, the most prestigious architect of his era. Now, with the skills of interior decorator John Fowler, the building could rise from dereliction and dust to become, for Aspinall and his customers, the most prestigious venue for gambling, where people could surely enjoy losing money. To achieve this, Aspinall had to find money. Where could he go?

'John's image was of this immensely rich man who gambled thousands on games of cards, ran a large home and zoo, and was written up in the newspapers in that way,' said John Burke. 'In truth, he was practically broke. He had assets, but no cash. He couldn't be seen to go around asking for financial guarantees. It would have damaged his wealthy cavalier reputation, and he'd worked hard at establishing that. He asked me to keep the facade intact.'

The Palladian mansion which was about to become the

Clermont Club was owned by Samuel Properties, a company headed by Charles Clore and Lord Samuel, who have said they 'missed' its development potential. They agreed to lease it to Aspinall for £12,500 a year over two decades. 'But they wanted guarantees,' said John Burke. 'They weren't keen on us being a gambling operation. They thought we'd go bankrupt in a couple of months and wouldn't be able to pay the rent.'

Finally, they made the unusual request for three guarantors. Aspinall asked John Burke to arrange it. Burke approached Tim Willoughby, Bernard van Cutsem and Richard Parkes, and they all agreed immediately. In return each of them received £1,000 in shares in the Clermont to be bought at face value. Yet much more money was needed to allow the skills of John Fowler, with the help of architect Philip Jebb, who'd been brought into the work through Dominick Elwes, to recreate the house's long-lost splendour. Aspinall planned to reinvent the spirit and sparkle of the Grand Salon and Club Room, and completely refurbish the house's interiors and the always admired, seemingly endless staircase.

'It had gone to rack and ruin,' said John Burke, 'and it cost a bloody fortune to return it to the very beautiful house which it was. To finance the whole thing, people were invited to lend £10,000, and for that they got the chance to buy £1,000 in ordinary shares.'

Investors included the Duke of Atholl, Jocelyn Hambro, Simon Fraser and many others. It was all officially registered at Companies House as a limited liability company. Yet, publicly, it appeared that Aspinall had created the Clermont Club. The reality was that this empire was built on credit, or, in the parlance of the tallymen of the time, on the never-never. It really was live or, rather, play now, pay later.

Aspinall was superb at what he did. John Burke says the king, who now had his castle, played a masterstroke: 'He lured over Pearson, the head doorman at White's. It was a touch of genius. All the big gamblers, the socially acceptable ones anyway, were members of White's.

'Pearson had worked at White's for several years,' explained John. 'He was well liked by the members and their guests, and, needless to say, he knew everybody who mattered as far as we were concerned in the social world of the capital. Somehow Pearson's presence inside the elegant front door of 44 Berkeley Square hinted at a connection between the Clermont and White's, and provided members with a sense of continuity. In terms of prestige, the Clermont Club now owed something to White's, while in return members of White's who gambled there frequently owed something to the Clermont.

'Then Mariani approached me. He wasn't very happy at Les Ambassadeurs and became our *chef de partie*. It is a most important job in a casino. He was in charge of the croupiers, of the gambling, and of talking to and looking after the customers, like a maître d'. Mariani was a great success – without a shadow of a doubt, the best *chef de partie* in London.'

Aspinall then had another moment of genius. He persuaded Jim Gore, the intelligent and popular head cashier of Martin's Bank, the con man's Coutts, to transfer to a similar responsible position at the Clermont. The man from Lower Sloane Street would be helped on busy evenings by Mr Money. Aspinall had known Mr Money for some years and was aware of his talents in getting around the foreign exchange regulations. He also knew that Mr Money fenced stolen jewellery, although he never spoke openly about it. Neither he nor John Burke was aware of his other underworld connections. Aspinall regarded Mr Money's foreign connections as another attraction for the Clermont, since their members often played the casinos of Europe.

Out of the recent past emerged Ian Maxwell-Scott, who became number three to Aspinall and Burke in the Clermont

Club Ltd. The fine dining and even finer wine at the Clermont was credited to Maxwell-Scott. And some of the better jokes. 'He told me that he felt he had gone back home when he went to the Clermont,' his daughter Cathy Maxwell-Scott, one of his six children, told me in February 2006. 'He was very happy there.'

The company secretary was the always affable chartered accountant Eddie Thomas. From a smart bridge club where he held the same position, Herbert Pretyman was appointed club secretary, and later a director. He was soon to be looking after close to 700 members. If anyone wanted a shopping list of the good and the great and the gamblers of Britain, then H.E. Pretyman had it. And the club president, the Earl of Carnarvon, tried to control it. 'Porchy' Carnarvon still delighted in seeing Jane Aspinall. For Aspinall, he added social cachet.

In the middle of all these handsome arrangements, a fiscal hand grenade was chucked at Aspinall. All his investment with Eddie Gilbert, around £150,000, had been wiped out by a calamity on Wall Street. Aspinall never complained, but it was a huge blow. He just accepted it, said John Burke. 'Gilbert had a company which boosted the value of the shares; it was a house of cards and it had to collapse sometime. It went sour and he got into all sorts of trouble.'

In fact, it got Gilbert into New York's notorious Sing Sing prison. John Burke recalls, 'John tried to help him whenever in every conceivable way. If John really liked somebody he could be a fantastically good friend. But why Eddie Gilbert? Some friends of John Aspinall expressed surprise at the fact that he had adopted Eddie Gilbert as one of his very closest friends. In private John would become, or used to pretend to become, extremely anti-Semitic; he'd say how much he admired Hitler and hated the Jews: there was something to be said, he felt, for Hitler's ideas about eugenics. "Broadly speaking, the

high income groups tend to have a better genetic inheri-
tance."

'It's amazing how much he owed to Jimmy Goldsmith and
people like Sydney Summer. Eddie Gilbert, of course, was a
Jew. I don't think John really meant it at all. It was probably
more of an act to impress people, to startle people. John was a
superb actor, a great performer. So was Gilbert, unflappable,
like Savundra.

'Gilbert approached John Derby to take a bigger piece of
the action after he got his first £20,000, but even Derby had
his suspicions. Derby didn't do it. He didn't fall for Gilbert, or
he, too, would have lost everything he put in. John Aspinall
was blind to Gilbert for some reason.'

But it can't have mattered. Surely Aspinall and Burke were
sitting on another gold mine? Far from it, said John Burke:
'Our games provided a financial bonanza from 1958 to 1961.
An absurd amount of tax-free money rolled in, especially to
John Aspinall. I, too, received and wasted plenty. John was a
really big spender: he kept two houses with their resident staff;
he had started to build up his collection of wild animals; he
had an expensive wife and some impecunious, greedy relations
and he enjoyed buying valuable antiques. When we were
forced to give up the private games and start the Clermont,
his income was seriously diminished – my gosh, it even
became taxable!'

It was a very different world for the gamblers. The over-
heads of running the club were vastly more than those of
staging private games once a week. The club games were legal,
but Aspinall and Burke could only make a 'table charge' that
produced a much smaller revenue for the house. Also, the
Clermont did not enjoy a monopoly of A-list gamblers. It
didn't have the proper cash reserve that a business like that
should have had. On the other hand, it was building up very
big assets in money owed, for in 1962 gambling clubs were

allowed to give credit. The club was owed substantial sums, by people who were good for it. Yet none of these debts were legally collectable.

'The bank was rather rigid about the situation,' said John Burke. 'We didn't have the sort of overdraft facilities that we needed. In that set-up it's important to have a financial back-up, because something can suddenly go wrong, and if you haven't got the cash to cover it you are in dead trouble. Yet, on a day-to-day basis, things were excellent. The club had a good membership, and the membership was growing, and growing the right way, with the right sort of people joining.'

The Clermont Club was patronized by men who thought they were going to transform Britain, rousing it back to colonial greatness from its post-war socialist torpor. It was a lair for aristocrats, players like Ian Fleming and was to become popular with a disaffected gang of right-wingers like Jimmy Goldsmith, Tiny Rowlands, Jim Slater and the Stirling brothers. All the names from the chemmy games – Derby, Devonshire, and the rest – became regulars. They now had a permanent and sumptuous home in Berkeley Square. At huge cost, Aspinall had created a comfort zone where his guests could waste their money and gamble themselves, as Tacitus said, into captivity. It was a social – and scientific – negative, albeit a fabulously luxurious one.

Indeed, despite being recently married, it became just like home for Lord Bingham, who would become the 7th Earl of Lucan in 1964. From the beginning he was as much part of the furniture as the luxurious armchairs and sofas that John Fowler had found and placed.

'Lucan had that awful thing, he had one little touch when he started the game,' said Mark Sykes. 'He had a huge win at the tables. Lucky? After that, gambling destroyed him. He was very good-looking. He was perfect in that period way. He was perfectly pleasant and agreeable for a long time, and had enormous stamina for drink. He was incredibly stupid. He was as thick as two short planks. He really was, didn't know what was going on.

'I would always see him there; I went for free meals with Jenny, Aspinall's half-sister. She was a charming girl. It was a rather pleasing atmosphere at the Clermont; almost everybody was in black tie and it attracted a social set, debutantes and the like.

'The amount of money that moved across the tables at the Clermont; in terms of money today, it would be millions and millions and millions a bloody day.'

Some of the members had an extravagant 'talent' for gambling and enjoyed doing so wildly in the gracious sur-roundings. Jane Aspinall would encourage attention, and gambling. According to a young socialite, Una Mary Parker, a few years later the Clermont acquired a reputation as a fast and louche 'alternative court', where young tycoons and age-ing aristocrats were gathered.

What 44 Berkeley Square also had to offer was a basement. John Burke says that he and Aspinall had no use for it. There had never been any talk of using it for anything but storage until Mark Birley approached them.

There were some plush nightclubs in London, but they were mostly threadbare affairs where often the piano-players seemed to believe the black and white keys had been switched around; Mark Birley, who would prove to be a genius at style and marketing, wanted to create something which would match the pleasurable ostentation of the Clermont. 'It has to have exclusivity,' he told John Burke.

A hands-on perfectionist, he got the mix precisely. He turned the basement into an English country gentleman's home – with added accoutrements. The bar could be a Chelsea drawing room, the panelled walls a clutter of cartoons, etch-ings and paintings. There were pictures of dogs everywhere:

spaniels, Jack Russells and whippets. Until he died in 2002, it was the job of one man to polish the club's brass pillars. He was known as 'Mr Brass'. In 2007, no one could recollect his real name.

A huge oil painting of Mark Birley's father, Sir Oswald Birley, watched over the guests as they sat on the red velvet sofas, gossiping and sipping champagne by candlelight. The Marquess of Londonderry had apparently not approved of his son-in-law's parents. His daughter, Lady Annabel, quotes him in her memoir as saying: 'His father was a bounder and his mother a whore.' His daughter responds in the book: 'This assessment was both monstrously untrue and unfair. Oswald Birley had been one of the most respected society portrait painters of the century and Rhoda was a well-known if some-what Bohemian hostess.'

Birley named the club 'Annabel's' after his wife, Lady Annabel Vane-Tempest-Stewart. It was an inspired choice. It gave the club the required aristocratic touch, like the linen from Ireland, the teaspoons from Denmark, the strict dress code and the accents as cut-glass as the decanters. Lady Annabel herself was a class-perfect asset in person as well as in name. The guests went all the way from A to Q, from the Aga Khan to Mary Quant, and every other Sixties name in the books; the Beatles met their first maharaja there, the Maharaja of Jaipur. Their friends included people like Harry, Viscount Hambleden, and Annabel and Simon Elliot, the sister and brother-in-law of Camilla Shand (later to become Duchess of Cornwall). 'Celebrities' at Annabel's were connected people – those like Princess Lee Radziwill, sister of Jackie Kennedy Onassis. The more the toffs turned out, the more people wanted to get into Mark Birley's hot new club and look at them, even dance with them, as the club had music – a newfangled idea called a discotheque – and plenty of girls.

Mark Birley's club complemented the Clermont, as

music and unaccompanied girls were not allowed in casinos. There was an internal spiral staircase which linked the clubs. There was no need to venture out beneath the striped canopy and up the precarious outside staircase into the dark, dangerous London night, risking more than your money. So, while the world glared bug-eyed at the goings-on of the rich and famous, and the newspapers reported the glitter and the gossip, the gambling went on.

'It was the perfect match for us,' said John Burke. 'People would come and play, go to Annabel's, and then, later, come back to gamble more. We had the best of both worlds.'

In *Annabel: An Unconventional Life*, Lady Annabel wrote that on her wedding night, in Paris, with Mark Birley, she found out about his quick temper. She asked him back to their room while he was gambling at Le Cercle: 'I learned you never interrupt a man who is running a winning bank.'

Yet John Burke, who for five guineas became, along with 699 others, a founder member of Annabel's (in 2006 there were 171 left), says Mark Birley was not a huge gambler in comparison to the Clermont regulars. Indeed, Mark Birley said, with a sly smile, on 3 August 2006, that he did not care to gamble at the Clermont. Why? 'I didn't trust it.'

Still, the gaming and dining club and the nightclub became the essential double for the cognoscenti of the Sixties. Annabel's and the Clermont were kept as exclusive as possible to heighten the appeal to those who could afford to play and pay. Membership procedure was the same as for gentlemen's clubs: candidates needed a proposer, a seconder and would then be passed by the club committee, but not automatically.

Peter Rachman could not get membership. Raymond Nash told me: 'Up until he died he wanted to join. He died before it officially opened, but he asked me to approach them about membership. They were very nice about it, but it was a "no".'

In practice, a rich aristocrat could walk through the door

with ease, and most people with the money to play just as easily. Money was almost always welcome at the Clermont – and always needed.

It was certainly needed at one point by Peter West, when strict currency control was still the law. He took all his money out to the casinos in Cannes, and lost the lot. He also hadn't paid his Carlton Hotel bill. He appealed to Jimmy Goldsmith to send funds. Mark Sykes recalled, 'Jimmy Goldsmith and Aspinall got £3,000, which was an absolutely colossal amount of money, over to him.

'The strict instructions were to take the money, go to the cash desk and go back to the hotel, pay the bill and come home. Unfortunately, between the cash desk and the door there were six roulette tables. He put £500 on each of them on even bets. They all lost. Everything.

'There was a very old lady watching all of this in some amazement. She exclaimed, "Nous n'avons pas vu ça depuis les jours des ducs grands russes. Le coup de suicide!" Which means, in case you lost me: "We haven't seen that since the days of the Russian grand dukes. The suicide coup."

'I think even Jimmy Goldsmith gave up on Peter West for a time after that.'

'Oh, "Westie" could be a problem,' said John Burke, 'but he was always a perfect house player for us: charming, urbane, just the right sort. People would want to sit alongside him, just as they did the lords and ladies. It was all part of the attraction. It's like people going to stupidly expensive West End restaurants so they might see celebrities. It was all part of the package.

'Another house player we had in the early days was one of Clive Graham's successors at the *Daily Express*, Charles Benson. He was a round, pink man. Charles loved gambling, but one night Aspinall caught him trying to steal a £1,000 chip, and that was the end of his employment.'

'The amount of money turning over at the Clermont was finite. Large amounts might be won and lost in an evening; nevertheless, because we were running a club, the money was not falling off the trees, not nearly as much as it used to.'

But John Aspinall was in need of even more cheques. John Burke explained the financial turmoil: 'The Clermont had a very exclusive membership. The reason for that, of course, was that to make money Aspinall was very much a hands-on proprietor. He always knew every detail of our cash situation. I was "de facto" financial director.

'The problem was, because of having to keep books and pay taxes, he couldn't skim enough off the top to pay for his lifestyle. He was spending like flowing water, and when you're into that it's not easy to shut the tap off; it's a difficult habit to break.

'Every day John came in and inspected the books and knew exactly who had won and who had lost; how much the table charges amounted to; who had paid, who hadn't. He checked things out very thoroughly. He was there, of course, every evening, himself. He started the game off, cracked a few jokes and then set about, as he had at our chemmy games, getting the action heated up. But no matter how hot that got, John could not make ends meet. His personal expenses or living costs, or however you care to describe them, were running away with him.

'He had to borrow money. He got around $200,000 from Ray Ryan, who was a benevolent man, always willing to help, to be kind.'

Ryan was also a hustler, albeit an extremely top-of-the-line one: he played his life and business extremely close to the edge, but was never malicious. He struck rich in the 1940s in the booming oilfields of southern Indiana, Illinois, and western Kentucky. He went on to become a huge land developer. He had the money to help. But it was a loan.

The money quickly ran out. Aspinall needed more. He borrowed heavily from Max Rayne, later the philanthropist Lord Rayne, who had made his fortune doing business with the Church of England commissioners, buying their property at cheap prices. Max Rayne had married, for the second time, Lady Jane Vane-Tempest-Stewart, a maid of honour at the Queen's wedding, and the other, lively daughter of the Marquess of Londonderry.

It was an intriguing marriage. Rayne was the son of a Russian Jewish immigrant, born in London's East End; his father a tailor, his grandfather a Jewish scholar. He knew Sydney Summers. He knew Billy Hill.

Bobby McKew recalls meeting Max Rayne at Nice Airport with Hill and Gypsy Riley. 'Gypsy couldn't get over the way Max talked, and said to him: "Where'd you get that funny voice from? I can't believe it! You don't sound a bit like yourself – or your brother. What a funny voice you've got now." But Max was fine. He'd had elocution lessons. He knew Billy from the old days, they had been close in their time.'

When he died, aged 85, in 2003, Max Rayne had established himself as an enduring philanthropist. He was a man who made money – and enjoyed giving it away: 'I do not believe there is any merit in amassing huge fortunes. If you've got it, it's very easy to give it away. It costs me more to give my time, and I'm prouder of giving that.'

When John Aspinall needed some help, Max Rayne gave it to him. John Burke said, 'Lord Rayne was very well set up. He had come from nothing in the East End; at that point neither I nor John Aspinall knew of his friendship with Billy Hill. Had he known, John Aspinall might have changed his mind about borrowing from Max.

'Max bought up lots of Church properties at bargain prices. He was cute, clever and, I suppose, a little guilty, which is why he kept giving his money away. Max Rayne loaned this money to John Aspinall on basically friendly terms, but being a business deal it was in a written agreement. Max held shares in the Clermont as security. It was rather pointless, because if things went well the written agreement would have ensured that he got his money back, but if things went badly the shares would have been totally valueless.'

Max Rayne's old friend Billy Hill knew about the whole operation; he knew what was going on in every casino in London. Indeed, Hill was operating, with an edge, in most of them, including the Olympic and the 21. He had even taken profits from Crockford's. He learned this unique form of larceny from his friends in the Union Corse. It was so good that there has never been a hint, until now, of what was going on. When the police, on occasion, did investigate at the big casinos, they could find nothing wrong.

All the time, the Clermont was a menacing glint in Billy Hill's eye. The other casinos were easier to work, for they had several chemmy tables and a socially wider clientele. Nevertheless, the Clermont, small and exclusive as it was, appeared to Hill as the jewel in the con.

Yet Billy Hill was still not entirely cognisant of the extent of John Aspinall's desperation for cash, or the gambler's paranoia that Ray Ryan would call in his loan. There was also the worry of the Clermont's missing guarantor. In August 1963, Tim Willoughby had tragically vanished at sea. All the people I have talked to have only fond memories of him, especially John Burke, who at that time, along with many others, fervently hoped Tim Willoughby would surprise them all and walk through the door having had some great adventure. It was not to be: no trace of him has ever been found.

Aspinall's costs at Howletts were spiralling as he became more involved with his growing animal kingdom. It seemed that his devotion to them was a manic motivation. What had started as something of a gimmick (Aspinall, in his Doctor

Dolittle moments, would bring a pet baby chimpanzee or miniature ponies down to the Clermont Club for the evening) had become an extremely expensive obsession. His wife Jane he left to her own devices. There wasn't time for everything. His expenditure was running at around £3,000 a week – about £4 million a year in 2007 – to fund his lifestyle.

John Burke, as financial director, was well aware of all the money problems, present and pending. He looked on with growing apprehension. 'It was a crazy situation – John was borrowing in one door and it was vanishing out the other. There had to be a day of reckoning. I dealt with the bank and I dealt with the general finances of the company and made sure there was enough money to cover the cheques and so on. But John had complete control. I was very much the number two, and John was the boss, the man in charge.

'The ideal solution would have been if John had agreed to cut back his own expenditure. But he never believed he could be wrong. It was lunatic arrogance. He was spending money at this stage that was not easy getting out of the company. If John had agreed to cut back, perhaps in a year we could have got things on an even keel.'

John Aspinall did no such thing. Instead, arguably his most cynical and sinister malfeasance manifested itself.

12. THE BIG EDGE

It was beautiful and simple as all truly great swindles are.

'THE OCTOPUS MAROONED' BY O. HENRY

'John, steal whatever you want, but don't rob the man who saved your life.'

When Ray Ryan walked out of the rigged game on 20 December 1963, the foundations of John Aspinall's life and aspirations were shakier than they had ever been. To clear up this nasty affair he would have to pay back Ryan in full. And very quickly. He had no idea what Ryan's reaction, on reflection, would be. He must have felt himself in a vacuum.

There was just so much he could take out of the Clermont: he'd tried and tried to skim off more, but his was now a limited company – and there were limits. Which is why he'd had to borrow so much from Ryan in the first place. He was like a cornered tiger. With his psychological make-up, all he could do was attack. For Aspinall, regarded by so many as the fun-loving, eccentric 'Aspers', was an almighty rogue. He created an image of himself, that he won and lost fortunes, that he gambled. He never gambled: he played games of chance. And he almost always hedged his bets.

John Burke had no early warning of Aspinall's plan to cheat Ray Ryan. He was told only a short time before, when arrangements were made for the upstairs game in the Salle Privée. When Aspinall explained that 'needs must', Burke understood just how panicked the owner of the Clermont Club had become. And he went along with it.

Mr Money witnessed all the events of that December evening knowing exactly who would be intrigued, delighted, to hear of them. The next morning at Moscow Road he eagerly divulged all his information to Billy Hill, who now became fully aware of Aspinall's desperation and of his failed scheme to avoid paying back Ryan.

That afternoon, Billy Hill and Bobby McKew had a talk at Moscow Road. Hill was quiet, but adamant that his number two should contact John Burke. Aspinall, he said, was now ready for the 'Big Edge'. Bobby McKew was still not certain about John Burke's reaction, but he could tell how serious Hill was about getting into the Clermont. He wasn't going to sit still.

'Billy had simply bided his time,' said Bobby McKew. 'From the moment Mr Money gave us the word about the Ryan fuck-up, he knew Aspinall would go for it. He'd have probably gone for it anyway, he was a greedy bastard.'

Still, Bobby McKew did not think John Burke would agree. Billy Hill asked him to arrange a meeting, and Bobby argued that his friend would not go for it, or recommend it to Aspinall. Billy just said, 'Do it anyway.'

There was no chance that Bobby McKew would not follow Billy Hill's instruction. The two Irishmen met at the Star, where John Burke had often sat in a corner having a drink while Billy Hill sipped his tea. The taciturn and careful McKew said only that he had 'some business' with Billy Hill and that he thought John should have a meeting with the crime boss. It would be of mutual benefit, he promised. It was a shock to John Burke, who knew that Bobby and Billy were friends but wisely had never inquired further: 'I found out for the first time that my old friend Bobby McKew not only worked for Billy Hill, but that he was a key figure in the proposed scam. It was important, because I trusted Bobby.'

Of course, for John Burke it was one thing to have a drink with the gangster; quite another to go into business with him. Burke was living in an elegant Mayfair town house, 4 Aldford Street, that had been the London pied-à-terre of the Aga Khan. His son Prince Aly Khan during his romantic excursions had entertained his conquests there (he said of society Englishmen: 'They call me a nigger and I sleep with their wives.') There was a secret panel where Aly Khan hid his drinks when his parents visited.

Tempted as he was to have a drink, John Burke wanted to keep a cool head for his visitor. He did not know what to think, or, indeed, what to say, to Hill. Bobby McKew had made him somewhat aware of the deal, but it sounded full of risks and dangers. Going bankrupt at the Clermont was one thing; going crooked a much more frightening prospect.

Billy Hill arrived dressed in a smart blue suit. He had a smile on his face as he handed John Burke his hat. Tea, he said, would be very pleasant. John Burke made a pot and brought it into the drawing room of his small but elegant house. The two men sat back in their armchairs. They could have been about to discuss the football results. They had a gossip, but the pleasantries ended quite quickly.

The conversation moved on to Ray Ryan. What a mess. Billy Hill did not think much of Signor Biondi as a card sharp. Indeed, he had arranged for Bobby McKew to drive one of his lads, Bobby Warren, over to Chelsea Reach to have a quiet word with him. Biondi, he said, would now leave the country.

The Italian had been a worrying embarrassment, but his most serious mistake had been not to ask Hill's permission for his misdeeds. Hill had interests in several casinos and did not want attention drawn to his activities. Indeed, if Aspinall wanted to make money, he was going about it all the wrong way. Hill got to the point: 'You are very foolish. If you want a job done properly, I'll do it for you.'

John Burke explained that he could not speak for his boss on this issue. He would tell Aspinall of their conversation, and, if necessary, arrange another meeting. There was cautious delight in Aspinall's eyes when he heard of Hill's approach. But he thought about it long and hard before making a move. If it went wrong, he'd be ruined. His business and social life would end. Howletts would have to be closed down. Yet if he didn't get more money quickly, his hopes and ambitions would be quashed.

Finally he agreed to go to John Burke's home for a meeting with Billy Hill and Bobby McKew. Again John Burke made tea for Hill, and opened his drinks cabinet. The discussion didn't take long; about half an hour. The conversation was amicable and did not dwell on the technicalities. Hill and Bobby McKew would deal with those. Aspinall simply had to go along with their plans and make himself lots and lots of money.

Desperate as he was, Aspinall was still circumspect before finalizing an arrangement with a powerful man renowned for violence and for keeping everything under his control. Aspinall contacted Sydney Summers, who, as we know, had been of great assistance in the past to him and John Burke. Aspinall, a dreadful snob who would never have entertained Sydney at his own home, respected his intelligence and his contacts, especially those in the police hierarchy.

They had a conversation about the Billy Hill proposal, somewhat absurd in a way, but which was to have dramatic financial consequences for many of the rich and famous. Yes, said Sydney Summers, Billy Hill was a scary man of violence, a tough character, possibly one of the most dangerous men around. But the wonderful paradox was that he was straight in his own particular way, even in his errant dealings. Everybody liked Billy, even some of the people he murdered.

'Is it something that will work for me, Sydney?' asked an increasingly anxious Aspinall.

Summers peered through milk-bottle lenses and nodded wisely. In his thick accent, he gave Billy Hill a glowing reference, 'Oh, yes. If he says he will do it and makes a deal, he will stick with it. Billy Hill is an honest crook.'

'After that,' said Bobby McKew, 'Aspinall grabbed at it with both hands; he was dishonest to his roots, so there was no trouble with his conscience.'

Or with his business expertise. He was no rollover on the percentages; everywhere else the deal with Billy Hill was 50–50, but Aspinall persuaded his new associate that with the amounts of money involved it should be 60–40 in Aspinall's favour. He was the one supplying the big golden pigeons. Billy Hill accepted this: 40 per cent of the riches was far better than nothing at all. It was agreed on a handshake at 4 Aldford Street.

The 'Big Edge' was brilliantly designed. John Burke regards it as 'psychologically and mathematically brilliant', and says in some wonder: 'Einstein would have been proud of it.'

Aspinall, no stranger to wagering with advantages, was in for one of gambling's most secret and sensational scams. He wanted the profit, but also wanted to minimize his personal risk, to distance himself from it, as John Burke explained: 'I put John and Hill together because I didn't want to be stuck in the middle of the bloody thing. John had said: "Burkie, I want you to deal with Hill, and here are my conditions . . ." I argued that I could do no such thing; how could I make deals if Hill responded with his conditions?

'John was the boss, and for many years I had always done what he'd asked. For the first time I didn't do exactly what he wanted; I didn't want to be in between two such dangerous men. John didn't like that at all.

'But in time, of course, I was the link. John never wanted

to meet Hill if he could possibly avoid it, so I used to go and see him. I was the intermediary. There was never any problem. We'd have a chat. It was happily easy for me to deal with him, but rumour had it that he was not always so polite.

'I don't altogether blame John Aspinall when he had been for years spending money like water, because money was coming in like water. It's hard to curtail. So when John did eventually decide to do business with Billy Hill, I acquiesced with these decisions. It would be hypocritical to say that I didn't.

'Obviously, morally, I should have taken a stand and perhaps even resigned. I saw that it meant financing John Aspinall's lifestyle through cheating rather than through stealing money from the Clermont – money that belonged to the shareholders and the taxman – in order to pay his bills. A choice between Scylla and Charybdis.

'Enough time has gone by to tell the truth. It is the whole truth and nothing but the truth. Clearly, when Billy Hill was alive and when Gypsy was still around, this would not have been a sensible enterprise. I got on well with Billy Hill at our meetings and I wouldn't have wanted to embarrass him with murder, especially my own. Seriously, it would have been a life and death matter. Now, I believe it is a part of history that should be shared. So, here goes.'

And a nightingale sang about Berkeley Square.

'I'm not suggesting I've grown a halo. I do this with no malice, but just to correct so many, many errors that have been put forward over the years. Not because people wanted to mislead, but because they did not have access to the true facts.

'They had John's stories, but that's what they were – stories. This is how it was. He was a very curious character, neither a saint nor a demon. In his own mind, he was entitled to rob in order to have the funds to do what was important in the world. That was what he believed.

'The Clermont, the glittering jewel of clubs, magnet for all the big names in the gambling world, took for a ride just about everybody who was unlucky enough to walk through its doors on the evenings when the financial outcome of the gambling was not determined by luck. It was grand larceny. But very clever.'

As the Christmas and New Year holidays ended in 1963–1964, preparations went forward to introduce the 'Big Edge' to the Clermont Club. There were clubs where the 'Big Edge' could operate every night, but the Clermont had a tight circle, an exclusive membership watched over by the careful 'Porchy' Carnarvon. Aspinall was intelligent and knew the risks involved. He allowed Billy Hill's boys to 'perform' once a week, at the most. He would brief them before every evening of cheating the Clermont members.

'It was so simple it was brilliant,' said Bobby McKew, who still shakes his head at the wonder of it. 'No one ever had an inkling.'

Aspinall had always been subtly manipulative about soaking, like a vampire, the wealth of all those he lured into his gambling dens. John Burke said, 'Aspers didn't care whose money he took. The psychology behind the cheating was twisting all the rules of fraud – you couldn't see the swindle for looking at it, hearing it almost. It was advertised, but all these aristocrats and tycoons, powerful men and women, would not believe what was happening. It was like stealing a wallet, snatching a handbag, but it was as though Fagin was in charge – they didn't feel a thing.'

The details of the method by which players were cheated have remained an underworld and gambling secret until now.

The normal method of cheating at chemmy was for the proprietor to employ a clever croupier like Louis the Rat who could do things with the cards, like arranging for a big winning bank to arrive at a fixed place, when the cards had been shuffled between each shoe. This was the simplest part of his legerdemain; a house player would win four, five, six, eight, ten coups the first time he got the bank.

Sometimes the cards were pre-prepared, known as 'the sandwich', and they were just inserted by sleight of hand into the pack and either the proprietor or one of his house players had a long bank and won a nice bit of money. That had problems, as John Burke explained: 'The main snag about that is that if it happens regularly, and people at the table are not complete idiots, the players want to know what's going on. They get suspicious.

'If it was going to work, which it did, it had to be smarter. And then the psychology was brought in. In brains versus greed there is no contest. All true gamblers, and even non-gamblers with a modicum of self-confidence, believe that a slightly uphill struggle as exemplified by fractional odds against can, by means of skill or even a little luck, be transformed into slight odds-on. And given the opportunity to bet at even money on a proposition that is mathematically odds-on, surely no proper man with red blood – or blue – in his veins would refuse to have a go.

'Betting with the odds in your favour is technically known as "value". I have always supported the idea that value ought to be taught as a separate school subject, or, at least, as a recognized brand of mathematics. The laws of probability and chance have a much stronger bearing on our affairs than any algebraic equation.

'Value is an essential component of risk assessment, which plays a vital role in our everyday life. The obvious examples of businesses that are dependent on understanding risk assessment and using it intelligently are insurance and book-making.

'But what if you take away most of the risk? What I am going to explain has never been described before. It is unique.

It is a system of cheating that is technically ingenious and extremely clever, both psychologically and mathematically.

'In gambling there are two types of people – winners and losers. An easy example – bookmaking. People backing horses. The bookmakers are risk assessors and make odds accordingly, in such a way that there is a percentage in their favour; assuming the money they take in is evenly distributed, for every £110 they take in they pay out £100. The bookmakers, who often have a bigger edge, win, and the punters lose.

'Poker is a good example. There are two kinds of players at poker. The player who plays to the odds; careful, tight play. He only risks his money when he thinks his hand is worth it. Then there's the open player who likes to play at every hand and bet freely, and comes in all the time even with a pair of twos, and might even play and draw four to an ace in old-fashioned draw poker. Of course, such a player, provided he pays his debts, is always extremely welcome. He's the guy you want in the game. He may have a lucky night, but on balance he's going to be a loser.

'At chemmy you have the same thing. This is universal to gambling. In chemmy it's not quite so obvious to see it, but it is very much there. I should know. I have been somewhat involved in the game. Each coup, each hand, is a contest between two parties. The bank, who has a shoe and deals the cards, and the person who goes *banco* and plays the hand against the bank. It's a straightforward contest.

'The bank has a built-in advantage. And that's official. After a long evening at Annabel's in 1963 with Basil de Ferranti, who headed his family's huge wireless and electronics company, I had the game analysed and computer-programmed by Professor Nigel Foster at the London School of Economics.

'Basil de Ferranti put the results through his company computers and they concluded that in chemmy, the bank's built-in advantage is roughly 1.78 per cent. Call it 1.8 per cent – the person calling *banco* has that shade of odds against him.

'The bank has that advantage because when the player who called *banco* asks for a third card, it is dealt face up. Depending on his hand, that gives the bank a small or big advantage because the bank now knows, mathematically, whether to rest or draw a card himself. During a playing session, this translates into 1.8 per cent in the bank's favour.

'The *cagnotte*, of course, has no effect on the mathematical odds of each coup. However, it means that because 5 per cent of the profit is deducted when the bank wins a coup, financially speaking, the bank is no longer a winner – all players now contribute to the house.

'However, with the *cagnotte* gone, the bank was always going have the edge.

'Or was it? There's always been a feeling among chemmy players that the person who just ran his bank and did nothing else was a mean player and was rather despised, whereas the open player who called *banco* all the time and bet freely, the Lord Derby figure, was the hero. He was the man every careful player and gambling promoter wanted in the game.

'The psychology behind the cheating was inspired. When the law changed and a table charge was substituted for the *cagnotte*, it meant everyone sat down and paid a certain amount for the privilege of playing a shoe of chemmy; the table charge was the same for all players. Whether you did nothing but wait for your bank and run your bank, or whether you bet freely, it cost the same amount to play in the shoe. This accentuated the difference between the careful player and the betting player. And, forcefully, the advantage of the bank.

'Mathematically speaking, the optimum procedure would be to sit quietly and when your bank came to you, run your bank and then sit quietly until it came around the next time. Like waiting for a train, *chemin de fer*, going around the railway:

deadly boring but mathematically correct. It's like someone today playing poker on computer against an anonymous somebody in Australia; it's not much fun. People who followed this rule, of course, were very unpopular and considered mean. Especially in the Clermont sort of games, where confident, outgoing people are there for fun, at a table chatting and drinking and trying to impress each other.

'The cavalier gambler's flourishes encouraged other people to bet freely. And the constant *banco* and *suivi* were music to the ear. The punter could have been shouting "lose" and "lose", because the statistical chance was that he would.

'As I said, prior to the "Big Edge" there was basically one form of cheating at chemmy: that was to give a good winning bank to somebody representing the house, the proprietor or one of the house players – the artificial banks known as a "sandwich" or a "sausage". Strange, then, if the proprietor or his friend or a house player had a winning bank every time. Even idiots would think there was something fishy about this. And the croupier was in on the cheating, and they had to trust the croupier not to talk, and it also lent itself to suspicion. Both were disadvantages.

'Is there a way of getting around it? Well, there is one way, but it sounds impossible.

'Could the winning be done by the person who goes *banco*? What if you turned the odds around? What if you could make the person calling *banco* odds-on? Apparently, the guy who is betting against the odds? Could he be created the winner by any manner of means?

'Eventually some genius, it must have been a genius, came up with a scheme to do it. That was the scam. That was the "Big Edge". A genius worked out a method whereby it wasn't the bank who won the money, it was the punter. It was the lunatic punter who everyone dreamed of having in the game and who was sure to lose; he was the person who won. That was the genius of the psychological end of it, and the mathematics of it are equally fascinating. God knows, whoever invented it had a special forte, something like the man who broke the Enigma code. It has never been discovered although thousands of people sat down at the tables and played with these cards for tens of thousands of hours. Nobody saw because it was so extremely subtle and so cleverly done.

'Now, the technicalities: in chemmy the cards are put in a wooden container known as a shoe, and they fit in exactly. The shoe is sloped and the cards come out through a brass mesh at the end, and behind the cards there is a heavy weight.

'The cards are held in tightly, with the heavy weight behind them and the brass mesh in front of them which they are pulled through one at a time; you can only get one card at a time. The effect of pulling cards through like this puts a slight curvature on the card.

'If you look at a pack of cards when people are playing bridge or poker, normally the cards are absolutely flat. Some people do have a habit of shuffling in such a way that the cards acquire a curvature. Yet there is no design to it. It is happenstance, what happens to the cards. But in chemmy a slight curvature is normal. You don't expect the cards to be absolutely flat, because they are not. That helps to explain how this whole thing can be done. Think of it like pulling a file from a rigidly packed filing cabinet. There will be a very, very slight bend to the file. Has to be.

'Our mastermind worked out a system whereby the cards could be distinguished. He discovered that there were only three possible changes in the cards. One, is that they came out exactly as normal, with that slight curvature from the shoe.

'Two, is that there is a slight adjustment made to the two diagonally opposite corners, right and left.

'Three, there is a slight adjustment made to the two diagonally opposite corners, left and right.

'That way you had three slightly different-shaped cards. When I say slightly, I mean extremely slight. So slight that none of the people playing the game for hundreds and thousands of hours would spot it.

'Except for the "readers", Billy Hill's people, who had perfect eyesight and were trained, practised for hours and hours at the cards coming out of the shoe. Instantly, and I saw them do it often enough, they could "read" the cards. They couldn't "read" the exact card and call the king of hearts or something, but they knew enough to have the edge. They could pick up the differences. They could put each card into one of three categories.

'What cards should you put in each category? There are ten values of cards, thirteen cards with four of them having a value of zero. King, queen, jack and ten are each a value of zero. The other nine are between one and nine. What way should they be apportioned into three? The answer they came up with, and somebody must have spent a lot of time working it out, was very clever.

'If we say A, B and C. A was a high card – nine, eight, seven. B were the lower cards – six, five, four, three, two. C were the zero cards and the ace.

'You have two cards, each of which has three possible clarifications – and, therefore, six possible combinations. In order of merit:

1: A and C, the best possible.
2: B and B, the second best.
3: A and A, third best.
4: B and C, fourth best.
5: A and B, fifth best.
6: C and C, worst.

'Clearly, an A and a C was the best hand, if the closest to nine is the winner. But an A and an A was not, as one might think, the second-best hand. The maximum would be an eight: two nines, eighteen, counted as eight happening one time in nine.

'Better off with a B and a B, which gives you twenty-five combinations, nine of which give you a nine or an eight. There are four chances at a nine, five at an eight. The odds are 16–9 against getting a "natural".

'The bank's hand and the punter's hand are classified in exactly the same way. What is important to know now is which is the better hand. Which is, mathematically, the best combination to hold in order to win the coup from the *banco*ing point of view. It's not difficult to work out that the best is a high card with a zero. So an A and a C is obviously the best hand. The "reader" knows the combination – it's like Eddie Chapman and the combination to a safe. If he gets it right, he's in the money.

'The well-trained "reader" reads each of the two pairs of cards as they come out of the shoe. He now knows who has the better chance of winning the coup – bank or caller – and therefore he can adopt the mathematically optimum strategy, either calling a bet or keeping quiet. Statistically, the bank will have the better hand five times out of twelve, likewise his opponent, while in one coup in six their cards will have the same rank. There would be situations when a canny reader might call *banco* with the inferior hand, hoping to lose for appearance's sake.

'The "reader" did not need to see the cards dealt on the table – he could "read" them as they came out of the shoe. That meant that if the *banco* was on his right, he had the option of going "*banco* prime", (taking the bank first) or, indeed, if the *banco* was on his left and likely to win, he could say in a friendly way to the caller, "a hundred with you for luck".

'Yet, and here is the brilliance of it, the "reader" knows which hand is more likely to win; he does not know which hand will win. If he did, it could be very suspicious. That's why it's so clever. The "reader" backs plenty of losers because things don't always work out, but he is betting with the odds in his favour.

'If the odds are in the favour of the *banco* he would go *banco*. If the odds were in favour of the bank he would keep quiet. In the course of a game of one hundred bets he will win, say, 60–40. That's profit. Perhaps he might win sixty-five and lose thirty-five. Maybe only win fifty-seven and lose forty-three. He would always have the edge.

'A simple way to look at it, as a non-gambler? There are two possibilities. One is mathematically more probable than the other, and you can back either of them at even money – so which one do you back?

'To put it another way, if you like, if it is mathematically 6:4 on (4–6) that a certain event will happen as opposed to not happening, and you can back it happening at even money, you would want to have a bet, wouldn't you?

'Now the character crying *banco*, the mad player, the lunatic if you like, is the winner. At the end of the game, of course, it needn't be obvious how much he's winning, because he doesn't win any big amount in one go and he can always put some of his chips in his pocket. He is the winner and anyone thinking about it would say: "Lucky bugger. Next time he plays he'll lose twice as much."

'There were ways of handling this situation intelligently. If it was spotted that somebody was winning consistently, a losing night or nights might be arranged. Someone else would do the winning, so that neither the house nor Billy Hill lost.

'It was the psychology of it that was so good. Punters wanted the daft guy going *banco* and *suivi* all the time to win. They knew he'd get his comeuppance, but it was great to see him win big coups. It was exciting, it turned them on. And that was good for business too.

'It was a superb concept, and Billy Hill was not just in at the Clermont, he was in many other clubs. That's the beauty of this thing. Billy Hill's man maybe has a hundred bets. Loses forty and wins sixty. It's so much better that way.

'By God, the inventor of this scam had a clear brain when it came to cheating the punters and gamblers who knew the system, pumped it like a money well. Psychologically, mathematically brilliant – can't say that enough times. They made millions.

'Mr Money, who acted as the money go-between for Billy Hill and Aspinall, took huge sums of money to Switzerland and turned them into numbered accounts at the Banca del Gottardo in Lugano.

'Millions.'

13. NEW CARDS, PLEASE

The reason he is called Sky is because he will bet all he has, and nobody can bet more than this.

'THE IDYLL OF MISS SARAH BROWN', DAMON RUNYON

While the scam was exceptional in its circumspect simplicity, it still required a skilled operator to oversee the mechanics. Bobby McKew was the man. A year after he returned to London from his French imprisonment he bought a printing company, the Dulwich Press in Herne Hill, and that had become part of Billy Hill's grand casino larceny. The main operational centre was a rented flat in Maitland Court, only a moment away from Bobby McKew's flat.

The 'Big Edge' relied upon the Clermont's customized cards being available for treatment before the night they were to be used. The cards were kept in a locked cupboard at the Clermont, and Aspinall would give several sets at a time to Mr Money to take to Billy Hill. Hill had a team of men on £200 a day.

'It was very good money for two reasons: it kept them at it and it kept them quiet,' said Bobby McKew. 'Billy knew when to work with expenses. He was never cheap, and no one complained. Or talked.'

At Maitland Court, the cards were given the 'Big Edge' treatment. In a room filled with cigarette smoke and activity, the smart Caro cards were put through a device like a small clothes mangle which an engineer had created for the sole purpose of 'customizing' them, giving the cards a unique 'look'. It was nothing sophisticated. Bobby McKew still smiles at the thought of it. 'You could have bought the machine in Hamley's, the toy shop in Regent Street – one of those children's mangles – and adapted it. But we had the machine specially made. It was a steel cylinder with thin tyre rubber around it. It was adjusted until eventually they got it just right. When it was right, it wasn't touched. That was the "Big Edge".

'It "marked" the cards in this special way. You couldn't tell anything had been done to them. You could fly them to the moon and back, and no scientist in the world could tell.

'When the cards came in they were wrapped in cellophane, and the packet was carefully cut with a razor blade. We'd take the cards out, put them in the roller and a seven would come out with that ever-so-slight curve and a two with an ever-so-slight curve the other way. And so on, throughout every pack.

'You had to go through each packet and be very careful to put them back in the correct order. It was a lot of work to make sure they were one, two, three, four and the rest of it: when the croupier opened the pack of cards – "new cards, please" – he would spread them out so that everyone could see. One mistake, and that's it. Somebody would notice.

'Mind you, there again, maybe not. The great thing about gambling people is that nobody watches anybody else's bets, they are only watching their own. It's a selfish business, gamblers are the most self-obsessed of people, up their own arses; their eyes are only on themselves. Nobody is going to look. People would get up and go and get a drink. They'd be talking to each other. Would they notice?

'But we never made mistakes. Every pack of cards was checked and rechecked. The cellophane, the seal, were put back on perfectly, using a cellophane machine I had at the Dulwich Press.

'It's just that the cards had gone through the machine, and the "readers" could spot a face card from a high card and a low card, and so on. The odds were irrevocably changed. The cards were bent. So to speak.'

It was a superbly clever operation, but the Clermont was an extremely difficult club for Billy Hill to work: there were only a small number of players, an exclusive bunch. A great deal of care was taken, and Billy Hill was highly intelligent about getting people into the Clermont – but only with John Aspinall's clearance and help.

Hill had many players 'on the books', some of whom had long hours of training as 'readers'; others who were sent in as back up. Yet not all were suitable for the Clermont; they operated at the bigger casinos where it was easier because people could walk in off the street. The Clermont 'readers' were hand-picked, and cover stories were developed for them. Mr Money established overseas bank accounts for them, and acquired glowing references. Billy Hill opened similar accounts for the Clermont 'players' in London. It was all for safety, for insurance against discovery, to show they had the money to play, but the references were never needed. They played on their good credit, 'staked', on paper, by Billy Hill. There were always two: one to play, one to watch and assist, on any evening.

The only exception to this rule was the Clermont. What Aspinall had insisted upon at the start was that he must meet, agree to and guide Hill's players and they must work alone. The first one he 'cleared' was a man called Bata – by lucky coincidence this was a name which suggested money, as Bata was a successful European shoe company, the Nike of its day. Bata was an expert, with experience of the top French casinos, especially the Aviation Club de France on the Champs-Elysées. It was there, six years earlier, on a trip to Paris with John Burke, that an audacious Aspinall had taken the bank at baccarat and had been wiped out for around £5,000. The gambler was now interested in much larger sums of cash.

Aspinall met Bata for a drink, introduced him to other members, and then proposed the newcomer for Clermont membership. In the middle of January 1964, the 'Big Edge' went into the Clermont. Or, rather, Bata did on his own. He was so good that he did not need an assistant.

The grand Clermont host, Aspinall briefed him on what table to choose, who to 'take', and whom to avoid cheating – usually a player in debt to the Clermont. But Bill Stirling and others like him were 'good targets'. Aspinall suggested Bata might 'try for ten grand'.

Aspinall wandered over to the cashier's office, where Mr Money was helping out that evening. John Burke was there, too. They were all apprehensive, first-night nerves.

They watched as Bata took his seat and a shoe began. Immediately, he had a run of the cards and the chips stacked up in front of him. Aspinall whispered to John Burke that it was going too fast. None of the other players, however, seemed in the least disturbed by this winning streak.

The pattern went on from that evening. Bata won more than £10,000 – but it didn't look like it, for much of the loot, as chips, was in his dinner jacket pocket.

When two of Hill's men played, chips were secretly exchanged between them. The non-player went to the cashier's office and cashed in the chips, always trying to get cash rather than a cheque in return. Still, if it was a large amount, it was always met by a Clermont cheque made out in the name of Hill's operative. The cashier would know exactly what had been cashed; and therefore so would Aspinall. If Mr Money was on duty, there was an added witness to the sums involved, should Billy require it. It was only a precaution, for nobody was inclined to skim off money from Billy Hill.

At the end of that first evening's play, Bata cashed in and

got a Clermont cheque in his name. He'd won a little less than £6,000. Or so it seemed to any casual onlooker. In fact, with the chips already cashed, the winnings were closer to £14,000.

The cheques went directly to Maitland Court, where they endorsed them for payment to the special account Mr Money had set up, with Billy Hill as a co-signatory.

Predictably, it was Mr Money who returned the next day with Aspinall's 60 per cent, £8,400 – enough cash to meet his expenditure for a couple of weeks or so. Aspinall, who was always paid off in cash, attempted to be nonchalant, but could barely conceal his excitement from John Burke.

From then on Aspinall enthusiastically played the ring-master of the 'Big Edge'. Mr Money would usually deliver Aspinall's share. Once, John Burke returned to 4 Aldford Street to discover that a thick package had been shoved through his door. It was a wedge of Scottish £100 notes (a total of £4,800), proceeds from the 'Big Edge' performing in Glasgow, being used to give Aspinall his cash share from the Clermont scam. John Burke received irregular payments from the 'Big Edge', and says that if he had insisted on a fixed percentage, Aspinall could hardly have refused. 'But I didn't need the money – John Aspinall did.'

As a director of the Clermont, John Burke was paid £10,000 a year – the equivalent of £200,000 in 2007, had the use of a chauffeured car, and signed bills at the Mirabelle, Annabel's and other fashionable restaurants and clubs, all of which were met by the Clermont. 'I was condoning the cheating but not getting a great profit from it. Maybe I was uneasy, but that said, if I had really needed the money I would probably have asked John Aspinall for a set cut.'

With the initial success, John Burke said the confident Aspinall was superb in introducing Billy Hill's gambling troops: 'John was a master of the art. He would say: "We've got this chap who has just inherited twenty million from his uncle . . ." – all this bullshit. "This is my friend who's just flown in from a big corporate deal in America / Hong Kong / China . . ." – John would just fill in the blanks.'

The scam had begun, big time. There were no slip-ups, except for one evening when the wrong cards were used instead of those treated by the 'Big Edge'. Nevertheless, even then the 'reader', a highly intelligent player, had a good evening and won a few thousand pounds.

But Aspinall did not warm to all of his new business partner's associates. One evening a supposed barrister turned up (wearing a dinner jacket in the early evening!), and was greeted by Aspinall. But this 'reader' was told to get lost. Aspinall thought him thoroughly unsuitable, especially because of 'the dodgy vowels'.

A bigger problem was Billy Hill's mistress Gypsy, who wanted to gamble at the Clermont. Aspinall went purple in the face at the thought of it. Bobby McKew recalls, 'She had a twenty-grand ring on her finger but she didn't fit the place. She was attractive and looked good, but there was something about her. People realized it. She wanted so badly to mix with those rich gamblers.

'If Gypsy had sat down and started her antics, the other players would have wondered what was going on. And her picture had been in the newspapers with Bill. She wasn't a lady. There was no way she could get into the Clermont in the middle of the scam and play.'

Still, she did make it into the downstairs bar for one drink, and that alone, said John Burke, all but gave Aspinall a nervous breakdown. Bobby McKew said wryly, 'But Gypsy got her money anyway. Billy would be splitting up the cash and he'd say: "I'm taking this £1,200 for Gypsy."

'I said: "What does she get for making the tea?"

'That didn't win me many points. I remember once Bill said: "Do you know, she's got fifty grand in Switzerland." I couldn't believe it. That amount of money! But, of course, she had. That was her bonus, bigger than any City bonus today. But Bill was raking it in, and so was Aspinall.'

So the scam continued at full pace every week at the Clermont, and never was there a hint of upset or disquiet from any of the members or their guests. Lord Derby would line up and shout his string of *bancos* and *suivis*, as would the Goldsmiths, the Stirlings, government ministers, European ambassadors, and other prestigious gamblers. They were totally unaware of the 'Big Edge'.

Not even James Bond knew what was going on. Bond's creator, Ian Fleming, cut a suave, stylish figure at the Clermont. John Burke liked him, despite 007's strange gambling habits: 'Bond's gambling is portrayed very poorly. Fleming lost a lot of money to us – he should have known better. But he liked the atmosphere and the girls, the edge to it all, so maybe he wasn't watching the cards. There are always people who are trying to lose money, and there are people who are there for the fun.

'One night when Fleming was playing at the big table in the Clermont, the club president, the Earl of Carnarvon, who, without understanding too much of our business, took a keen interest in the financial affairs of the club, advised me in his best stage whisper: "Give you a tip, Burkie, specially clear that fellow Fleming's cheque; he's got a dicky heart, might drop dead any moment."

'A few weeks later Ian Fleming had a fatal heart attack. "Porchy" Carnarvon was subsequently pleased to learn that all cheques paid to the Clermont by Fleming had been safely cleared in time.'

Which was the spectacular spin to the 'Big Edge': the heavy losers were always good for the money. If they lodged a cheque with the cashier, it would be honoured. It was a marvellous moneypot of ill-gotten gains, and Billy Hill was stirring it.

At the top tables with the toffs – those described by author Brian Masters in *The Passion of John Aspinall* as 'the best roll-call of rich and exclusive London society of the 1960s' – were the players from Maitland Court. It was a smooth operation, and Bobby McKew said: 'There was never a problem with the cheating at the Clermont because Aspinall was clever and did not let it be overdone, but sometimes there was trouble at other clubs with the scam. Once at the 21, the police got involved. The owner, Meadows, wasn't in on it, but the cashier and a couple of croupiers were. The police knew something was going on, because Billy played there. Even I did, a couple of times, and I never gambled unless it was crooked and I knew it.

'Some of the top people from the Yard came in and took all the cards away in a bag; they were going to get forensic experts to have a look. They came back and said: "Nothing wrong with these." That was in the 21, using the same card scam as at the Clermont and elsewhere.

'If cards were "clocked" – with a certain dot that indicates it's a six or a king – you can tell what it is. There are infrared methods, too; if you wore dark glasses you could read the cards coming out. But these cards weren't marked. That was another wonder of it.

'At the Clermont nobody noticed. They seemed to love losing money. Gamblers are like that. I told a friend of my wife's about a bent game. He'd lost £15,000.

'I said to him: "It's crooked. Don't go gambling there again."

'He nodded. The following week he went in and did about another ten, twelve grand. I don't suppose he believed me. Or just didn't want to. Gamblers!

'Some gamblers go in knowing they are going to lose. Billy Hill went in knowing he was going to win. Couldn't fail. The Union Corse, through his old friend Marcel Francisi (he was shot dead some years later, eight or nine bullets, think it was a machine gun), had brought the system to him, and he played it to the full. He worked it in every other major gambling club in England. Took a fortune.

'From the Aspinall deal and all that Clermont Club affair, Billy must have taken his share of what today would be at least £10 million. It was like robbing Fort Knox or the Bank of England. Just a lot easier. It was sweet. And not one of the victims ever knew what was going on. No one did. Millions and millions, tax free, into numbered accounts, Gypsy's purse and God knows where else, no questions asked.'

Aspinall never showed any concern for those he was mercilessly ripping off. For John Burke, there were moments of disquiet: 'I remember having a pang of conscience on hearing Aspers explain to the night's "reader" before a big game that he was to sit to the left of Major Derek Wigan, who had been having a good run, and concentrate on making him a big loser. I did not know Derek Wigan well, but I always saw him as a considerate, courteous gentleman, and hearing Aspinall describe him to his stooge as "detestable" forty-odd years ago is something that I cannot, but wish I could, forget. Perhaps that incident helped to give me a slight nudge in the right direction . . .'

14. COPPER-BOTTOMED

Que sera, sera – Whatever will be, will be.

DORIS DAY'S HIT SONG, 1956

As the 'Big Edge' settled into a reliable routine, John Aspinall began to spend the money as swiftly as Billy Hill delivered the cash to him. He had the upkeep of zoos and his town house in Lyall Street, Belgravia, to pay for, and his financial needs seemed to grow by the day. While Aspinall showed no qualms about cheating his members and his supposed friends, John Burke, although he insists on his culpability in the scheme, suffered disquiet. He also got lucky: his conscience was aided by a massive coup on the London metal market.

He'd gambled in copper on the London commodities market with the help of his friend Geoffrey Marriott. He'd met Marriott, by all accounts a dashing, charming man, in Dublin in the late 1940s, and they became great friends. After the war Marriott married Maura Ryan, the sister of Eddie Chapman's lover, the film star Kathleen Ryan, but it had a tragic conclusion when, driven by alcohol and drug addictions, she killed herself.

When the two old friends met again in London in 1960, Marriott was married to Anne from Amsterdam: 'They were good friends of Liliana and me. Geoffrey's job was copper buyer for Pirelli Tyres, when copper was a very important component in the manufacture of tyres. He was also a close personal friend of Sir Ronald Prain, who was the chairman of the Rhodesian Selection Trust which controlled the Rhodesian copper mines; he was the number one man in the world of copper, and his inside knowledge was invaluable.'

All the financial news said that there was overproduction of copper and that the price would drop. It did, but then the copper producers said they would not sell copper any cheaper. Still the financial pundits insisted that there was too much copper, not enough buyers and too many sellers, and the price would collapse.

Sir Ronald Prain told Geoffrey Marriott, and therefore John Burke, that the copper producers would make a stand and hold the price. But because of all the doom reports about the price, copper could be bought forward on the commodity market cheaper than the cash price. It is known as backwardation. It was very unusual: normally when you buy a commodity – gold, silver, copper – six months forward, the price is higher, if only to factor in the effect of inflation.

In the summer of 1964, John Burke, who had huge credit with Rudolf Wolff, was able to buy forward, on paper with no money exchanged, 1,500 tons of copper at a few pounds less per ton than the cash price. He had done this before, and he and Geoffrey Marriott had made steady profits, every three months turning over a few thousand pounds.

Suddenly, the situation changed. There were problems in America, a big strike in Chile. Instead of there being a surplus of copper, there was a shortage. Many speculators who had sold short heavily on the London Metal Exchange now had to buy back quickly in a market controlled by sellers. The price of copper exploded. It went up and up and up. John Burke was astonished, and remains so.

'We thought we were going to turn over a few thousand; instead we turned in a massive profit. After a few other profitable speculations, I walked away with somewhere between

£300,000 and £400,000, which was a nice amount. Quite a few millions, in today's money. Mr Money introduced me to the Banca del Gottardo in Lugano, where I opened an account. My one-time seven-figure Swiss franc account has, alas, dissolved into thin air.

'My relations with John Aspinall were not brilliant at this stage and I was also a bit worried. We were in this ridiculous situation with Billy Hill, and if it ever came out we would be in serious trouble. It was a highly criminal operation.'

This was forcibly brought home to Burkie in late 1964, when he had a nervous few days after he was approached by a friend, a highly placed lawyer and member of the club. He told him the authorities were investigating the Clermont. John Burke's informant was connected enough to know about such matters, but too discreet to pass on all the details. John thought it might be to do with government officials' habits – something MI5 took an interest in, or, more probably, currency exchange schemes – what would be called money laundering today. He never found out. He told Aspinall, and the investigation went away: 'John had the sort of friends who could do that.' Even so, for John Burke it was the final push he needed.

He sought out John Aspinall and told him: 'John, I wish you the best of luck but I feel I must bow out.'

Aspinall was furious. He felt betrayed. 'Burkie! You can't go!'

'I must.'

'Well, don't go now, stay till the end of the year.'

John Burke agreed to stay on for that time. Ian Maxwell-Scott heard of John Burke's decision to leave, and sought out his friend. They went for a drink at the Star, and Maxwell-Scott said that he, too, wanted to leave Aspinall. He, too, found the situation intolerable. He asked John Burke's advice: should he resign?

Ian Maxwell-Scott was on a generous income from the

Clermont, but also had a large family and the upkeep of Grants Hill House in Uckfield, Sussex. Without the job, the gambler would find it difficult to make ends meet.

John Burke, who talked Ian Maxwell-Scott out of leaving, himself got out of the Clermont about twelve months after the 'Big Edge' went in at the club.

'I officially resigned as director of the Clermont and moved on. I hadn't grown a halo. I said nothing about the "Big Edge". If I had, there would have been a huge scandal; the Clermont would have gone bust; the shareholders, many of them friends of mine, would have lost all their investments; and the directors, of whom I was one, would probably have been in for some heavy flak.'

As far as John Aspinall was concerned, the until-then always supportive and loyal John Burke was the forgotten man. He might as well have been dead. Aspinall ruthlessly wrote his friend out of his life:

'In John Aspinall's eyes, I had done something unforgivable. I was an outcast. I was a traitor. I had walked away and deserted him in his hour of need. I'd behaved in a despicable way. No Zulu warrior would dare to behave like that towards his great hero, the Zulu leader Shaka. The unfortunate warrior would have been banished to the most inhospitable corner of the kingdom. John never changed his mind. Once the idea was there, he wouldn't ever think back and rethink it.

'There were rumours that all was not above board in London gambling clubs, and no wonder, considering how much money was changing hands. I never made an effort to re-establish the friendship with Aspinall, because he told a couple of people that "One or two things strange happened when that fellow Burke was here, as he was friendly with gangsters."

'It was a rather rotten thing for Aspinall to say about his ex-friend and partner, but I suppose he saw it as his way of getting out of a tricky situation. He couldn't say it to too many people, of course, because anybody who understood anything about the running of a gambling club would realize that for anyone to infiltrate the Clermont Club from the outside and take a lot of money without the proprietor knowing would be not only impossible, but utterly ludicrous.'

Ironically, a few months later John Aspinall used John Burke's departure as the opportunity to cut his links with Billy Hill. He decided that he need not give away 40 per cent of his dubious earnings. He sent word to the gangster through Mr Money that he believed things were becoming too difficult for the 'Big Edge' to continue at the Clermont. Hill was practical about it. Without Aspinall's connivance with the 'readers', the scam could not operate. He'd got into the Clermont and taken a fortune from it. There were other casinos to rip off. Why try and pressure Aspinall, who was not an easy knockover? Why make a noise?

Yet Aspinall's financial needs, as ever, were still growing. The 'Big Edge' might have left the Grand Salon, but in its place he introduced another scheme. John Burke said, 'John simply began another scam to make money directly for himself. It was devilish and cunning; he employed a really first-class "mechanic" croupier, somebody who was streets ahead of even Louis the Rat, but almost in the same class as Bruce the Australian.

'There was a lot of money owed to the company; many members had lost vast sums of money, largely because of the Hill activities. If a recognized player had gone too far, got in too deep and reached the limit of his credit, he might want to withdraw from the game for a while. He'd plan to clear it all off; it might take a year or so, but before he did, John would go to him and say: "Hey, this is what we'll do – you can continue to play, but play for me. You enjoy playing. You're popular at the table, people like to see you sitting down there, and you lend an atmosphere to the place . . ." All that sort of bullshit.

'The deal was that if the player won he took 10 per cent, and if he lost it cost him nothing. It looked like a very good deal, and John would present it extremely well to people like Lucan who were on the books owing the Clermont a lot of money. The player would agree, and John would say: "Well, there's a big party next Wednesday, why don't you come Wednesday night." He would make one condition. He would say: "By the way, the only thing I would say is don't go calling *banco* all the time, just have the occasional bet. But run your banks for the maximum all the time."

'Apart from anything else, this was the right strategy because now we were not taking the *cagnotte*. There was a table charge, which is the same for every player at the table. So the odds were in favour of the bank and against the punter. It was the correct mathematical strategy to run your bank and bet as little as possible.

'What happened during the game would be that, at the right moment, the person who was playing for Aspinall would get a massive bank, a run of ten or twelve winning coups. It would happen perhaps twice in an evening. This croupier was a genius. But the person with the lucky bank was a regular player – not a "house" player – so there were no questions about it. In the Clermont, the big winner was someone of unquestioned integrity.

'John's man would be a big winner at the end of the night; say he won fifty grand, John would say, "Take £5,000 for yourself," and the person would very probably say: "Oh no, knock that off what I owe the company." Of the fifty grand, forty-five would go directly into John's pocket and the other five grand would go to the club.

'Good business all round. And of course, there's no danger of exposure, because neither party would talk about it and admit that was the way it was happening. And John's player thought it was just a behind-the-scenes deal with him; only John knew about the mechanic sending the winning banks to the correct seat.

'It would all go unnoticed, and John could use it to his advantage, saying: "How lucky so-and-so was with his win last night. Good player." It was clever!'

With the gaming laws of the UK changed in 2007 and Britain starting to look like one great casino, John Burke is a more than interested observer:

'It's as though we were going back to the gambling fever of Regency days, although today gambling is democratic and much of it is run by computers, not croupiers. There's a great history to upper-class gambling in England, and there's also, of course, the English working man who would go into the pub and play darts for a pint of beer and later visit the betting shop. Then there's that bunch of people who think gambling is wicked. And another bunch who want to take the gamblers for a ride, make money, lots of it, out of them.

'There is no question that a gambling bonanza is happening in Britain, with the online betting – I use Betfair – and the casinos. The casinos will be like corner shops in no time.

'The future of gambling? I have not gambled in a casino in London for twenty years. I would charitably assume that everything is now completely above board and that the people who are running the industry are men of undoubted integrity.'

He paused, thought for a moment, and with a smile added, 'Although it might be wise not to ignore, or indeed forget, the time-honoured proverb concerning the leopard and his spots . . .'

15. THE RETURN OF BRUCE

Never give a sucker an even break.

W.C. FIELDS, 1941

In 1972, Bruce returned to London.

Mark Sykes believes Lord Derby had won huge amounts of money at the Clermont, or that was what he was told. John Burke believes that it was a hugely successful businessman who had been a big winner. It is not very important who is correct. What is more disquieting is that the big winner became an even bigger loser, thanks to Bruce the marvellous card mechanic; the man who could work magic with any pack of cards.

The winner – whether it was Derby or another man – enraged John Aspinall. His run of luck had gone on all evening and into the early hours of the next day. There was no mechanic at play for Aspinall, just the house players, who, like the members, were getting their cards by chance, not by sleight of hand or direction from the croupier.

Aspinall wanted his money back. Badly. He said to the winner: 'How about a private poker game?'

It was agreed that a game would be arranged in two weeks' time at Aspinall's house in Lyall Street. Aspinall was so desperate for the return of the money that he wanted the best mechanic he could get, and someone who would be unknown to the membership of the Clermont.

Mark Sykes received a telephone call from Peter West. West asked if he knew someone who was absolutely top quality, an international card sharp, to come and play poker for the house. It was urgent. The game was in two weeks, very short notice.

Mark Sykes told West that he knew the perfect player: Bruce the Australian. He was really good. But he was in Tasmania.

'We'll pay all his costs,' said Peter West, adding: 'He's just got to get here for this game. It's vital.'

Mark Sykes called Bruce on that faraway island to tell him that his talents were urgently required for a special game. The money for a first-class air fare and expenses would be wired to him. Over thirty years ago, it took Bruce three days to get to London. On arrival, he went to stay at a little hotel in South Kensington. It was there that Mark Sykes introduced Bruce to Peter West and their arrangements were made. Mark Sykes 'was very well looked after'. Bruce was to be paid £25,000 for his help: there was, it seemed, never any question that the big winner was going to go down.

Indeed, Bruce won all the money back for Aspinall. The details of the game were kept quiet. All those involved were absolutely discreet and never told the exact details: whether it was one session, or over one day and into the next.

And there could have been more than one victim at the table. Aspinall would not have been keen to have their names known, because no possible good could come of it. It might do him serious damage or hamper future operations.

Aspinall said to Bruce: 'By the way, don't ever mention the names of the people who subscribed so generously to us.'

Bruce played his part, which is why he may have dissembled, telling a white lie to his good friend Mark Sykes and naming John Derby as the big winner, and subsequently big loser.

It completed the circle.

Bruce stayed around for a week and played cards with his friends, including Mark Sykes, who recalled that Bruce had a problem; he used to drink. 'Even when he was ripped he could make the cards do whatever he wanted. That is the most unbelievably, incredibly difficult thing even to think about doing. You've got to know where every single card in the pack is. You've got to try and remember. It's an astonishing feat.'

John Burke recalls that it was Bruce who taught John Aspinall one or two simple tricks of the trade at poker; how to arrange the cards in such a way as to take off some gullible young man. Not much had changed since his first encounter with John Aspinall in the Jermyn Street offices of the entertaining master of the understatement, Sydney Summers. Yes, Aspinall was good with the cards, John Burke confirmed.

'But Bruce was spectacular. You want four aces? You want a straight flush? Anything you want, you got it. Even following Mr Dooley's advice about always cutting the cards doesn't help in those circumstances.

'Cheats, as Sydney said, have the "Big Edge".'

POSTSCRIPT: GUYS AND DOLLS

Nobody's perfect.

JOE E. BROWN, THE LAST LINE OF *SOME LIKE IT HOT*, 1959

Lord Lucan has had a bad press. In contrast to what has become the established view, many people liked him and enjoyed his company. It was only later, when his marriage was in tatters and he lost custody of his children, that drink and his sorrows made him difficult and obsessive. But friends, especially the Clermont set, he had. One of the most loyal was Ian Maxwell-Scott. Lucan had become a house player for Aspinall – a titled shill at the Clermont Club, a man of unquestioned integrity. Just the sort of player Aspinall required.

Lucan may not have been the most intelligent of men, but he was not a complete fool. He knew cards: he'd played bridge at the Hamilton Club with Stephen Raphael, and was an experienced gambler. He had played at the Clermont almost constantly from the opening night. Instinctively, he knew something was wrong with the gambling at the Clermont: the constant run of coups, the big winners. It's not clear whether he confronted Aspinall about it, but Ian Maxwell-Scott told John Burke, with whom he remained close friends all his life, that Lucan had approached him. Maxwell-Scott said Lucan was distressed by the cheating and 'had a lot of problems with it'.

John Burke said: 'In the 1950s, John Bingham had a dead-end job in banking, but he loved gambling. He lost money, but he became one of the Clermont's house players in the late 1960s.

'What helped send him off his head was the ongoing despair when he found out about the mechanics, the bent croupier, the cheating scheme. Bingham was an honourable man – cheating at cards! My God, to him, it was despicable. When he discovered what was going on he was terribly troubled by it. It only messed up his confused mind even more.

The madness took over totally on 7 November 1974, when Sandra Rivett, the nanny to Lucan's three children, was killed.

Lucan had quietly entered the five-storey mews house, opening the door to 46 Lower Belgrave Street with his latchkey. His wife Veronica and his children were upstairs, watching *The Six Million Dollar Man* on, television. After the programme Lucan knew his wife would send the children off to bed and then go to the kitchen in the basement to make tea. On the stairway to the basement, he took the light bulb out of the socket. Then he went down the stairs to the darkness of the kitchen and waited.

True to form, after the TV show, 'Lady Lucan' walked down the stairs, having tried but failed to turn the light on. At the bottom of the stairs, her estranged husband hit her over the head with a ten-inch-long piece of pipe. She fell to her knees and was bashed on the head again and again. Lucan had planned the murder, his alibi and the disposal of Lady Lucan's body. But then he heard her voice from the top of the stairs, saying, 'Sandra, Sandra.'

Nanny Sandra Rivett, like her employer just five feet two inches tall, had changed her night off so that she could see a boyfriend later in the week. Fate had dealt Lucan a joker, a case of mistaken identity. He had killed the wrong woman.

Shocked, enraged, bewildered, he went up the stairs at a pace and began to attack his real target: his wife. He hit her with the pipe, tried to strangle her and stuck gloved fingers into her throat and eyes. Lady Lucan fought back, grabbed him between the legs and squeezed hard. She then managed to quieten Lucan and, moments later, when he was distracted by the appearance of his daughter Lady Frances, she escaped and ran down Lower Belgrave Street to raise the alarm at a pub called the Plumber's Arms. From there the Lucan saga unfolded.

Mark Sykes told me: 'I can well imagine him murdering the wrong woman by mistake; it was just the sort of thing he would do.'

It now seems that the Lucan mystery may never be solved. The 3rd Earl of Lucan, John Bingham's great-great-grandfather, directed and was disgraced by the disastrous charge of the Light Brigade, which resulted in massacre in the Valley of Death at Balaclava, during the Crimean War. Infamy and many questions still surround the 7th Earl of Lucan.

What we can clear up here is that Lucan did borrow £10,000 before the killing. It was not from Jimmy Goldsmith or Aspinall, or any of their so-called 'set'. It was from a group of moneylenders in Mount Street, near the formerly intimidating premises of the Mount Street Bridge Club. When Lucan vanished after the murder of Sandra Rivett, the guarantor of the loan, John Burke's good friend Richard Parkes, had to pay over the £10,000. John Burke recalls:

'He did so without a quibble. Richard was such a man that he never said a public word about it. He knew the pressures that were on Lucan. He thought he could use the money to pay debts and sort himself out.'

In 2005 it was suggested in print that a certain 'Mr X', a 'secret' man with a facility for international money dealings, especially in Switzerland, had arranged for Lucan to escape from Britain and then, some time later, had him killed. The theory was built around an interview with the late Susan Maxwell-Scott. Her daughter Cathy said in 2006: 'My mother did talk to the writer, but she was very ill. I don't think anything that was suggested was true, and I've grown up with the whole Lucan business.'

An underworld figure who was said to have facilitated the murder of Lucan said in January 2007: 'I never met Lucan, which means I never murdered Lucan.'

Yet Susan Maxwell-Scott was the last person to see Lucan alive. Her husband was staying at the Clermont when Lucan, only a few hours after the killing of Sandra Rivett, appeared at Grants Hill House in Uckfield. He was distraught. He wrote some letters. He babbled. He left.

Not too long afterwards, Susan Maxwell-Scott, a devout Catholic who took such things more than seriously, had a Mass said for Lucan. John Burke said: 'As far as she and Ian were concerned, Lucan was dead then. Mass was not a trivial thing for them, not some token gesture. They knew he had gone. They would never have had a Mass otherwise.

'Did he kill himself? Was he killed? I don't know how he died, but I believe he did. Susie wouldn't have done that unless she knew for certain he was dead. Ian always said Lucan was dead.

'Lucan was a friend of mine. He was also an unlucky gambler. In every sense.'

Aspinall played on the Lucan mystery from the beginning. On 8 November 1974, the day after Sandra Rivett's murder, Aspinall's friends (but not, expensively for *Private Eye*, Jimmy Goldsmith) gathered for lunch. The *Eye*, under the editor of the time, Richard Ingrams, stated that Goldsmith had been present at the lunch. Goldsmith took it as an accusation that the lunch meeting was to talk about helping Lucan escape, and that the magazine was implying he had therefore conspired to obstruct the cause of justice. He went on to issue sixty-three writs against the satirical magazine, which launched the 'Goldenballs' fund to defend itself against Goldsmith's legal onslaught.

The day after Aspinall's lunch, newspapers suggested the implausible, the impossible and the incredible, including the theory that Lucan had begged Aspinall to feed him to his tigers. Aspinall, who went to great lengths to promote a conspiracy theory and to imply that he had been an integral part of it, was interviewed on television and said that if Lucan showed up he would embrace him; this was tribal loyalty, the Zulu rules which he insisted upon from his friends. Aspinall was asked if he was proud to be the friend of a man who had murdered a woman and attempted to kill his wife. Aspinall said: 'If she'd been my wife, I'd have bashed her to death five years before, and so would you.'

The Clermont set had their fun at the expense of the police investigation. Detectives got short shrift when they tried to quiz members at the Clermont and Annabel's. Lady O. was reported to have ended a telephone conversation with the police: 'Got to go and give Lucky his food. He's down under the tiger cage.'

Another story – but remember Aspinall's imagination – goes that when the police arrived at Howletts' they were told by the butler: 'I'm sorry, Mr Aspinall is having dinner.'

'But we're the police.'

'I'm terribly sorry. I've been told not to disturb Mr Aspinall.'

'We have to see him now.'

Eventually, they were led into the dining room. Seated at the table were John Aspinall, his wife, Lady O., and a gorilla.

There were many strange events and stories following the

murder of Sandra Rivett. One involved the American who had introduced Signor Biondi to Aspinall. He knew Lucan and played backgammon with him. The day before the murder, Lucan had sent the man a cheque to pay a backgammon debt. When a writer expressed surprise at such a detail, he was told: 'Those gamblers. Their sense of integrity is devoted more to each other than even to their families, particularly the ones who are addicted.'

Loyalty was essential. Those like Dominick Elwes, who supposedly broke the code, were ostracized. Elwes, the court jester of the crowd, made the mistake of selling a painting he'd done of the 'Clermont set' to the *Sunday Times* colour magazine. It was published in the inside pages to illustrate a superb investigative article by James (*White Mischief*) Fox. The picture depicted Lord Lucan, John Aspinall, James Goldsmith, Charles Benson, Stephen Raphael, the Earl of Suffolk, Peter West, and Nicholas Soames, the grandson of Winston Churchill.

On the cover was a photograph taken twenty months earlier in Mexico of Lucan, and, next to him, Lady Annabel, the lover of James Goldsmith and mother of his two children. Goldsmith lost the plot. He went crazy with rage. Elwes was 'out' of the crowd. Mark Sykes told me what happened next:

'When he found himself cut off from the company that he adored, my poor, sad cousin committed suicide. He was my fourth cousin. He was a depressive, but one of the reason why he killed himself was that he had been thrown out of the Clermont lot and told to "piss off" by Goldsmith and the others. Basically, they gave him the boot. They thought he had given a story or something to the *Sunday Times* and been paid a lot of money. They were all in it, and they thought it was disgraceful.

'They didn't think that the poor bugger had to get a few quid together. I saw him on the evening he topped himself.

At his funeral, Aspinall had the nerve to make a sententious speech. Dominick and I shared a little squat, rugby-playing Welsh cousin called Tremayne Rodd who is now Lord Rodd. He went up and gave Aspinall the most useful punch in the face you have ever seen in your life. Aspinall sat down in the road. He did. Aspinall had the grace to say: "None of my gorillas have ever done that to me!" It was brilliant.'

After he died, it was revealed that Dominick Elwes, although short of money, did not sell the photographs to the *Sunday Times*. It was Lady Lucan who made that arrangement.

Another suicide victim was the brewery heir Mark Watney. In the early days of the Clermont, he had an affair with Jane Aspinall. 'The Spirit of Park Lane' had been encouraged by Aspinall to flirt with his customers, but it seems she did more than flirt. Aspinall did not openly berate her about the affairs, one said to have been with an animal-keeper at Howletts, another with a well-known aristocrat.

Jane and John Aspinall were estranged by 1964 and divorced in 1966. In their bitter divorce Aspinall retained custody of the children, and Jane Aspinall was all but banned from contact with them.

Aspinall did not forget what he saw as her betrayal. Some years later, Mark Watney bounced a cheque for £1,000 with the Clermont. Aspinall had him 'posted', disgraced, as his bad debt had been made public. In reality, it was a trifling sum to Aspinall, and the cheque would have been honoured by the Watney family, if not, later, by Mark Watney himself.

Watney, who had other personal problems, found it all too much. He killed himself, shooting himself in the head, at the Star in Belgravia. The apocryphal story says that Watney had a gentleman's manners, and pulled a plastic bag over his head before pulling the trigger.

For Paddy Kennedy it meant there was less mopping up.

After Watney's death, the publican checked his credit book and saw that Watney owed £200. 'What the hell,' he told his customers, 'we might as well wipe that out and let him go with a clean slate.' He opened a bottle of the house champagne, Krug, and toasted the beer heir's departure in what he always called a 'glass of Krugelberry wine'.

After the divorce, Jane Aspinall pawned some jewellery at Sutton's in Victoria. It was found to be stolen, and the police began inquiries. They could not locate her, but it was easy to find John Aspinall. When quizzed he quickly replied: 'Lord Timothy Willoughby gave my wife a present of some jewellery.'

Of course, Tim Willoughby, a man of good name who had guaranteed Aspinall's lease on the Clermont, was dead. In that, he served John Aspinall's purpose. It was a cynical ploy: Tim Willoughby was not a dealer in stolen goods, nor did he have an affair with Jane Aspinall, which was the implication of Aspinall's remark to the police.

Until the upset of the Salle Privée, Ray Ryan had also served Aspinall's purpose. He had been repaid with interest by John Aspinall, and Ryan added the funds to the already considerable investment he had in the Mount Kenya Safari Club – the 1,256-acre game ranch he created with the Hollywood actor William Holden, a little more than one hundred miles from Nairobi.

John Burke met up again with Ray Ryan in 1967. 'I assumed that Ryan would very much give me the cold shoulder. On the contrary, he was extremely friendly. He'd made his own inquiries about what had happened at the Clermont, and he knew that it wasn't my idea. I wasn't even consulted about it, and I had nothing whatsoever to do with Signor Biondi. Ryan even invited me and Liliana and our daughter Daniela to be his guests in Kenya in the first week of of 1968. It was a wonderful holiday. Magnificent chalet.

I remember going to the races in Nairobi, and we saw the Kenya Derby.'

He never saw Ray Ryan again. On 18 October 1977, Ryan went to a health club in his home town of Watertown, Wisconsin, as he often did. When he finished his workout, the 73-year-old Ryan walked outside to his new Lincoln Mark V coupé.

A bomb was linked to the ignition of the car. Ryan turned the key and the car exploded. The blast killed him instantly. It took two days to locate and collect all of the pieces of his body and the car – one piece was found 377 feet from the scene.

In 2007, three decades after the killing, the murder has still not been solved. Clearly Ryan upset the wrong person or people at the wrong time.

The Mafia have often been mentioned in connection both with Ryan's death, and with gambling in London. Ryan had been subjected to a US Government Internal Revenue Service (IRS) investigation before his death. There was a suggestion that the Mob bosses believed he might have said too much.

In the mid 1960s they were taking an interest in Billy Hill's gambling territory. By then the Clermont had established itself as the Beautiful People's gambling mecca. The Mafia wanted their own establishments, and that's when Bobby McKew again met some men with vowels at the end of their names. At the time he had an interest in a couple of London clubs, including one of the first discotheques:

'I met them with Billy because they couldn't really do anything in London without his cooperation. They wanted someone to run their club, the Colony. I was talking to Billy and I said that the ideal person would be Paul Adam. He'd be a marvellous "front" because he was Princess Margaret's favourite bandleader, played in the Milroy and was the housewife's choice. He was tall, handsome, a very good-looking man.

'The Americans, two men who never gave their names – dark suits, white shirts, very smart-looking men, with beady eyes – were staying in a hotel off Conduit Street and came over to see us. The oldest had close-set eyes. He looked at you and he could freeze you just by doing that.

'I asked them: "Drink?"

'They both growled: "Club orange."

'Paul was there and had had a few and he was pissed, and he kept pulling up a girl's skirt. The Yanks were annoyed, and the next day when we met they said: "He drinks. He's not for us."

'Which was when Billy told them: "You need an Englishman. You've got to realize the Mafia here is the police. If you haven't got an Englishman who can deal with them, it won't work."

'The Mafia guys were from the Midwest, tough guys, and didn't quite believe all this, and they said: "We'll put our guy in, there's no question about that."

'Bill said: "They won't reign long there."

'He was right. They put in George Raft. Raft lasted about six months, if that, at the Colony. They had an interest in a few other places, including the Mount Street Bridge Club, the one where Jack Buggy was carpeted. Raft was provided with a chauffeured Rolls-Royce and a Mayfair penthouse for his time at the Colony.'

In 1978 I spoke several times with George Raft, who, trying to live up to the part, wore a corset under his dinner jacket at the Colony. His last big movie had been, yet again, playing a gangster in *Some Like It Hot*, Billy Wilder's superb 1959 confection with Marilyn Monroe, Jack Lemmon and Tony Curtis. Now aged 83, Raft was once again in the gambling business.

Every morning at 10 a.m. he turned up at the offices of the Riviera Hotel-Casino on Wilshire Boulevard in Beverly Hills. His job was to promote the casino and help lure gamblers to Las Vegas. It was all rather sad. He'd stare out from beneath his silver toupee and wave to passers-by who peered in the windows at him. He was the $500-a-week 'ambassador of goodwill', a role like the hosting work he performed at the Colony Club.

He'd never talked in detail about the Colony Club, the Kray twins, or his lifetime ban from Britain (then Home Secretary Roy Jenkins had banned him for life in 1967). Along with eight other Americans – men with those vowels at the end of their names – he was considered to be someone 'whose continued presence in the United Kingdom would not be conducive to the public good'.

'What did I do?' he asked me. 'I'm still very hurt, very bitter. What was my crime? I'm not a member of the Mob, never was. Rocky Marciano had organized the whole thing. He picked me up at my hotel in London one Sunday afternoon and said we were going to meet some poor kids in the East End of London. So, I met the Kray twins. I had my picture taken with them, but I didn't know who they were. No, no, they didn't look like poor kids. No, sure they didn't.

'I admit I was wrong, but I couldn't get any work after the London business. I liked to gamble, I once had twenty racehorses and I still go to the races, to Hollywood Park and Santa Anita. I lost a fortune. But it was that club in London that finished me off. They just wouldn't let me do that job. I'd hardly got to London and they kicked me out.'

Bobby McKew simply nods at the story: 'We never fell out with the Mafia over the Colony. In fact, they paid more attention to us over other matters. They understood we knew what we were talking about. We had even more clout.

'The next ones who did come in were the Playboy Club, Hugh Hefner, who had Victor Lownes running it. I went up there once or twice and in the lounge there were half a dozen people, all drinking, and they were all policemen. Plain clothes.

'They were American, which just shows you that you could get around it. I don't know how they managed it, but they did it anyway. That was the late 1960s, and they were more relaxed about the gambling.'

And there were more clubs. Mark Sykes and Eric Steiner ran the Pair of Shoes at four different London locations. It was a moneymaker, said Mark Sykes. 'Eric organized what he called "junkets" for high rollers from Las Vegas, who were flown over to London and stayed for a week at the Dorchester, all expenses paid. The American gangsters in Las Vegas sent over planeloads of people who would gamble at the Pair of Shoes.

'It was staggering business. It was wonderful. All these people would come over and they all took over the floor of our casino. These people would open with credit of 250,000 bucks each, and the gangster guy at the other end would guarantee the money. We were paid everything in two weeks. No money changed hands. All markers went into the accounts and within two weeks we had the money. Tremendously efficient, the Americans.'

In the late 1960s, Eric Steiner offered to sell the Pair of Shoes for next to nothing to John Burke, but he turned it down. By 1977, John Burke and Liliana had divorced and he had married again, to Gigi, a Swedish girl: 'I married in a Catholic church on St Stephen's Green in Dublin and in a Lutheran church in Stockholm. Not bad for an agnostic.'

They separated in the mid 1980s and divorced in 1989. With Gigi he had three children, James, Janina and Richard.

In 2007 he had retired to a remote part of Ireland with his partner Caroline Gray.

Nancy Gillespie, who was divorced from Prince George Sapieha in 1960, continued to amuse smart dinner parties with her stories. Now married to Michael Lambton – an early and besotted devotee of Christine Keeler – she was living in London, where we talked many times in 2006. She thought her husband might be in Austria and added, with a wink: 'With a girl, you know. He always liked the girls.'

Her memories of the past are as sharp as ever. 'When I was at the *Express* I was walking into the front hall one day when Beaverbrook walked up to reception. He saw me, but didn't say anything. I went to the editor John Junor's office and said to him: "Do you know where Lord Beaverbrook is?"

'He said: "Yes, he's in Florida or Jamaica."

'I said: "No, he's not, he's in the front hall."

'He said: "Don't be so ridiculous."

'I protested. I told him what Beaverbrook was wearing. He made sure everybody was at their desk when Beaverbrook did arrive. Beaverbrook gave me a big wink. He hadn't missed a trick. I was a very attractive girl in my youth.

'There were some characters around. I knew Jimmy Goldsmith very well. I once lent him £3. It was at a party in Oxford. He said: "Nancy. Have you got any money on you?"

'I said: "Who, me? Not much."

'He only wanted £3 for a taxi to get him back to the Randolph. He was always very grateful. Naturally, I got it back. He, too, was ruthless, but he wasn't like Aspinall.

'I met Ava Gardner, and she became a great friend. My husband Michael Lambton had a flat in Onslow Gardens, and Ava had a flat beneath. That's how I met her. She got ill, and then sicker and sicker. She rang me up in the winter of

1989 and asked if I could come around; she said that she felt so ill she wanted to go back home to America, and she said: "You'd better ring Frank and ask him if he can fetch me."

'I said: "Frank?"

'She said: "Frank Sinatra."

'She gave me his number and when I rang up I said: "I'm ringing for Ava Gardner, she's in a bad way and she would really like to speak to Mr Sinatra."

'The voice said: "Is she drunk?"

'I said: "No. She's not drunk, she's ill."

'Sinatra said, "I'll send for her straight away."

'He sent a plane for her. It was not many months before she died, back in London. I think he always loved her dearly. She was the love of his life.

'Lots of people have gone. John Burke, who was a good friend of Peter West, and I went to Peter's funeral. Aspinall was there. He didn't want to be there, but Jimmy Goldsmith was paying for it all. Peter West adored Jimmy. At the graveside, Jimmy said: "What do I do now?"

'I said: "Take a handful of earth and throw it on the coffin."

'He said: "Are you sure?"

'I said: "Yes, I'm sure."

'Aspinall marched up to me: "What did you tell Jimmy to do?"

'I said nothing; I was very rude to him. And he didn't like me either.'

John Burke recalls the 1996 funeral: 'Jimmy Goldsmith and Peter were always close friends; in their last years they became inseparable. So Westie was able to enjoy the good things of life, which he appreciated, while Jimmy had an intelligent, amusing companion who was also a loyal friend. Jimmy died only a year later.'

Sir James Goldsmith – 'Sir Jams' to *Private Eye*, which

he had sued over the Lucan affair – was 64 when he died on 20 July 1997. He left a fortune. Estimates put it at £1.8 billion, but that was just a guess. As it had to be when Billy Hill died at his Moscow Road flat on New Year's Eve 1983. Frankie Fraser said, walking down Browning Street in 2006, that he knew Hill was 'a goner'. Fraser had been in prison ('when wasn't I?') when Hill had visited him: 'He said the docs had told him he'd die if he didn't give up smoking, in four years, probably two, maybe three. They didn't know for sure, but he was taking a ball of chalk. I told him he should just quit the fags.

'He said: "Frank, I can't do it. I can't do it."

'See, such a tough guy, but he couldn't quit smoking. Says something.'

Ian Maxwell-Scott died from a heart attack in November 1993, and his wife Susan Maxwell-Scott, the last person known to have seen 'Lucky' Lucan, died in September 2004.

In 2007 Michael 'Dandy Kim' Caborn-Waterfield was working on his memoirs. He has quite a story to tell. He met the Kray Twins in Tangier, ran guns to Cuba, upset Joan Collins with a naughty story about her one-time husband Anthony Newley and launched the Miss Topless World beauty contest with Lord Patrick Lichfield as photographer and Earl Alexander as musical director.

He has seen everything and everyone: he evaded a naked Pamela Digby Churchill Hayward Harriman, 'a true redhead, she was aflame, mop, collar and cuffs'. He loved and managed Diana Dors from her teenaged starlet days to her tragic early death from cancer in May 1984. He was the last person to talk to Dors' distraught husband Alan Lake, vainly trying to stop him killing himself. On the way he helped Greg Dyke rescue then struggling TV-am, befriended political Mr Fixit, Lord Goodman, founded the Ann Summers chain of High Street sex shops, wrote a bestselling sex manual, and made movies with Stewart Granger, Anthony Newley and Petula Clark. He only married once, to the beautiful *Vogue* model Penny Brahms by whom he had his daughter, Campbell.

Bobby McKew, like Oscar Wilde, could resist everything but temptation. And boredom.

He was kicking his heels, working the gambling clubs and other schemes with Billy Hill in the 1960s, when towards the end of the decade he linked up with Richard Leigh, the heir to a baronetcy. Neither of them was interested in titles – just money: Swiss francs, and lots of them.

A clever technician, Bobby McKew recruited a team of expert printers and a camera operator. For three weeks they worked to originate the plates to forge Swiss franc notes, each of which carried a face value of around £10. He said: 'They wanted to know how many to print and I thought we might as well go for one million. Should have said ten. Had I been left alone, I would have solved Britain's balance of payments problem.'

And he might have. After the scheme was discovered, Swiss bankers called the forgeries the finest they had ever seen. They were so good that the Swiss government had to change its note-printing methods. It all ended in tears, and jail, because the gang did not have a distribution system as good as the forged notes. And somebody talked, just as the next few millions were being printed.

Interpol worked with Scotland Yard: forgeries were found in Munich; £50,000 worth were used to buy Swiss watches; and thousands more passed to a man, identified in court as 'Syd', to pay off 'Dogs of War' mercenaries in Biafra. The distribution was haphazard and traceable, and led to the Old Bailey in 1970.

Bobby McKew was fined £10,000 and jailed for five years. He served three at Albany on the Isle of Wight. 'I just had to get on with it. There's a great class system inside. If you are "in", you don't get any aggravation from the screws or the other inmates. Most people don't want trouble, especially if you're in there for a long stretch.

'In jail in France, they didn't know what to do with me. For a long time I was the only Englishman in the jail. They treated me fairly. In Albany, which is a much tougher nick than Parkhurst, we sat apart from the petty thieves and the burglars. I'd eat with Charlie Kray and one of the Train Robbers; I can't even recall which one now: there were a lot of them inside at one time or another. There was an upper echelon, and wc were left alone.'

While he was in Albany, it became clear that his mother Iris was dying in South Africa, where she had moved to be close to his sisters Joy and Paddy and her grandchildren. He asked to see the governor and requested compassionate parole to visit his mother. The governor looked at his record, told him it read 'like the Debrett's of crime', and denied the request.

Also during his prison term his marriage of fourteen years ended, although in 2007, thirty-five years later, he remains close and friendly with his former wife.

After Albany, he moved to another island, the sunnier one of Ibiza. He did some 'transport work', for which read smuggling, there, but had no intention of going behind bars again: 'I'd much rather be outside prison sweeping the roads than inside with a million waiting for me. Anyone who does something knowing it will get them into prison is an idiot. It's a ridiculous place, a total waste of time.'

He wrote the novel *Death List*, which reads chillingly like reality. He was encouraged to do so by the actor Stanley Baker, to whom the book is dedicated. Baker planned to turn it into a film, but died from cancer before this could happen. His long-time friend Richard Harris's production company took up the option.

Bobby McKew, Harris and his brother Dermot Harris were discussing the project in New York in the mid 1970s when they were invited to dinner with Frank Sinatra. When they sat down to eat it was at Umberto's Clam House in New York's Little Italy, with Sinatra and Mafia boss Joe Pagano. 'They made a point of putting me in this corner seat,' said Bobby McKew. The seat was the one where, on 7 April 1972, Joey 'Crazy Joe' Gallo was gunned down in a Mob hit. 'Sinatra thought it was a huge joke.'

After another meeting in Los Angeles with executives from MGM, Bobby McKew went on to an awards dinner. When the studio bosses realized who he was, he got all but a standing ovation. 'They all hated Jack Warner and wanted to applaud anyone who had ripped him off.'

For all sorts of reasons – Hollywood ones – *Death List* went off the boil, only to be heated up again in 2006 when a studio in Los Angeles optioned it for a six-figure sum. 'It would be nice to see it get made, for Stanley and Richard, for they encouraged me.'

In 2007, he remains close to people from his past, including Charles Richardson. Together with Richard Harris, they were able to help out the House of Windsor and save the Royal Family from embarrassment.

Harris, who had enjoyed romantic encounters with Princess Margaret, learned that actor-gangster John Bindon was offering for sale lurid pictures of the Queen's sister. Bindon had played the villain as something of a violent artful dodger in television series and films. In Chelsea and Caribbean circles he was better known for his ability to hang beer mugs (one to five, depending on who tells the story) from his erect penis.

Bobby McKew is matter-of-fact: 'Bindon was a right prick. A year or so after Richard's affair with Margaret ended, Richard phoned me sounding tense and said he needed to see me urgently. He told me he had just been to see the princess, who'd been told that Bindon was trying to find out how much he could get by selling pictures of them together in compromising situations. All involving Bindon's famous body part.

'She was aware that Richard and Bindon knew each other, and hoped Richard could help. They were embarrassingly explicit photographs taken on Mustique, where she had her Caribbean home, and she was paranoid about them being made public.

'I knew Richard had met Princess Margaret in the 1960s, but I didn't know they had been to bed together until he told me in the early 1980s. They got together again while he was playing King Arthur in *Camelot* in London in 1983. She went backstage to see him and later instructed one of her staff to invite him for tea. They obviously hit it off again, for he was invited back for more tea.

'When the photograph business started Richard could have spoken to Bindon himself, but he'd fallen out with him. He asked me to see Bindon to find out how much he wanted for the pictures. I'd met the guy several times, but I didn't think he would take me seriously. I said: "There's one man Bindon respects and tips his forelock to, and that's Charlie Richardson. Why don't I ask him?"

'I'd introduced Charlie and Richard shortly after Charlie was released from prison in August 1984 [he'd been jailed for twenty-five years in the 1960s 'Torture Trial']. Richard liked anyone with a brain who was worldly and able to converse on several topics, and he found Charlie fascinating, stimulating company.

'"Do you think he'll do it, Bob?" he asked me.

'I said: "I'm sure he will. For two reasons. He loves the Royal Family and hates a bully, which is what Bindon is."

' "Ask him to find out what Bindon wants for the photos and I'll pay it," Richard said. "And tell Charlie I'll pay him for his trouble."

'The next morning I explained everything to Charlie over a cup of tea. He reacted the way I thought he would, and a couple of days later contacted Bindon, who invited him to his flat in Belgravia. Apparently, Bindon was quite lairy, boasting he was going to sell the photos for nothing less than £100,000.

'I don't know everything that was said, but I do know that when he is asked to do something important, Charlie does it. And I know he can be very persuasive. Finally, Bindon agreed to hand over the pictures for £5,000. That evening, Charlie arranged to meet Richard and me and arrived with a sealed brown envelope.

'Richard looked to make sure the pictures were inside, then dropped the package on a fire in the corner of the pub. He gave Charlie an envelope containing £5,000 in notes, and said: "That's for Bindon. Now, what can I pay you for yourself?"

'Charlie shook his head and said: "It's nice of you, Richard, but I don't want anything. You were only doing someone a favour. And I'm happy to have been able to do one for you." '

The renowned actor Jared Harris, son of the Limerick-born Richard, commented: 'When my father told me about the affair, he said he told Princess Margaret that he was only doing to her what her sister and those before her had been doing to his country for three hundred years. She told him: "But you're doing it much better." '

Bobby McKew said, 'It's weird how Margaret and Richard were linked: she died in February 2002, and then in the October he passed away. Marvellous characters, in their oh-so-different ways.'

John Aspinall had gone before them. At Eaton Place he had given a home to a mini-zoo, before buying Howletts and thirty-eight acres of Kent on which to establish a refuge for hundreds of animals; he opened the collection to the public in 1975. Later he added the nearby estate of Port Lympne and its 275 acres. Both zoos are unorthodox in approach, encouraging close personal relationships between staff and animals, and today are run as a charity by the John Aspinall Foundation.

John Aspinall carried out pioneering work on the preservation of endangered wild mammals, yet his legacy as a zoologist is controversial thanks to his belief in close bonding with the animals. He frequently appeared in public scarred and bruised after being mauled by one pet or another. Five keepers were killed and at least one seriously injured by Aspinall's animals, while a young boy lost an arm to a chimpanzee. Yet John Aspinall, the Zulu warrior, was proud that his zoos had achieved eight elephant births, fourteen black rhinos, seventy-five gorillas, twenty-five leopards and some 400 tigers. He claimed to have more black rhinos than Zambia.

His casino career was also colourful. He sold the Clermont for £700,000, but lost his investments in the 1974 stock market crash. This forced him to start all over again by launching, with financial help from Jimmy Goldsmith, Aspinall's Club in Knightsbridge, which became the the Aspinall Curzon in Curzon Street. With Goldsmith's sage advice he made an enormous amount of money – £90 million – when he sold it in 1987. In 1992 he opened yet another gaming club, again called Aspinall's, and in 2007 it was run by his family and was regarded by those who know as the smartest and most socially aware casino in London.

He died from cancer on 29 June 2000. After his ten-year marriage to Jane Hastings ended in 1966, he married Belinda 'Min' Musker, a granddaughter of the 2nd Viscount Daventry; when they divorced in 1972, the same year he took his wedding vows again with Lady Sarah Courage.

The affable Claus von Bülow, who was 80 in 2006, was a

great friend to the gamblers. In 1966, he married the former wife of Prince Alfred von Auersperg, who became Martha von Bülow, known as Sunny. Claus von Bülow was charged with trying to kill her with an insulin overdose in late 1980.

In 1982, he stood trial in Newport, Rhode Island, was found guilty and was jailed for thirty years. Two years later the conviction was reversed on appeal. At a second trial in 1985, a jury found him not guilty on all charges. John Burke sent him a telegram which read: 'Well done on a winning suivi.'

Von Bülow's appeal lawyer, the celebrated American lawyer and lecturer Alan Dershowitz, wrote a book which in 1990 became the movie *Reversal of Fortune*, for which Jeremy Irons won an Oscar as Best Actor, starring as the melodically voiced von Bülow.

Families? What did Philip Larkin say?

A grand character, Mark Birley had three children with his wife: Rupert, Robin and India Jane. Tragically, Rupert vanished while swimming off the coast of West Africa in 1986. Many explanations have been offered over more than twenty years: everything from an accident to the theory that he was a spook and was whisked away to Moscow; that one probably had more to do with the fact that he spoke Russian than with a Soviet ship being seen in the ocean near Togo on the morning of his disappearance.

Robin Birley, tall and charming like his father, immaculately dressed and mannered, was also almost lost to his parents. When he was 12, his mother took him to Howletts, John Aspinall's zoo, where he was mauled by a pregnant tiger. His mother thought him dead, but nine hours of surgery saved him; he endured much reconstructive work to his face.

He and his sister revamped Annabel's on its fortieth anniversary in 2002. They were helped by their half-brothers Ben and Zac Goldsmith and their half-sister Jemima Khan, ex-wife of Pakistan cricket star Imran Khan and, later, companion of actor and Annabel's regular Hugh Grant.

Artist India Jane Birley and her brother were involved with the running and overseeing of most of their father's businesses. In 2003, Robin Birley was put in charge of Annabel's, but in September 2006, then aged 48, the son of the man who created Britain's most exclusive nightclub renounced that role. The gossips went to work.

By October that year, it appeared that father and son had been engaged in an almighty row. One reason, according to gossip, was Mark's disapproval of some of the 'celebrities' the club was attracting.

It was reported that Robin's half brothers Zac and Ben Goldsmith had offered to buy Annabel's and reinstate Robin Birley, but Mark Birley, supposedly, did not want the club run by a Goldsmith. The estrangement got even messier in October 2006, when Mark Birley was absent from Robin's wedding to Lucy Helmore, the former wife of singer Bryan Ferry.

The members and staff at Annabel's, used to scandal and intrigue, hoped that family relations would quickly become more amicable. Yet, it was pointed out, all those involved are stubborn.

As Paddy Kennedy himself was. In the end he refused the help of friends, and died in a charity nursing home run by publicans. Even there, he was said to be a rascal.

One big rugby game weekend in 1965 after the Profumo affair, John Burke was with a group of politicians in the horseshoe bar of the grand Shelbourne Hotel on St Stephen's Green in Dublin when Paddy Kennedy arrived with Christine Keeler on his arm, and announced: 'I've brought Christine over to reshuffle the Irish Cabinet.'

The Star Tavern is still there at 6 Belgrave Mews West,

and they do a fine pint of Fuller's and decent pub food. It's unlikely that the legendary deals of the past go on there any more.

Deals such as Billy Hill's proposal in the upstairs room to fund the Great Train Robbery, using the proceeds of a bullion raid; yet Bruce Reynolds, who did much of the robbery's planning there, rejected the offer. 'It was simple business,' said Bobby McKew. 'Bill wanted the lion's share of the haul, at least 60 per cent. They didn't go for that. They made other arrangements.'

The Great Train Robbery, a £2.3 million heist, went ahead on 8 August 1963, at Bridego Railway Bridge in Buckinghamshire.

Today, the Star doesn't have that Kennedy edge either; no longer a place where people would drop in just to listen to the landlord swearing. Which he did, to great glee, when the fish in his display tank kept vanishing. Kennedy was convinced that someone was stealing the goldfish that he got from a shop in Kensington High Street. He just kept buying more, and didn't spot that one of his fish was getting fatter. Eddie Chapman had slipped a piranha into the tank.

And piranhas, or perhaps sharks, lead us to the Clermont and Annabel's of 2007, for there's been much frenzied feeding there and elsewhere. Especially by the government. New Labour appeared to be turning the UK into one big casino in 2007, with a new Gambling Act which was to come into force in September of that year. It was claimed that the National Health Service would require more money to treat gambling addiction.

Although gambling is not as socially smart as it was in the 1960s, plans were under consideration for the Millennium Dome to become a gambling temple, and it appeared that just about every town would have its own casino. Also, while

the American authorities were all but outlawing online betting, Britain's Department for Culture, Media and Sport
(DCMS) was lobbying the Treasury towards the end of 2006
to get a better tax deal for online betting and gambling
companies.

That summer Richard Caborn, the Minister then responsible for gambling, visited the headquarters of PartyGaming
and 888.com in Gibraltar. At the end of October 2006, Tessa
Jowell, then Secretary of State for Culture, hosted an international summit for politicians to talk about gambling regulations. She held it at Ascot racecourse. United Nations and
European Commission representatives were invited, along
with executives from major credit card companies.

Caborn also had meetings with Mark Davies, the managing
director of the punters' much-loved Betfair, the online betting
operation. The plan was to establish Britain as the 'world
leader in online gaming'. This would, argued the government
officials involved, protect the punter. Others, like Mike Atherton in his 2006 book *Gambling*, claimed that the Gambling
Act of 2005 would threaten 'an area of life that has been
regulated and crime-free' for decades.

John Burke smiled when he read that. 'Crime-free and
gambling is, I think, a superb example of an oxymoron.'

The transformation of Britain into Las Vegas, something
begun so long ago with the outcome of *Regina* v. *Aspinall,
Burke & Osbourne*, was analysed in the *Evening Standard* on
15 January 2007 by the writer and seasoned gambler Matthew
Norman. He suggested that this might well be Tony Blair's
legacy. He wrote: 'It is the first government policy in memory,
across the developed and democratic world, designed to
increase human misery.' He believed it would lead to a rise in
poverty, opportunistic crime, domestic violence and 'other
life-destroying social ills'.

The Macao-factor in the UK, the deregulation of gambling, was estimated by some to point to the industry doubling in size, and the money involved being close to £100 billion by 2008/2009. Certainly at the end of 2006 the London casinos, fast overtaking Monte Carlo as the most popular in Europe – places like Crockfords on Curzon Street and Park Lane's Les Ambassadeurs (sold in 2006 to Indonesian businessman Putera Sampoerna for more than £100 million) – were vastly popular.

The Clermont was less so, but the signs were that business was improving – which was good news for Quek Leng Chan, a Malaysian lawyer and a billionaire, who in August 2006 bought the club for somewhere around £30 million from Grosvenor Casinos. He clearly likes a gamble. His game is not chemmy but *punto banco*, a variant of chemmy in which everyone can participate in the betting.

He won out over bids from more familiar Clermont surnames. Zac and Ben Goldsmith, the sons of Jimmy Goldsmith from his marriage to Lady Annabel, and their friend and partner Ben Elliot, failed in their attempt. As did Damian Aspinall, the son of John Aspinall and Jane Hastings. Damian Aspinall has a daughter, Freya, with the MTV and *Big Breakfast* television presenter Donna Air, and runs his father's estate Howletts. The couple met at a dinner with Tara Palmer-Tomkinson in 2001, when she was 21 and he twenty years older. He has two daughters, Tansy, 17 in 2007, and Clary, 14 in 2007, from his marriage to Louise Sebag-Montefiore.

John Aspinall's son was reported to be worth around £42 million in January 2007. As well as the expansive Kent estate, he has a enviable town house in London. He made his takeover bid for the club his father founded with another famous son, Jamie Packer, whose late father was the great gambler and Australian media baron Kerry Packer. Like his own father, Damian Aspinall is a determined man. With Jamie Packer he has opened a casino called 'Aspers' in Newcastle, to great success. The partners plan to launch a chain of 'Aspers' casinos across the UK.

'Aspers' is still gambling.

Bibliography

Allsop, Kenneth. *The Angry Decade*. John Goodchild Publishers, 1984, originally, 1958.

Atherton, Mike. *Gambling, A Story of Triumph & Disaster*. Hodder and Stoughton, 2006.

Blond, Anthony. *Jew Made in England*. Timewell Press, 2004.

Evans, Sir Harold. *Downing Street Diary: The Macmillan Years, 1957 to 1963*. Hodder and Stoughton, 1981.

Fabian, Robert. *Fabian of the Yard*. The Naldrett Press Ltd, 1950.

— *London After Dark*. The Naldrett Press, 1954.

Fallon, Ivan. *Billionaire: The Life and Times of Sir James Goldsmith*. Hutchinson, 1991.

Fleming, Ian. *Casino Royale*. Jonathan Cape, 1953.

Foreman, Freddie, with Lisners, John. *Respect, Autobiography of Feddie Foreman*. Century Books, 1996.

Fraser-Cavassoni, Natasha. *Sam Spiegel, The Biography of a Hollywood Legend*. Little, Brown, 2003.

Goldsmith, Lady Annabel. *Annabel: An Unconventional Life*. Weidenfeld and Nicolson, 2004.

Haggard, H. Rider. *Nada the Lily, A Tale of the Zulus*. Longman, 1892; Wildside Press, 2001.

Henessy, Peter. *Having it so Good, Britain in the Fifties*. Penguin/ Allen Lane, 2006.

Hill, Billy. *Boss of Britain's Underworld*. The Naldrett Press, 1955.

Keeler, Christine, with Thompson, Douglas. *The Truth at Last*. Sidgwick & Jackson, 2001.

Masters, Brian. *The Passion of John Aspinall*. Jonathan Cape, 1988.

Morton, James and Parker, Gerry. *Gangland Bosses, The Lives of Jack Spot and Billy Hill*. Time Warner Books, 2004.

Owen, Frank. *The Eddie Chapman Story*. Allan Wingate Ltd, 1953.

Read, Leonard, with Morton, James. *Nipper Read: The Man Who Nicked the Krays*. Futura Paperbacks, 1992.

Reynolds, Bruce. *The Autobiography of a Thief*. Bantam Press, 1995.

Richardson, Charlie, with Long, Bob. *My Manor*. Sidgwick & Jackson, 1991.

Sandbrook, Dominic. *Never had it so Good: A History of Britain from Suez to the Beatles*. Little, Brown, 2005.

Thomas, Donald. *Villains' Paradise, Britain's Underworld from the Spivs to the Krays*. John Murray, 2005.

Index